W9-CZU-793

# Green Politics

*Also by James Radcliffe*

THE REORGANISATION OF BRITISH CENTRAL GOVERNMENT

# Green Politics

## Dictatorship or Democracy?

James Radcliffe
*Senior Lecturer in Health Policy*
*Staffordshire University*

Consultant Editor: Jo Campling

First published in Great Britain 2000 by
**MACMILLAN PRESS LTD**
Houndmills, Basingstoke, Hampshire RG21 6XS and London
Companies and representatives throughout the world

A catalogue record for this book is available from the British Library.

ISBN 0–333–73941–8

First published in the United States of America 2000 by
**ST. MARTIN'S PRESS, INC.,**
Scholarly and Reference Division,
175 Fifth Avenue, New York, N.Y. 10010

ISBN 0–312–23138–5

Library of Congress Cataloging-in-Publication Data
Radcliffe, James, 1952–
Green politics : dictatorship or democracy? / James Radcliffe ; consultant editor,
Jo Campling.
p.   cm.
Includes bibliographical references and index.
ISBN 0–312–23138–5 (cloth)
1. Green movement.   2. Political ecology.   3. Environmental policy.   I.
Campling, Jo.   II. Title

JA75.8 .R33   2000
324.2'187—dc21
                                                                99–053562

This book is printed on paper suitable for recycling and made from fully managed and sustained
forest sources.

10   9   8   7   6   5   4   3   2   1
09   08   07   06   05   04   03   02   01   00

Printed and bound in Great Britain by
Antony Rowe Ltd, Chippenham, Wiltshire

*To an Angel*

# Contents

# List of Tables

# Acknowledgements

I would like to thank those activists within the green movement who gave so willingly of their time. I would also like to thank Dr Michael Watson at the University College of Wales, Aberystwyth, who first introduced me to the environment as a political and spiritual issue as an undergraduate and master's student in the 1970s. Thanks are also due to Jo Campling for her advice in the development of this book. Sheila Berrisford and Jean Edwards in the International Relations and Politics Division at Staffordshire University should also be mentioned for their help in some of the typing.

JAMES RADCLIFFE

# Introduction

The development of green politics has been seen as a major revolution in social and political thought. It has also bred a form of political activity which is intimately linked to ideas of personal transformation and a change in lifestyle. Its rise and influence on mainstream politics is so significant that critics have sometimes referred to a green establishment, and are critical of the way in which green issues are so readily accepted and used in educational establishments. Earlier efforts to lift environmental issues into the popular consciousness were not so successful. However, the association of a new political movement with a particular science and a spiritual revival has been unique in recent years and this association has also resulted in a series of contradictions. The title of this book refers to a question of whether these contradictions also involve the political structures suggested to resolve the ecological crisis.

One of the issues considered in this work is whether green politics is a new phenomenon. In general, green politics has become a catch-all term in which any political group or action concerned with the environment finds itself covered. However, the traditions of interest in the natural environment stretch back into political history way beyond the areas discussed below. However, the terms used are varied and need to be explored.

In Britain and the United States earlier concepts of conservation and environmentalism had existed before the development of green politics and the equally recent concept of political ecology. These terms need disentangling as they may help to identify different types of political action, from a reformist position to more radical life-style politics.

According to the Oxford English Dictionary, Conservation is:

1. The act of conserving; preservation from destructive influences; decay or waste; preservation in being, health etc.
2. Official charge and care of rivers, sewers, forests etc.; conservancy.

The environment on the other hand is defined as:

1. The action of environing; the state of being environed.
2. That which environs; especially the conditions or influences under which any person or thing lives or is developed.

Even within these brief definitions there is an apparent distinction between a defensive, protectionist approach contained within the concept of conservation and a concern with an active influence on development within the idea of environment.

However, while these two concepts are still in use the more recent utilization of ecology as a political term is linked to a sense of the inadequacy of conservation and environmentalism. Again referring to a definition from the *Oxford English Dictionary*, ecology is:

> The science of the economy of animals and plants, that branch of biology which deals with relations of living organisms to their surroundings, their habits and modes of life, etc.

While this definition is fairly limited, the inclusion of humanity as a part of ecology has led to the development of a radically different approach. However, there was also a more political reason for its increasing adoption, particularly in the United Kingdom. Increasingly, governments have adopted the environment as a part of the mainstream, and consequently those who deem government activity as inadequate to the crisis see ecology as providing a wider ideological foundation. From the early 1970s there was a rejection in some quarters of the concept of environmentalism in favour of ecology.

> We must repudiate the term 'environmentalism'. It is too far gone to be rescued, now the D. of E. [Department of the Environment] has described the proposed airport at Foulness as the 'world's first environmental airport' ... [it] can be described as environmental only by those who regard that adjective as synonymous for odious, squalid and natural ... Ecology tells us that the ecosphere is not an assemblage of academically watertight compartments, but is a single system, composed of interconnected sub-systems which have evolved as a single behavioural process.
>
> (Allen, 1972)

The change in name of the People Party in the UK to the Ecology Party in 1972, was significant for this reason, as indeed was its later adoption of the name Green Party in the 1980s.

Allen saw environmentalism as being politically compromised by its co-option into official use, while ecology was conceived as a discipline with something to teach humanity about the natural world and our place within it. In addition, it was argued that scientific ecology countered the reductionist trends in mainstream, positivist science.

When the traditional reductionist approach of piecemeal analysis fails to achieve long-term solutions then it is time to consider a more holistic approach in which interactions of the pieces and ways of dealing with the situation as a whole are also considered. This is what ecology as an 'emerging new integrative discipline' is all about.

(Odum, 1977)

Within this perspective it will be contended that there are strains and contradictions, for while Odum may argue for a way forward out of reductionism, the potential for scientific ecology to be used as the basis for a wider critique is also present. The distrust of positivist science was linked to a more radical attack on rationalist approaches which were dominant from the age of the Enlightenment. Some have rejected the scientific method and sought a new relationship with nature through a spiritual renewal or sense of affinity with the non-human world.

Through the use of scientific ecology as a new science or the adoption of a non-rational ethical approach there is the potential to revive alternative ways of viewing the world. The science of ecology is holistic and green ethics can appear absolutist. At the same time supporters argue in favour of non-western perspectives on the world in opposition to western dominance. The problem facing green politics is that while there is an increasing consensus on what an ecologically sustainable society may look like, there is no common ground on how we may arrive at such a society. In addition, if the western model of scientific rationalism is dominant and is supported by powerful interests, how is one to arrive at a society radically different from the present system and the intellectual enterprise supporting it.

The present text attempts to consider some of the major issues confronted by the green movement and assess the concepts preoccupying a range of authors and some activists. The issues confronting industrialized society will form the main focus as the green movement developed out of a sense of dissatisfaction and frequent revulsion from the products of industrialism. The questions of technological change, economic growth and subsequent alienation of humanity from the rest of nature are at the heart of the debate. The associated social movements of feminism and animal rights are also considered as they in turn have had a significant impact on the ecological debate. There are interesting areas of debate and conflict between these perspectives as well as between writers on green issues, to such an extent that apparent areas of intolerance have arisen between different wings of the movement. These conflicts are also evident in some of the debates between grassroots activists.

The structure of the book aims to follow through some of these debates and bring out some of the contradictions. In particular, the association of the green movement with the ideal of a decentralized society hides a basic contradiction in that there is a desire for stronger international agreements and governmental regulation to tackle environmental degradation. This is made even more problematic in that the search for an environmental ethic may promote a moral position which is too narrow, with the environment providing the benchmark for all other aspects of our social and political life.

The first chapter will consider debates over the nature of industrialism and the role of technological change, economic growth and the use of resources. These were born out of the early concerns with pollution and resource depletion, and although the predictions concerning limits to growth have proved to be overly pessimistic, the basic ideas are still central to the green movement. The second chapter moves on to look at how green thinkers have debated political solutions to these ecological problems. Early beliefs in the immediacy of the crisis led to the prediction of authoritarian solutions, while as the time scale has lengthened more writers have debated the idea that an ecologically sound society has to be small scale and decentralized. A more sophisticated debate has developed on the relationship between ecological thinking and democracy. This has resulted in a complex analysis of whether or not the primacy of ecological ends take precedence over democratic processes when the outcome of such decisions may be damaging to the environment.

The third chapter is concerned with the alienation of humanity from nature as the root cause of our present ecological crisis. Most notably, the role of reason and the scientific method emerging from the Enlightenment was identified as the basis of that alienation. If this problem is at the heart of the crisis then green thinkers have moved on to try to develop an ethical theory concerning how we should relate to the non-human world. Chapter 4 considers a range of problems tackled by such ethical writings with the aim of revealing the difficulties involved in such a project.

These ethical considerations and the critique of alienation were also a focal point for eco-feminists who provide one of the most stimulating challenges to mainstream ecological thinking. Chapter 5 assesses some of their ideas and also links them into the concepts of post-modernism. Post-modernism has some of the same issues at its centre as green thought, most notably its criticism of reason and the scientific method as part of the modernist project. However, there are significant question marks against going too far in identifying green thought as a postmodernist concept in its purest form. This is equally the case with the ideas emerging from writers on animal rights and the animal liberation movement. Chapter 6 explores these ideas and assesses the reasons for conflicts between green thinking and animal rights when on the surface one would expect them to be natural allies.

The rest of the book moves on to assess some of the practical problems linked to the political arena surrounding the environment. Chapters 7 and 8 cover the role of international conferences and the green movement in much of the industrialized world. The history of international conferences on the environment is one of slow but steady progress, but one which can be frustrating to the green movement. The green movement itself is wide-ranging and engages in both pressure group activity and party politics. The review of the green movement inevitably touches only the surface of the extraordinary growth and development across the industrialized world. However, some trends are identified as part of this review before going on to consider in more detail the development of part of the green movement in the United Kingdom.

The last two chapters are based on interviews with a number of activists in the late 1970s, and contrasts these with some of the ideas developed by green thinkers in the first half of the book. In addition, some consideration is given to the way in which the movement has developed in the United Kingdom. While some of the groups examined in the 1970s are still in existence, there has been a tendency for them to develop closer links with government and this has led to some frustration amongst younger activists. The more recent challenge emerging from New Age lifestyle groups with their moral and spiritual concerns returns the movement to the ideas of the 1970s counterculture. As such, the green movement may be developing into a new phase as we emerge into the new millennium.

# 1
# Industrial Society Challenged

From the beginning, the basis of the ecological challenge to industrial society centred on the two core issues of *technological development* and *economic growth*. The basic association assumed between the two was that technological developments allowed an increase in labour productivity by increasing capital input and sophistication, which promoted the efficiency and profitability of individual units of labour giving rise to economic growth and increased prosperity. This increased prosperity allowed individuals and institutions to save and invest in capital equipment, research and development, which in turn created technological innovation and gave another spin to the wheel of progress. Ecologists questioned these assumptions initially by introducing the problem of limits, both to the idea of growth and to technical change, which gave rise to political questions. As Dryzek noted, the 'environmental discourse' began in the developed world as part of the critique of industrialization (Dryzek, 1997, p. 12), a critique that made it distinctive from other political ideologies, including liberalism and Marxism.

The role of technological development and its place within the ecological crisis was central to the debate between Barry Commoner and Paul Ehrlich. The basis of their disagreement was the emphasis Commoner placed on technology as the main element in the crisis, which to Ehrlich seemed at the expense of other factors of equal importance, notably the rate of population growth and the degree of individual affluence. Of Commoner, Ehrlich stated:

> …he continued, and continues to insist that the only significant factor in producing the environmental crisis is technological error.
>
> (Pole, 1973)

Ehrlich considered that technology, population growth and affluence interacted with each other to create the crisis. Commoner concentrated on the problems created by technological change and the reasons for the displacement of one technology by another. He developed the idea that in order to achieve greater profitability and control over the market industries had developed new, more ecologically damaging technologies. For this reason he downgraded the other areas of concern including economic growth which he argued was a popular 'whipping boy':

> The rate of exploitation of the ecosystem, which generates economic growth, cannot increase indefinitely without over-driving the system and pushing it to the point of collapse. However, this theoretical relationship does not mean that any increase in economic activity automatically means more pollution. What happens to the environment depends on *how* the growth is achieved.
>
> (Commoner, 1974, p. 266)

A major criticism was the way in which energy forms had developed, resulting in a continued expansion of electricity generation for many end-use activities. The nature of the system of production based upon private enterprise and its need for profit generated the need to produce a source of energy that would have a high demand and a high return.

Indeed it was the 'crucial link' between 'pollution and profits' which Commoner (*ibid.*, p. 266) spoke of which was at the centre of the synthesis between the environmental concerns of the counter-culture and the political ideas of the New Left. Commoner's criticisms were centred upon a socialist analysis of capitalism, which had its roots in Marxist economic thought. In particular, he approached the issue using the Marxist concept of the falling rate of profit, a problem which was severest in the area of energy development and especially so in the case of nuclear power technologies. Commoner pointed out that, particularly in the United States, the costs of development had been borne by the public while all the benefits went to the private sector (1977, p. 111). He saw the public taking the risks at both ends of the production line, in that they invested in research and development and also endured the physical risks incurred due to environmental degradation. The private industries on the other hand received the benefits of a developed technology and increased profits resulting from the improved productivity of labour due to increased capital input. However, the cost and level of capital investment had reached a point where there was a decline in capital productivity. Consequently, the 'growth in output is now very largely due to the rise in *labour* productivity' while the other factors of production remained static or declining (*ibid.*, p. 229).

Energy technologies had developed so that capital was increasingly taking over from labour, this necessitated growth simply in order to generate the profits required for continued capital investment. The reason for the emphasis on energy technologies in the 1970s lay in the energy crisis, but also in the position of energy as the source of humanity's ability to shape their environment, and, even more basically, as the source of all life on earth. Industrial society was based upon the transformation of fossil fuels into usable heat, increasing the strength of humanity in its physical relationship with the rest of nature. These fuels were such that they were the most vulnerable to depletion of all the materials used. Indeed, they have contained within them all the elements of the ecological crisis, both in its physical nature and in its most obviously political sense. Ehrlich argued that energy consumption was 'the best single' measure of affluence, technological development and ecological impact (Ehrlich *et al.*, 1973, p. 219). The increasing costs of fossil fuels led to the search for new fuel sources by all parties, and this new importance in our economy led to a generalised feeling that we were in a period of transition towards a 'post-industrial society' (see for example, Bell, 1976; Gershuny, 1978).

While this emphasis on energy, as a resource issue, was central to these debates the role of industrialization as a wider ideological concern was evident and was to continue after the energy crisis was apparently over. Indeed, for Milton (1996, pp. 139–40) the critique of industrialism was central to the green case for cultural change. In her view there was a 'myth of primitive ecological wisdom' which was superior to the growth centred and ecologically destructive culture of industrialism. This myth was built on the idea that such primitive cultures were less destructive because they required so little and therefore made less impact on the earth. Milton criticized this position because it ignored the anthropological literature that showed industrialism was not alone in seeing prestige as being linked to conspicuous consumption and wealth. Rather, there was a need to look elsewhere for the reason for ecological damage and the nature of technology and associated political structures were a possible route.

## Energy paths, technology and industrial society

With the widening of the ecological debate there developed a feeling that humanity could make a reasoned decision between alternative futures. Within the area of energy technologies, Amory Lovins saw this as a choice between 'hard' and 'soft' energy paths. The major distinction he made was that of flexibility in industrial, social and political structures. The decision to opt for a 'hard' energy path precluded other options, whereas a 'soft' path involved the integration of a number of approaches to achieve a balance based upon numerous local initiatives, building a complex picture of energy production.

> The distinction between hard and soft energy paths rests not on how much energy is used, but on the technical and socio-political *structure* of the energy system, thus focusing our attention on consequent and crucial political differences.
>
> (Lovins, 1977, p. 38)

This was one of the most important questions which the ecological approach had opened up in relation to the nature of industrialized society; whether, and in what way, does the technology of a society, and especially the technology of energy production, affect the social and political structure of a society?

Lovins' was criticized as being over deterministic, and his belief that the two alternative energy paths both rule each other out and dictate particular types of social and political organization was central to this criticism. The danger of 'soft' technologies being co-opted into hierarchical and authoritarian social structures was not examined.

> … while particular technologies *lend* themselves to particular social and political structures, the connection is not *automatic*.
>
> (Martin, 1978, pp. 10–13)

This problem was seen to arise with the introduction of new technologies, both complex 'high' and the so-called 'appropriate' technologies, to the developing world. It was not a simple situation where highly capitalised technology was the only offender, 'alternative' technologies could be as well. For example, biogas plants were introduced which increased the value of dung and undermined the economies of the poorest villages:

> The point is not that biogas plants are inherently bad…but that they cannot be introduced thoughtlessly, without new forms of social organization.
>
> (Norman, 1978, p. 22)

The development of this line of thought was also evident in the criticism of central and eastern European states. David Dickson examined the historical development of technology within the western capitalist system and argued that the development of industrial techniques within a hierarchical society resulted in the adoption of those techniques which reinforced the established hierarchy. These aspects were not just of a technical nature, but included shop-floor organization, beginning with the introduction of the factory system itself. The machines which came to be introduced reinforced this system, especially with the advent of large scale division of labour and mass-production.

> These tactics inevitably included the need for increased social control on the part of capital, and the authoritarian relationship that this implied became crystallized in the machines that were introduced.
>
> (Dickson, 1974, p. 79)

The aim of maintaining hierarchical structures led to the adoption of productive techniques which were dependent on them (*ibid.*, p. 87).

Dickson, therefore, considered technical change to be as much a necessity as social change. In viewing socialist societies, the question of the 'betrayal' of the revolution or the emergence of a 'new class' were seen as products of the lack of a thorough-going revolution in the technical aspects of society. The end of capitalist economies and the placing of the means of production in the hands of the state as a transitional step towards a communist society, failed due to the continued adoption of capitalist technologies and working practices. Indeed, for some ecological writers this was the inevitable result of the adoption of Marxism as a creed and due to its stagnation as an 'ideology of development which is but a comic caricature of nineteenth century bourgeois scientism' (Roszak, 1974, p. 21).

Enzensberger considered that the challenge posed by the new ecological awareness led to a re-examination of certain aspects of Marxism.

> To begin with, one must examine critically the concept of material progress which plays a decisive part in the Marxist tradition. It appears in any case to be redundant in that it is linked to the technical optimism of the 19th century.
>
> (Enzenberger, 1974, p. 22)

For Enzensberger, there was a need to analyse capitalism as a productive form rather than simply as a 'property relationship', and this would enable the ecological crisis to be analysed from a Marxist perspective (*ibid.*, p. 21).

This 'revisionism' obviously did not find favour with more orthodox Marxists. For Etienne Balibar the new 'ideologies' were attempts to preserve the status quo and to resolve any crisis situation to the bour-geoisie's own advantage by presenting the situation as something which was 'inevitable'. The questioning of the role of science, technol-ogy and the nature of progress was a diversion from the social causes of the crisis of capitalism. Concepts such as zero growth and the harmful-ness of science and technology were a 'mechanical inversion' of the myths that had sustained the development of capitalism.

> whereas throughout the historical period of its economic rise and political dominance, the bourgeoisie above all developed rationalist ideology and philosophies, exalting the advance of knowledge or advance through knowledge, this tendency is inverted in the epoch of its crisis and decay.
>
> (Balibar, 1978, pp. 4–5)

Consequently, the commitment to economic growth and an ideology that stressed humanity's supremacy over nature was just as much a part of planned economies as it was in the West. Therefore, as Eckersley (1992, p. 23) noted, the green critique of industrialism included the systems of 'state capitalism' just as much as purer, free-market capitalist economies. The problem of discussing the crisis of capitalism or indus-trialism outside of related social forces was also relevant in the criticism of both Commoner and Lovins. There were other elements to the crisis than technological issues and the problem of 'technological determinism' was to be guarded against (Dickson, 1974, p. 13).

The work of the futurologist Daniel Bell revealed the problem of con-centrating on technology. The development of a technocratic society in which theoretical knowledge became the organizing principle was, for Bell, an inevitable change with the coming of a 'post-industrial' society. The change in the position of the intellectual elite was bound up with the nature of the society's technology, where complexity took control of the machine out of the hands of laypeople. For the critics of such developments this was, by its nature, anti-democratic, allying a complex, high-technology with the requirement for large capital investment and the proliferation of experts.

Bell was optimistic, for he saw the future as a projection of the pre-sent in that the values of future scientists were deemed to be the values of today's scientists:

> Science itself is ruled by an ethos which is different from the ethos of other major social groups (e.g. business, the military) and this

ethos will *predispose* scientists to act in a different fashion, politically, from other groups.

(1976, p. 359)

Bell held the view that this meritocracy was innately benevolent due to the concern of science for the search for 'truth', as opposed to the business ethos of the search for profit. A critic of Bell pointed to the likelihood that 'the 'intelligentsia' stratum' which carries and develops such (theoretical) knowledge will end up serving, rather than transforming, American capitalist goals (Ross, 1974, p. 331).

Bell's view of the future was unacceptable to many ecologists, particularly in relation to the form of technology developed in industrial society. This was a major criticism by ecologists of the implementation of nuclear power and other 'hard energy paths'. It was seen to distance production decisions from the eventual consumers, and its highly complex technology and high capital intensity limited the role of the individual worker:

> At the same time it provides an opportunity for the further centralization of control – a cause close to the heart of many technocrats. Because of the security problems, nuclear technology requires increased secrecy and a semi-militarised work force.
>
> (Elliott, D. *et al.*, 1978, p. 44)

For this reason the alternative of a 'soft' energy path contained certain common features of an ecologically sound future. The development of 'soft' energy technologies were seen as permitting technology to be controlled by individuals and local communities:

> A low energy policy allows for a wide choice of life styles and cultures. If, on the other hand, a society opts for high energy consumption its social relations must be dictated by technocracy and will be equally distasteful whether labelled capitalist or socialist.
>
> (Illich, 1974, p. 16)

For this reason alternative technologies were seen as being not only non-violent in their actions upon the earth, but also democratic. Simplicity was looked for, not as a substitute for quality, but in order to allow understanding on the part of the user. In this way, Illich argued, the aim was to allow the user to develop their tools for the uses they were to be put to. The relationships between energy's form and its end use were brought along a closer path of alignment in their development.

Lovins saw the possibilities arising from the increased use and substitution of solar energy in all its forms as diverse:

> its diffuseness is a spur to decentralization and increased self-sufficiency of population … and by limiting the density and absolute power at man's disposal it would also limit the amount of ecological mischief he could do.
>
> (1975, p. 84)

It produced the ideal synthesis of reduced environmental damage and democratic control, a 'Demo-technology' as opposed to an 'Aristo-technology' (Stavrianos, 1974), and gave the development of these techniques a key place in the ecological movement. Skolimowski warned activists that such a development of alternative technology groups within the movement as a whole must not get out of hand. He saw them under-mining the development of a coherent philosophy because they had become too concerned with the technology rather than the core values (1976, pp. 702–3). For Skolimowski the role of ecology as a critical tool in examining society was not limited to a discussion of technology. Waste was seen to be a symptom of a deeper malaise in western industrial society which was essentially anti-democratic and potentially authoritarian.

## Capitalism and industrialism

The environmental destruction wrought in central and eastern European socialist societies may have highlighted the problems of industrialism as such and created by the technologies and methods of work developed within capitalist social structures. The next question we must ask is whether the structure of capitalism means that an ecologically viable system would be incompatible with its continuation.

Robert Heilbroner saw the possibility of maintaining capitalism, at least in the short and medium term, through rational planning. He appreciated that this may be anathema to laissez-faire purists, but reminded them that the presence of governmental intervention had always been with us as a way of defending private property and ultimately the market (1977, p. 29). Paul Ehrlich also believed that a major requirement was to prove to Marxists that capitalism could survive the ecological crisis even with the difficulties resulting from the need to 'de-develop' (Ehrlich and Ehrlich, 1970, pp. 322–3). Ehrlich suggested that the reason for the adoption of harmful technologies was brought about through the growth in population and affluence (Ehrlich and Pirages, 1974, p. 15). This concern with rising expectations and materialism was linked to the problem of growth in industrial production. For Ehrlich this was a spiritual malaise but one which could be affected by a change in social and political organization and, although capitalism had led to the present situation, this was a distortion of its true nature:

> ...industry in the United States is dominated by oligopolies. Today, free enterprise means freedom to stifle innovation and to manipulate markets out of self-interest, there are not enough competitors to make the invisible hand work.
>
> (*Ibid.*, p. 85)

Ehrlich saw the solution to the ecological crisis lying with a spreading of resources and a return to the 'golden age' of capitalism and perfect competition. Heilbroner, on the other hand, considered the expansionist drive and the concentration of economic power as essential parts of capitalism and of a capitalism which would continue to develop in this way for some time to come. Indeed, the medium term future comprised the replacement of the nation-state by powerful multinational corporations:

> We must begin by recognising that the fundamental process behind the rise of the multinational corporation is growth, the urge for expansion that is the daemon of capitalism itself.
>
> (1977, p. 70)

But, equally importantly, when looking into the 'long run', Heilbroner saw the expansionist drive inherent in capitalism coming up against environmental constraints. These problems were of such magnitude, and the dynamic of growth within capitalism so important, that the result must be the end of capitalism.

It was this inner dynamic of growth, inspired by the profit motive of privately held capital, which was seen as the great revolutionary power of capitalism as a social and economic force. But in a finite world and due to its lack of social responsibility, this was the very factor which resulted in capitalism's unviability (Stoneman, 1972, p. 64). This problem was identified by Garrett Hardin as the 'Tragedy of the Commons' (1977). The basis of this concept was that, given common property, each user of that property will consider the benefit he, as an individual, can attain from its use. The problem the user will foresee is that he cannot be sure that other individuals will take no more than an equal share of the grazing land. Self-interest will result in the individual placing as many grazing animals on that property in order to secure as much use as possible because of this lack of certainty concerning the behaviour of others. The result was the destruction of the pasture through overgrazing, or 'exceeding the carrying capacity'. For Hardin the carrying capacity of the earth was coming under stress because of the 'freedom to breed', which was 'intolerable', because the earth's resources, particularly air and water, were deemed to be free resources, or 'commons'. The increasing use of these resources for dumping the effluent of the human species was considered a major problem, one which was limited when the human population was small but was now leading to an imbalance.

Hardin argued that the blame for the overuse of the commons did not lie with capitalism and its urge for growth but in man's nature which rested on 'self-interest'. His solution was to establish a system of 'Mutual Coercion Mutually Agreed Upon' (*ibid.*, p. 26), an authoritarian solution as he dismissed appeals to conscience as being based on hypocrisy and self-interest. On the one hand we appeal to an individual's conscience and attack them as irresponsible if they do not accede, and on the other hand we attack them if they do, because they are foolish and all the rest will continue to exploit the commons.

Hardin took a rather simplistic evolutionary line, contending that if we appealed to conscience and the above was true, then all those with a conscience would eventually disappear due to lack of descendants, while those without a conscience would multiply:

> To make such an appeal is to set up a selective system that works towards the elimination of conscience from the race.
>
> (*Ibid.*, p. 25)

A close look at these arguments shows they fail on a number of counts. Firstly, the idea of the elimination of conscience by breeding is too simplistic to be taken seriously. It discounts the numerous factors involved in the make-up of an individual, both environmental and genetic. Secondly, the appeal to self-interest is inherent to capitalism, it is viewed as a traditional concept of man's make-up and is looked upon as that element of personality which is the driving force behind the 'invisible hand'. The premise of self-interest was not fully examined by Hardin and the possibility of its being overturned was not considered, whereas the ease with which conscience is eradicated was. Thirdly, the basis of the idea of the commons was that there was no real society, it was abstracted away into a mass of individuals whose only interaction was through competition, the very heart of capitalism. Further, Hardin used examples of 'mutually agreed coercion' from the past in order to analyse future possibilities for action and reform. In the specific instance of common grazing land from which he developed his whole argument, he stated:

> ...we abandoned the commons in food gathering, enclosing farm land and restricting pastures and hunting and fishing areas.
>
> (Hardin, 1977, p. 28)

But there was no accurate historical analysis, for in this case enclosures were the action of a minority of wealthy and powerful citizens, which caused inequities and hardship for the poor, not a system of mutually agreed coercion. In a democratic society concerned with the rights of all its citizens and an increasing desire for equitable arrangements in the face of declining growth prospects, there would need to be a more refined approach to the idea of 'mutually agreed coercion'.

However, the green position on industrialism, as with the issue of energy paths, also presents a critique of the political consequences of technology. While authoritarian solutions such as those presented by Hardin have declined the critique of industrialism has emphasized the nature of modern society as inherently anti-democratic. John Barry (1999, pp. 209–10) has noted that many green writers have contended that the process of industrialization and economic growth has resulted in anti-democratic structures and processes. The real Tragedy of the Commons was not so much the issue of the resource depletion that led to the need for change, but the adoption of enclosures as the solution to the problem. It was the privatization of common goods, or their commodification, that ensured the political and economic framework of industrial societies was authoritarian. Consequently, much of the activity of green pressure groups was targeted at existing state institutions and processes that were identified as profoundly undemocratic. In particular, opening up decision making in science and technology to democratic debate was a significant good.

Part of the problem was the association of technological change with the scientific worldview and concept of progress. The link between these three issues led to a political system based on hierarchy and domination. It also linked together the ideologies that emerged from nineteenth-century industrial society, whether it was *laissez-faire* capitalism or Marxism, in their belief in the benefits of technological progress. Dryzek (1997, p. 132) noted how they all 'believed in the essential idea of history moving in the direction of social improvement'. For Dickens

(1996) this process was linked with the 'humanization' of nature as a particular project of the scientific endeavour. The process of science was involved in the reduction of nature into its component parts in order that they could be manipulated and controlled. In this way, the process allowed the industrialization of nature and its increasing transformation into a commodity:

> The main problem as regards production in such forms as genetic engineering and the new reproductive technologies is that they are founded on myopic forms of abstraction which deny the importance of organisms as a whole and their wider social and ecological connection...In this way, industrial production not only becomes insulated from the vagaries of the weather but further separated from human labour and public accountability.
>
> (1996, p. 130)

This took the analysis further from the narrow problem of secrecy and authoritarianism associated with the military uses of nuclear power and its knock-on effects on civil society. The scientific problems associated with new technologies were those of the control and dissemination of information in society as a whole, in particular the consequences for democratic accountability in the economic sphere. The existence of liberal, representative democracy constrained as it was to the political sphere of action failed to penetrate the underlying causes of ecological degradation and the anti-democratic forces at work in industrialism.

  This position presented a significant distinction between radical ecologists who identified green thought as something new, and those concepts more consciously embedded in the traditions of political thought such as eco-socialism. Eckersley (1992, p. 121) noted how eco-socialists contended that deep greens neglected the issue of ownership by concentrating on environmental degradation 'rather than on who owns and shapes' the means and relations of production. For Pepper (1993, p. 221) this meant that ecology should be part of the tradition of Enlightenment thought and not a rejection of rationalism. While deep greens may see industrialism itself as the cause of non-democratic and authoritarian processes, Pepper contended that it was capitalism as a form of industrialization that caused the associated problems of social injustice and ecological damage:

> [Eco-socialism] cannot consider 'nature's needs' aside from those of humanity, and just as it considers that a communist society cannot,

by definition, be ecologically unsound, so it would assert that a proper ecological society could not countenance, by definition, social injustice.

(1993, p. 222)

As a strong anthropocentric position such an approach would 'prioritize human over non-human needs' when necessary.

John Barry identified a more thoroughly green position when he contended that this would result from a politics less dominated by the demands of industrialism and economic growth. Such an approach would result in a reduction in the role of the state due to the simplified social and economic relationships that would emerge:

> If we understand modernity in terms of its industrial and democratic components, then the green democratic position can be viewed as suggesting that there can be a contradiction between the industrial modernization of society and democratic modernization.

(1999, pp. 209–10)

Both the deep green position and that of eco-socialists, while possibly disagreeing on the anti-democratic consequences of industrialism as such, both agreed on the centrality of economic growth to industrial development and capitalism. Indeed, it may be contended that the radicalism of eco-socialism and the deep green analysis of industrialism meant that they both shared a view which attacked the reformism of much 'shallow green' or reformist thinking. However, Zimmerman has noted how deep greens have identified the 'interlocking' nature of the economic, social and political aspects of modernity contained within both liberalism and Marxism (1997, p. 233). As such the critical issue of economic growth, and its importance to both these traditions of modernity, has played a central role throughout the evolution of ecological thought.

## Problems of growth

For critics of economic growth a central issue was the productive process and the nature of growth as a tool for assessing the wellbeing and quality of life in a society. The possibility of questioning the makeup of economic growth was urged because of the fear of resource limitations, but Daly contended that there were social and moral reasons for moving to a steady state long before the arrival of ecological constraints (Daly, 1973, p. 117).

The steady state was an attempt to move the systemic analysis of the energy flows within a natural eco-system into the eco-system that included humanity. The aim was to establish that humanity's relationship with the environment was one of inter-dependence rather than dominance, and that the requirements of humanity were linked to his/her relationship with nature and the constant flow of energy within the earth and its atmosphere. Odum discussed the position of humanity as an element of an eco-system in which, as the system became more complex, more energy was dedicated to its maintenance rather than to growth and development (Odum, 1971, p. 442). For this reason Odum stressed the need to develop a 'space-ship economy' and shift the emphasis of our activity onto the 'quality of the capital stock and human resources' rather than quantity.

However, the question arises that if we do halt at a maintenance level at what level will that be and do we remain at our present global state of extreme economic and political inequality? Singh stated that such a decision would not be tolerable:

> it would be crass impertinence merely to plead for the institution of a stabilised and non-growing economy which would go on reproducing itself forever after.
>
> (Singh, 1976, pp. 34–5)

Consequently, a steady state was unattainable if such a state was based on the continued use of fossil fuels and the products of the petro-chemical industry.

The rejection of economic growth brought about serious criticism from supporters of growth, as seen in the debate between Mishan and Beckerman. Mishan assessed the problems of the external diseconomies suffered in industrial nations that resulted from economic growth. The major area of concern which touched upon resource depletion was the decline of areas of natural beauty due to the advance of transportation and the associated growth of tourism (1969, pp. 176–80). This objection opened Mishan up to the accusation by Beckerman of being in the grip of a 'middle-class obsession' with mass intrusion into previously remote holiday spots (Beckerman, 1976, p. 40).

Beckerman argued that many major aspects of pollution were being controlled by the development of technologies and that it required growth in order to allow these to be developed and to be employed economically. For Beckerman (1979) it was the existence of economic growth that had helped improve the environment and shifted our social objectives towards less immediate social goals. The problem of external diseconomies, which firms had passed on to the public in the form of pollution, led to the introduction of legislation in order to reduce or eliminate the problem (Beckerman, 1976, pp. 125–7). But he argued that such developments could only be associated with economic growth. He acknowledged that the 'anti-growth' movement had increased our awareness of the problems of inter-generational responsibility. But he was critical of the way in which too great a concern with future generations would lead to inactivity in relation to present day problems.

Ridgeway agreed with this view and saw ecology as having supplied liberal-minded people with a safe and peaceful solution which would supply them with,

> a way of seeming to remake society, limiting the growth of capitalism, preserving the natural resources through pollution control, developing a more coherent central state: in short establishing programmes and plans for correcting the flaws in what many perceived to be a fundamentally reliable, sound political system.
>
> (Ridgeway, 1971, p. 13)

For Ridgeway this enabled ecology to be co-opted into the status quo, resulting in the creation of an ecology 'industry' (*ibid.*, p. 16).

Beckerman insisted that there was every reason to rely upon the price mechanism to resolve the issues of resource depletion and pollution. This was,

> the same as for any product, material or otherwise, the supply of which *at the initial stage* cannot keep pace with the rise in demand: the price rises. This tends to slow down the rate of increase in demand, as well as provide a further stimulus to increases in supply or the development of substitutes.
>
> (*Ibid.*, 1976, p. 224)

He conceded that this would mean a slowing of growth in the developed nations. However, Pirages pointed out that the operation of the price mechanism, allied to the increasing capital requirements for both the exploitation of traditional fossil fuels in harsher environments, as well as new fuels such as coal shale and tar sands, would lead to increasing inequities. While Beckerman attacked ecologists as having regard only for their middle-class comforts and amenities, Pirages stated that the use of the price-mechanism in this case was equally disregarding of the poor:

> The assumption is that economic and political 'muddling through' that has supposedly served industrial societies well in the past will

continue to do so in the future...But the consequences of such action would be severe, particularly to the poor who would be left with little purchasing power in a stagnant market place.

(Pirages, 1977, p. 5)

Pirages contended that while zero growth may no longer be the issue, the question of the kind of growth we require and the problems of the distribution of resources were crucial. As growth declines due to ecological limits, conflicts over the distribution of the wealth produced by this growth will increase (*Ibid.*, p. 11).

It is here that the problems of growth and the nature of technology come most directly to act upon one another. If the criticism of technology discussed earlier is valid, that it is spurred on by and in turn reinforces a hierarchical and centralized society, then growth has acted as a lubricant to increase the effectiveness of this centralization. The decline in growth rates forced a re-examination of the distribution of wealth and the relationship between labour and the means of production. In addition, ecologists considered that economic rationality was 'thoroughly anthropocentric; nature exists only to provide inputs to the socio-economic machine, to satisfy human wants and needs' (Dryzek, 1997, p. 113).

This issue was also addressed by Dobson (1995) who made the distinction between radical greens and ecological modernizers in their approach to growth. For the modernizers there was the possibility of 'decoupling' economic growth and environmental degradation. Such an approach involved a concern with intergenerational responsibility, and saw that the failure to protect the environment simply placed a burden on future generations. Modernizers argued that environmental protection was a spur to economic growth through the development of new industries and the global market place would ensure that the most successful products would have the highest environmental standards set by the most successful economies.

However, Dobson noted that radical greens questioned whether industrialists, or indeed consumers, were interested in intergenerational issues. Secondly, they would contend that whether environmental protection adds to economic growth or not depends on what criteria were employed in the measurement of growth and the relative value placed on environmental amenity. Finally, the idea that products with the highest environmental standards will be the most highly prized depends on the nature of the product and the global acceptance of environmental standards. Radical greens would point to the 'export' of pollution as multinational corporations switched their productive capacity away from countries which might be applying strict pollution controls to those with more liberal regimes:

> Ecological modernizers might argue that it is part of their agenda to ensure this sort of legislation, but one suspects that tough environmental standards are more likely in places where there is already an 'environmental culture'.

> (1995, p. 207)

For radical greens the development of an ecological or environmental culture was one that only a far reaching critique of the nature of industrial society, and humanity's place within nature, could address.

For writers such as Keekok Lee (1993, pp. 109–10), one of the failures of the industrial project was that it was impossible for all the worlds population to share in the good of that project. Lee argued that the inequality in the utilization of the world's resources was a major limit on the potential for global industrialization. He noted that on 1980s figures the USA had 6 per cent of the world's population but utilized almost 40 per cent of global resources. The prospect of global industrialization on the scale of the USA was therefore impossible. In addition, the levels of pollution such a society would produce would be unimaginable and because of the nature of economic growth the developing world in particular would forever be playing 'catch up' with the USA. Developed countries would not stop their economic growth while the rest of the world attained some form of equality.

An additional problem arising out of such limits concerned the political structure associated with industrialization. Eckersley (1992) argued that the ideals of liberal democracy were dependent upon a 'frontier setting' in which there was an expanding supply of resources and wealth with an associated trickle down of goods to substitute for equal distribution. However, as resource constraints begin to exert themselves inequalities will become more evident and the possibility of greater distributive justice will recede. In order to maintain their own position the most powerful beneficiaries of the system will seek to impose a more authoritarian solution on the rest of society:

> Indeed, the classical liberal defenders of individualism and laissez-faire economics are seen by emancipatory ecopolitical theorists as apologists for the very dynamic that has led to the 'tragedy of the commons'. And, as the survivalists had shown, the logical sequel

to this dynamic is authoritarianism from above rather than self-limitation from below.

(p. 24)

However, Goodin (1992) asserted that the 'trade-off between economic growth and environmental protection owes more to the rhetoric of environmentalists themselves than to the arguments of their opponents' (p. 99). For Goodin the failure of environmentalist critiques of economic growth centred on a failure to analyse what contributes to growth. Consequently, what was required was firstly that economic measures of growth take account of the externalities of the productive process through a form of 'let the polluter pay' system. It may well be that in arriving at a more environmentally sound analysis of what constitutes growth particular industries may find their profits severely curtailed. Secondly, we must analyse the details of growth figures as we should not establish the erroneous belief that we achieve something beneficial through sacrifice. It was not necessarily the case that we always gain environmentally when we cease a particular productive process, as the full consequences of such a reform may not be self-evident. More importantly, introducing a more ecologically sound measure of what constitutes growth and constraining industrial activities through environmental legislation does not always necessitate sacrifices in economic prosperity and well-being.

John Barry (1999, p. 160) has also contended that for greens there was the need to re-establish the relationship between decisions affecting the economy and the political process. He noted that for greens the necessity of capital accumulation and the drive to economic growth within a global, capitalist economy led many ecologists towards an anti-capitalist position, but also identifying the need for 'socially re-embedding the economy by democratically managing it'. For Lee (1993) the definition of what constituted indutrialization created a significant problem for the development of an environmentally sound society. Industrialization comprised the following components that were also significantly linked to a definition of capitalism:

1. the industrial mode of production,
2. high universal consumption,
3. indefinite exponential economic growth,
4. mass production involving a division of labour and a simplification of tasks, and

5. productivity and efficiency through the lowering of costs of production, notably through the transfer of costs in the form of externalities.

These factors together created problems for the development of an environmental society in that they were dependent on the degradation of nature and the exploitation of other humans and animals, resulting in the general impoverishment of life and a lack of true democratic structures.

## Conclusions

The critique of industrialism and economic growth, whether capitalist or otherwise, raised the issue of sustainability. The view that environmental problems cannot be tackled through the development of new technologies led to the perception that social and political change was essential. The issue of sustainability was often associated with the problem of maintaining some form of economic development, most notably in the developing world. However, such a view was subject to challenge by radical or deep green writers in particular. John Barry (1996, pp. 117–8) contended that sustainable development was a largely economic conception which concentrated on bridging the gap between human demands on resources and the supply-side problems of ecological scarcity. Consequently, this was a classic economic problem of supply and demand which when removed from the socio-political contexts could result in the use of anti-democratic means to ensure that the main economic problem was resolved without challenging existing patterns of distribution.

   In addition, there was no questioning of the end product of our economic activity and the use made of the earth's resources:

> Sustainability … is concerned as much with the ends of our use of the environment as with the ecological means to economic development.
>
> (Barry, J., 1996, p. 117)

Adams made a similar distinction in his discussion of sustainable development and green development. Sustainable development was identified as having within it a basic naivete in that its concerns were centred on an adjustment to existing patterns of trade which would entail a number of reforms. These would involve: increased capital flows to the developing world; dealing with the externalities resulting from productive processes being based in developing countries; and reforming capital investment to ensure adequate technology transfers (Adams, 1990, p. 62).

Green development was more radical and 'eclectic' in its approach to change. Adams assessed the work of Friberg and Hettne in which the focus of development would be based on a culturally defined community, and centred on self-reliance, social justice and ecological balance (*ibid.*, p. 72). Consequently, it moved beyond the simple economic 'tinkering' associated with mainstream concepts of sustainable development, but was still subjected to criticism from radicals within the development movement itself.

This concern with sustainability in the developing world was an essential part of the overall pattern of thought linking industrialism and limits to growth with the need for a radical review of the social and political systems associated with modernity. The ecological challenge to industrial society was centred on the resource constraints and pollution resulting from, and eventually inhibiting, economic growth; the social and political consequences of an over reliance on fossil fuels; and the doubts over the idea of technological progress. The evolving debate over the nature of growth and the consequent move away from a concern with zero growth has also had an impact on ideas concerning the political nature of an ecological society. The connection between energy forms and political structure, while subject to challenge, also raised the question of whether a sustainable society will be more decentralized and democratic than a technocratic state. As the sense of ecological crisis has receded in comparison with the fears of the early 1970s global issues such as the erosion of the ozone layer and climate change dominate the agenda. The idea that an authoritarian solution to the ecological crisis exists has also receded and an apparently decentralized political structure is more in favour. However, the potential for a reemergence of crisis and a consequent transfer of sentiments towards authoritarian solutions once again was also evident in the writings of a range of green theorists. It is to the debate over centralist and decentralist social and political structures that we now turn.

# 2
# Centralism versus Decentralism

The previous chapter centred around the relationship of technology to social structure, the nature of economic growth and the questioning of their role within a finite world. The result was to see that society had to take account of both these factors and control their substance in order to achieve a desirable future. In essence the demand of ecologists is that humanity must actively participate in the directing of the technological and economic development of his/her future rather than reacting to circumstances or 'muddling through'. This entails the creation of an ecological society, and means we must enquire into the structure of such a society, in particular its political structure; for if decisions are to be taken about technological developments and the nature and distribution of resources, we are in the realm of politics. This requires that we ask who makes the decisions and how they are to be enforced. Within the ecological debate this centres upon the centralist–decentralist division.

## Centralism or 'ecological dictatorship'

The centralist argument began by considering the magnitude of the problems the new environmental awareness revealed and considered that because of this, large forces would have to be mobilized to fight them. The most pessimistic of these was, perhaps, the position held by Robert Heilbroner, for with the acceptance of environmental limits to the growth of capitalism he saw the emergence of social disputes over resources. These disputes presented threats to democratic institutions:

> The likelihood that there are obdurate limits to the reformist reach of democratic institutions within the class bound body of capitalist

society leads us to expect that the government of these societies, faced with extreme internal strife or with potentially disastrous social polarisation, would resort to authoritarian measures.

(1975, p. 90)

As we have seen earlier with Heilbroner, he saw the continuation of capitalism for some time to come, with the increase both of state regulation and the economic power of multinational corporations, and to maintain the class privileges which underlie our society. Although he saw the final demise of capitalism as it reached environmental and social limits to growth, the resulting society would be largely authoritarian:

In the face of extreme distributional tensions on the one hand and potentially lethal consequences of private economic activity on the other, the extension of public authority must reach into and displace private decision making, not only in the determination of incomes but in the choice and means of output.

(1977, p. 87)

This belief that distribution of wealth and the nature of industrial production will eventually become decisions made by a number of multinationals and by governments, was central to Heilbroner's view. Further, the collectivist state which he envisaged had to institute a massive degree of intellectual control on its citizens as well, for Heilbroner conceived of the situation as being so acute that we would have to substitute a society which was 'tradition-oriented' and static for the present dynamic society. Thus it would require the abandonment of 'intellectual heresy' and the search for scientific knowledge outside of set parameters. The major reason for this was that the complexity of our society would require a central role for an intellectual and skilled elite, and the mass of the population would have to be kept in the dark concerning disagreements between scientists (*ibid.*, p. 26).

For Heilbroner a democratic and decentralized society was only possible in a distant future. Ophuls, although also establishing an authoritarian system, saw this more as a transitional state on the way to a decentralized future. He contended that the industrial world had enjoyed an unprecedented political and economic freedom based on the abundance of resources and the large rates of economic growth. He considered the political theory of Locke and noted that references to the open expanses of the New World were the basis of Locke's conception of private property. This great abundance allowed the establishment of the Frontier philosophy of American capitalism. Orr and Hill, in their criticism of Ophuls, considered that this association between abundance and democracy was reminiscent of De Tocqueville, who in viewing America found that the abundant wealth of resources was a 'lucky circumstance' which allowed for stability (Orr and Hill, 1978, p. 458).

Ophuls considered Hardin's concept of the 'Tragedy of the Commons' and concluded that the only way to avoid ecological ruin was the establishment of the 'Hobbesian Solution' of a strong state. He argued that the only major difference between the political philosophies of Locke and Hobbes was that of scarcity (Ophuls, 1977, ch. 4). The return of scarcity, in the form of ecological scarcity at a level neither Locke nor De Tocqueville could have envisaged, revived Hobbes conception of political power as the means to ensure the 'safety of the people' (*ibid.*, p. 155). Essentially Ophuls agreed with Hardin's sentiment that 'Injustice is preferable to total ruin' (Hardin and Badin, 1977, p. 28):

> Better that we should choose Brave New World and try to make it as benign as possible than to continue along the path of non-politics; for this would surely earn us – quite justly – the enmity of posterity.
> (Ophuls, 1977b, p. 171)

Thus, like Heilbroner, Ophuls did not see the present democratic institutions and economic structure being able to cope with the ecological crisis.

Ophuls may be criticized on the same grounds as those utilized by Macpherson in criticizing Hobbes. Macpherson argued that Hobbes, in his attempt to discover man's true being within the 'state of nature', gave to man desires and attitudes which he had attained in civilized society:

> Hobbes' state of nature or 'natural condition of mankind' is not about 'natural' man as opposed to civilised man but is about man whose desires are specifically civilised; that the state of nature is the hypothetical condition in which men as they now are, with natures formed by living in civilised society, would necessarily find themselves if there were no common power able to overawe them all.
> (Macpherson, 1962, pp. 18–19)

These men were 'specifically' civilized in that they fit a particular model of society, which Macpherson termed the 'Possessive Market

Society'. This society had specific attributes which fulfil the require-ments of Hobbes to establish the need for a sovereign to govern 'the war of all against all' which is the nature of man's lot:

> Only in a society in which each man's capacity to labour is his own property, is alienable, and is a market commodity could all individuals be in this continual competitive power relationship.
>
> (*Ibid.*, p. 59)

This model of society was one of emergent capitalism and, like the idea of the tragedy of the commons, placed greatest emphasis upon man as a competitive rather than a socially cooperative being.

The political theory held by Ophuls and Hardin was essentially a view of the political process in America as comparable with the eco-nomic system:

> Muddling through is therefore a highly economic style of decision making, well adapted to a pragmatic, laissez-faire system of politics. Moreover it has considerable virtues. Like the market itself, dis-jointed incrementalism promotes short-term stability by minimising serious conflict over ultimate ends … (but) because decisions are made on the basis of immediate self-interest, muddling through is almost tailor-made for producing policies that will generate the tragedy of the commons.
>
> (Ophuls, 1977a, pp. 191–2)

If the economic system was creating the onrush towards an ecological catastrophe it must be abandoned in favour of planning for ecological goals and so must the political system surrounding it.

Heilbroner considered an increase in planning and market control by both government and multinationals as necessary to sustain capitalism. As the technology of production had become more complex and the need for larger capital investment developed hand in hand with this trend, so economic power became more centralized. This centralized eco-nomic and political state will find itself entering a new area of conflict, rather than the traditional capital/labour conflict, 'between capital, and the scientific-technical elite' (1977, pp. 44–50). Heilbroner, therefore, was in the same area as Daniel Bell and his conception of the nature of a Post-Industrial Society. Both writers saw a future where political decisions would be taken to control the economic direction of society, and that within this the role of the holder of expert knowledge would increase.

But there was an essential difference between the view of change in Daniel Bell and that held by the centralist ecologists. The latter considered such a development as necessary in order to change the direction of our industrialized societies in the face of increasing external threats resulting from the misuse of resources and the pollution of the planet. This was especially so for Ophuls and Hardin who considered that the need to replace 'muddling through' was a conscious act in the face of ecological crisis. Bell saw such a development as the evolutionary change emerging from the development of capitalism in society based upon the secondary, manufacturing, sector of the economy, to that of the tertiary, service sector with the 'subordination of the corporation' to the political sector (1976, chs. 2–4).

Heilbroner also foresaw the movement away from an individualistic to a communal ethic, although he held less to the idea that a liberal society would be maintained, instead there would be the establishment of a 'statist religion':

> What is crucial in the 'statist religion', as I foresee it, is the elevation of the collective and communal destiny of man to the forefront of public consciousness, and the absolute subordination of private interests to public requirements.
>
> (Heilbroner, 1977, p. 95)

The element of convergence, which seems to arise from these two different analyses, can, to a large degree, be seen to centre upon the question of the role of an expert elite developing within society. By posing both an increasingly sophisticated technology and major ecological problems, which are seen to be arriving at a specific historic juncture, these analyses placed a spotlight on the problem of a planned society and the position of the planners in relation to the rest of society. This was a situation examined by Ophuls, although his leaning towards a centralist solution led him to particular arguments.

Ophuls discussed what he termed 'Technology's Faustian Bargain' through his analysis of the writings of Alvin Weinberg, director of the Atomic Energy Commission's Laboratory at Oak Ridge, California, and the work of Saint-Simon. Studying Weinberg entailed discussion of the desirability or not of using nuclear energy, especially the problems it posed of waste. The concept of the Faustian Bargain was that, as a price for the abundant energy released by nuclear technologies we shall have to suffer the imposition of abnormally static political institutions and a 'priesthood' of technologists to maintain the reactors and dispose of the wastes. He equated this institution with the Catholic Church, thus reminding one of Heilbroner's 'statist religion'.

Similarly, Saint-Simon's proposals included the need for a scientific elite who would determine the requirements of our society and bring about the integration of society and technology. Ophuls concluded that such a society was needed because nuclear power was vulnerable to social instability and a stable system was essential (1977a, p. 158).

The result of this hard energy path was, therefore, a question of 'quis custodest ipsos custodes?' If this was so, does Ophuls propose that an ecological society would oppose such a development? By opposing the complexities of modern technological systems and the growth of nuclear societies does the ecological society propose anything different, a way out to a more democratic alternative? Ophuls basic answer was 'no'. While giving a nod in the direction of a future democratic and decentralized society, he considered the dangers which are before us as both too difficult and too near at hand for such a society to develop in the 'short-term' and proposed a very different 'transitional' society:

> Thus, whatever its level of material affluence, the steady state society will not only be more authoritarian and less democratic than the industrial societies of today – the necessity to cope with the tragedy of the commons would alone ensure that – but it will also in all likelihood be much more oligarchic as well, with only those possessing the ecological and other competencies necessary to make prudent decisions allowed full participation in the political processes.
>
> (*Ibid.*, p. 158)

So, for Ophuls the decision we are left with is rather more a choice of technique than one of political structure. The difficulties associated with both the advanced technological and the ecological solutions to the problems of scarcity, are such that a rigid, authoritarian society was the result, at least in the medium term.

A rather more moderate assessment of the situation was that put forward by Ehrlich and Pirages in 'Ark II'. They felt that the problems of economic growth and materialism were due to a dysfunction in the capitalist economy brought about by the emergence of large-scale enterprises wielding centralized economic power. Essentially, they saw the capitalist system as being correct and harked back to an age of small firms and the ideal of perfect competition as the solution. They rejected the belief held by others that it was in the nature of capitalism to expand its capital base and centralize its ownership in fewer hands.

Equally, Ehrlich and Pirages felt that the political system of the United States was basically correct but because economic power had become centralized, vested interests came to dominate the political scene. This situation needed to be challenged in order that society could change direction (Ehrlich *et al.*, 1973, p. 279).

It was this hope for change that concerned Ehrlich and Pirages in the development of ideas for reforming United States political agencies. But equally, their aim was to 'defend existing political institutions against a popular onslaught' because they considered that the possibility for reform could only come by developing an elite with an ecological awareness that could put these principles into practice. The major problem they saw was that developing ideas of participation too early would be more dangerous than even our current trend. The concept of 'power to the people' was dismissed because they foresaw the solutions required to solve ecological problems would be too difficult for the average person to accept. This was particularly the case with the redistribution of resources and the social changes that this would require (Ehrlich and Pirages, 1974, p. 133).

Ehrlich's proposals included the establishment of a planning branch of government to take on the task of supervising the future of society along ecological lines. This would be established after removing present vested interests and replacing them with a 'new oligarchy'. But this argument had within it major problems which had not been fully thought out. For if they were correct in assuming that the American political system was failing to respond to crisis, because it had been captured by vested interests and it was unlikely these could be separated from political decision-making, then the possibility of reforms occurring at the centre were remote. Added to this, if the majority of the American people are at present against the necessary changes in social structure and the distribution of resources for whatever reasons, then it was equally unlikely that candidates proposing such changes would be successful at the polls. Ehrlich and Pirages, therefore, cut off the two major avenues for reform within the political system because, while on the one hand they asserted their belief in the American system, on the other hand they condemned its present state. The feeling one is left with is that only a catastrophe of some magnitude would bring about adequate change, and lead to the installation of expertise in government, thus pointing Ehrlich and Pirages in the direction of a centralist, planned society.

This tendency towards the support of a new alternative expertise was inevitable when the assumptions which underpinned their ideas are taken into account. Orr and Hill listed four assumptions implicit to all these authors:

1. That an authoritarian state can cope with its own increased size and complexity;
2. That it can muster sufficient skill to exert control over the external environment; and
3. That these conditions can be maintained in perpetuity.

A fourth and crucial assumption (was) that we have no practical choice.
(Orr and Hill, 1978, p. 461)

One may add to this a further assumption, that such an oligarchy would be well-intentioned (Stillman, 1974, pp. 53–8).

The questions of size and complexity were central to the ideas surrounding demands for increased authority by centralized expert government. But the criticism was whether such an elite would be able to cope with this increase in power. Heilbroner believed it would be problematical, though in the short term he felt that the structures in the socialist systems of the time, reacting slowly to the challenge initially, may have been more able to confront it (Heilbroner, 1975, ch. 3). To some extent the feeling was that, with large-scale ecological problems to cope with, only large-scale institutions could act successfully. The role of government in planning the economy had increased in scale along with these problems and therefore, at the very least transitionally, the future would be dealt with in a similar manner.

## Decentralism or 'ecological democracy'

The decentralist argument must, therefore, begin at this point. For its proponents among the major problems in the crisis was the size and complexity of industrial society, of the ecological damage caused and of the institutions that created it or have been established to cope with it. For this reason one of the most influential works was 'Small is Beautiful' by E.F. Schumacher. Schumacher considered that technology and economic growth were dissociated from the needs of humanity and that the original roles of technology and economic growth as means to a humanistic end had been lost and had become ends in themselves:

> Ever bigger machines, entailing ever bigger concentrations of economic power and exerting ever greater violence against the environment do not represent progress; they are a denial of wisdom.
> (Schumacher, 1974, p. 27)

For Schumacher, the problem of the place of the individual within the ecological system and how this affected his/her quality of life was of great importance.

'A Blueprint for Survival' was much more explicit in defining the way in which a change towards a decentralized system could be established and how this would affect ecological sustainability. However, the process that was to be adopted contained within it some limited authoritarian elements. Essentially the reforms promoted by Goldsmith and his team were a combination of political and personal change. Firstly, restraint in personal consumption enforced by legislation and the police as well as personal transformation. Secondly, a small scale community allowing the integration of employment and beauty. Third, decentralized communities that would be invigorating places to live in as well as more ecologically sound, and finally, their small scale would greatly reduce environmental impact (Goldsmith *et al.*, 1972, pp. 50–3).

Within these arguments there was an attempt to answer those criticisms aimed at the technological determinism of the supporters of alternative technologies such as Lovins. If we agree with Dickson's argument a political transformation was an essential supplement to the introduction of alternative technologies (1974, p. 99). The problem to be confronted was the method by which the transition from the present system to a decentralized society should be carried out. Returning to the centralists' arguments, their position was based upon an analysis of present trends and attempting to guide such centralizing tendencies inherent in present society towards a system more favourable to maintaining the ecological balance. The desire of the decentralists was to work more immediately towards a decentralized system, considering the problems of size and centralist control to be a major element within the crisis. This meant that the structure of policy-making was being questioned just as readily as the policies pursued. The argument of the centralists essentially recommended the maintenance of expertise as the deciding factor in the access to political power. Decentralists questioned the role of experts and their relationship to other members of society and proposed that they be subjected to democratic control.

The social-ecology of Bookchin contended that our present society had developed adequate technologies for the development of a just and equal society in which a 'face-to-face democracy' could emerge and ensure that technology was flexibly applied to the needs of that society (1974, p. 106). Bookchin also considered that technological achievements would result in a world of abundance:

> All but hidden from society, the machines would work for man. Free communities would stand at the end of the cybernated assembly line with baskets to cart the goods home.
>
> *(Ibid.,* p. 133)

This would place him in the camp of the technological optimists but for a number of factors, basically his belief that the problems of scarcity have political causes allied to the nature of capitalism, which demands 'production for productions sake'. He considered ecological damage to be the result of inappropriately applied technologies, and a major part of his response was concerned with re-establishing humanity's consciousness of its dependence upon nature and the need to manufacture socially desirable goods. The problem of complexity associated with industrialized society was solvable because it was founded upon a false analysis:

> Modern society is incredibly complex, complex even beyond human comprehension, if we grant its premises – property, 'production for the sake of production', competition, capital accumulation, exploitation, finance, centralization, coercion, bureaucracy and the domination of man by man.
>
> *(Ibid.,* p. 136)

The solutions to these problems lay in a popular, anarchistic, revolution in which power would lie with 'the armed people in permanent assembly' *(ibid.,* p. 169).

This position was almost diametrically opposed to that of Ophuls and Heilbroner both in its political solutions and in the premises it based itself upon over matters of technology and scarcity. Also it was at the extreme end of the decentralist position, but its importance lay in the way ecology was approached from a revolutionary angle. It raised the question of whether expertise and complexity within industrial society was the result of the nature of a hierarchical system, both within corporations and governments rather than determined by technology.

Another equally radical conceptualization of the problems facing modern society was that developed by Ivan Illich. Illich was less strictly an ecologist and more a radical critic of industrial society who saw

ecological breakdown as a symptom of a greater malaise. But his criticisms of the professionalization of society and the related problems of
size are important, both as questions to be answered by the centralists
and a reminder to the supporters of appropriate technology of the
need for structural change.

Illich questioned the idea of enhancing the role of an ecological elite
as well as the development of present trends into what he termed
'managerial fascism'. He perceived that the development of an 'anti-
growth elite' would merely be the pawns of the 'growth-optimizing
bureaucrats' who would remove our society even further from the possibility of attaining to his concept of a 'convivial society' (1973,
pp. 122–3). This notion of a convivial society was one in which technology served 'interrelated individuals rather than managers' and
therefore limited the use of technology (*ibid.*, p. 12). A convivial society is a communal society in which technology is limited in order that
it may serve humanity's needs and be under the control of all members
of the society. In moving towards this form of society Illich believed
that we would experience a future of developing crisis, and that only
through this crisis that the true power structure could be exposed and
undermined. However, he did acknowledge that the society emerging
out of this crisis could be authoritarian as much as it could be democratic (*ibid.*, pp. 124–5).

Both Illich and Bookchin foresaw a period of revolutionary violence,
and it can be inferred from Dickson that he, too, failed to see any real
possibility of a reformist trend succeeding. In criticising Schumacher's
approach Dickson stated that, the assumption was that humanity would
rediscover its 'innate common sense' and live an ecologically sound
existence, ignoring the reality of political power (Dickson, 1974, p. 200).

One criticism of the debate on the move towards a decentralized society was by Allaby who contended that much of the debate about
'utopian' communities had been carried on between anarchist and
Marxists of a previous generation (Allaby, 1977, pp. 34–8). Allaby argued
that the concept of political oraganization along decentralist lines was
becoming clearer because they were increasingly perceived to be practical and desirable by activists in areas of politics which may not have as
their original aim an ecological society (*ibid.*, p. 244).

The concept of participatory democracy was one which was at the
heart of the decentralist thesis and was antagonistic to 'expert' government. The belief was that the individual was the best judge of his/her
needs and that a community should be responsive on a day-to-day
basis, which required small-scale communities. But although Allaby

saw forces acting within the political spectrum along-side the ecological movement promoting such concepts, the problem was how these trends would meet the challenge of those installed in advantageous positions within the established system?

Robertson contended that, on the one hand people would aim to liberate themselves from their dependence on such things as governmental institutions and people in the public sector would aim to help individuals in this task:

> Increasingly they will aim to enable people … to develop their own autonomy. In thus helping others to liberate themselves, they will *decolonise* the institutionalised economy.
>
> (Robertson, 1978, p. 56)

This was an extremely optimistic conception of the future when humanity will come to realize its 'innate common sense' all will be well. Although Robertson did acknowledge the role that would be played by 'reactionary', 'cynical' and 'routine practitioners' he was in the end confident that both through propaganda and example, a predominantly 'Sane, Humane, Ecological' (SHE) future would emerge (Robertson, 1978, ch. 1).

Ronald Higgins was equally voluntaristic, but his conclusions were pessimistic (1980, pp. 22–4). He expressed doubts about the ability of democratic institutions to cope with ecological problems, particularly because of the 'paradox' of democracy which 'calls for popular action, not the right one' (Higgins, 1980, p. 162). Because of this, political institutions, both in democracies and totalitarian states, suffer from what he termed the 'Seventh Enemy', political inertia. This enemy included a moral blindness, which essentially entailed the projection of our unconscious evils on to others (*ibid.*, p. 181). The problem of political inertia was, for Higgins, to be countered by the actions of individuals in concert and by establishing pressure groups and self-help groups to counter the forces working against the ecological structure of society and the needs of the individual:

> The movements for worker and consumer participation and for self-help in fields like housing, education and health embody the convictions that we all have the capacity to make more of our own decisions.
>
> (*Ibid.*, p. 218)

As with Robertson, therefore, Higgins relied on the changes effected within the individual consciousness, a 'reawakening of the religious', but against a background of a disintegrating world picture. By acknowledging, perhaps more realistically than Robertson, the problems presented by power and the institutional supports for the maintenance of a centralized and unequal system, Higgins saw only a vague chance of success and it would be brought about by the collapse of the present system. This desire by Higgins and Robertson, and also Schumacher, for a new consciousness was not uncommon. But, as Kraft (1977, p. 189) pointed out, while the new consciousness was developing more traditional political action was required to develop ecologically sound policies.

As part of this process Bobrow saw the need to effect 'continuing changes in the distribution of money, power and information across persons, classes and institutions' (Bobrow, 1977, p. 200). Within a reformist model, the only manner in which an ecological society could be popularly sustained would be through 'substantial steps to equalize the standard of living in terms of which persons are expected to be moderate and restrained in their mutual appetites (*ibid.*, p. 204).

Obviously this would make appeals to established elites difficult, and while those in favour of a centralized system would be tempted to quote this in favour of their arguments, Bobrow added the rider that the economic and resource requirements of their coercive methods would be intolerable. We are left with the alternative of 'coordinated action on a global basis resting on increased recognition of the set of realities which impinge on the successful pursuit' (*ibid.*, p. 216) of an ecologically desirable future, a policy which both Higgins and Robertson would appear to agree with. But it was a policy which posed the obvious question of who was to coordinate the global action demanded, as well as the problems associated with participatory democracy and the method of transition to such a system.

Cook and Morgan contended that proponents of such systems have to confront, in these smaller societies, the same problems and dangers confronting mass-society. They ask whether or not 'participatory democracy could very easily degenerate into some sort of plebiscitory democracy, in which popular participation is only a matter of acclamation politics – the enthusiastic ratification of elite decisions by the popular assembly, (Cook and Morgan, 1971, p. 32). The concept of participatory democracy released people from accepting the definition of efficiency in purely economic terms and made possible the consideration of other goals and values. Thus the Elliotts saw the question of participatory democracy centering not just on the problem of organization but also on the conception of the 'quality of life' and how we define it.

Until now the issue of a centralist or decentralist system has been examined on the grounds of the means by which industrial societies can respond to the perceived crisis and the manner in which the technology which is a part of that crisis is to be controlled. Further to this a question must be asked as to whether ecology as a science gives any clue to a decision one way or another. Odum's scientific ecology was significant in the way it attempted to give some emphasis to the idea of seeing humanity as an element in an ecological system. However, sociological data was linked to political units rather than natural ecosystems and Odum suggested that social structures based around natural watersheds would be preferable (Odum, 1971, p. 512).

The idea of a watershed is that of a system within which a natural self-regulating ecology can exist. Sam Love took this position to its logical conclusion and suggested the division of the United States along purely geographical and biological lines which he termed 'bio-regional' and contended that the Indian boundaries were very close to this, so that:

> Perhaps the White Man's lines on the continent of North America will turn out to have been a mere historical aberration lasting only a few short centuries.
>
> (Love, 1977, pp. 318–9)

But this was limited in its effectiveness, for as we have seen, the feeling of crisis led to an authoritarian conclusion at times and the possibility of analysing ecology to reach such different conclusions was possible. Speaking about the analysis of social systems from the point of view of an organic structure the Elliotts noted that the use of an organic metaphor could equally lead to a centralized, hierarchical system as to a decentralized society (Elliott and Elliott, 1976, p. 208). An example was Goldsmith who argued for the establishment of an authoritarian neo-feudal system in which a 'natural' hierarchy was established within a decentralized system:

> Undifferentiated individuals competing for the same ecological niche cannot cooperate in any way…Competition is a means whereby a hierarchy is set up. In the right conditions…the competing individuals eventually arrange themselves so as to constitute a hierarchy and learn to accept their respective positions within this hierarchy.
>
> (Goldsmith, 1974, pp. 124–35)

Stephen Cotgrove commented that Goldsmith's view suggested that 'aggression, hierarchy and ritual are all natural and therefore good' (Cotgrove, 1976, p. 28). The difficulty with Goldsmith's conception was that by accepting such competitiveness as natural to man and ruling out co-operation, he perpetuated not just competition and aggression but the continued spiral of acquisition. It is difficult to see how these factors can be adequately controlled within the decentralized system he proposed given that he attempted to make these elements in humanity ritualized virtues of that system.

## A victory for democracy?

From the above it can be seen that while the ideal proposed by early ecological writers was a decentralized system based upon communities and technologies less damaging to the environment, the problem of the transition to such a society was open to wide variations in approach. While it may be true to say, as Goodin does, that decentralization has become a defining characteristic of green political thought, this has not been arrived at without continued debate. There are still strong authoritarian elements contained within the moral imperatives argued by some green activists, so much so that the denigrating term of 'eco-fascists' has been utilized by their opponents. Consequently, there are still debates as to whether ecological ends are compatible with democratic means. Saward has stated that,

> democracy should be understood as responsive rule…If governments, to be democratic must respond to the felt wishes of a majority of citizens, then greens have little comeback if a majority does not want green outcomes.
>
> (1996, p. 93)

However, he went on to argue that for democracy to persist then the conditions which ensure its survival must exist. These might include the appropriate environmental conditions which may take precedence over the wishes of a majority at any one particular time. Consequently, Saward argued that ecologists much recognize that they are watering down democracy in favour of the greater demands of the environment. For Saward democracy is one particular social value and 'there are other reasonable values people will promote, values which may clash with democracy in theory and in practice' (*ibid.*, p. 94).

The existence of an argument in favour of a more centralist, authoritarian strand still frequently harks back to the Hobbesian state discussed by Ophuls. The quality of Ophuls analysis still places this as a benchmark for critiques of the centralist solution. De Geus (1996) presented the argument of supporters of the centralist state as comprising four main parts:

1. The environmental consequences of individualism as exhibited in the 'tragedy of the commons' requires a collectivist state solution;
2. Industry and trade are powerful actors in modern society and only a powerful state could counter their influence;
3. The state is needed to enact rules and laws which support companies that move towards more environmentally sound activity when under normal market conditions such a move would disadvantage them in respect of their competitors;
4. The state can act as an impartial judge concerning polluting activities and is central to the development of expertise to make such judgments.

For de Geus, however, Ophuls' argument was flawed on each count as he overlooked a number of important issues. Firstly, de Geus stated that the assumption that the individual was the main polluter was a misplaced target. The much greater responsibility of industrial companies and governments would mean that environmental regulations affecting these major polluters could be enacted without the infringement of individual rights and that this could receive the approval of a majority. Secondly, for de Geus constraints on individual choice in the use of certain goods was not a constraint on their freedom. Rather he defined freedom as the ability to participate in the political process as a 'positive' freedom and to have legal constraints placed upon the state limiting its ability to infringe individual privacy as a 'negative' freedom. Finally, de Geus accused Ophuls of equating a strong state with an absolutist state. This, he argued, was a misconception as an absolutist state acts on behalf of a limited and powerful group 'unconstrained by constitutional conventions' while a strong state can be conceived as acting on behalf of the whole society, enacting environmental regulations (1996, pp. 193–4).

Equally, for Mills (1996) the problems facing Ophuls and Hardin were centered on a Hobbesian view of human nature whereby without a strong state there would exist a 'war of all against all'. In addition, their analysis of political and state systems was ends-centered, concentrating as it did on the need to escape the doom-laden predictions of 1970s ecological thought. Mills, however, argued that the dangers encapsulated in such an absolutist state were much greater than those involved in the adjustment of democracy to the need to tackle environmental problems. Indeed, he stated that the argument in favour of increased authoritarianism can be turned against itself:

> The greater the problem, the more severe the risk, the more pressing the imperative, the more necessary it becomes that democracy becomes extended, entrenched, and practiced.
>
> (*Ibid.*, p. 98)

Mills argued that the more severe the problems then the more difficult it would be for an authoritarian group to manage, based as it would be on limited information and having to coerce the public. Consequently the political system adopted should be more process-orientated allowing for greater participation and flexibility.

Also of importance in the development of the environmental case was the role of rationalism and scientific knowledge. The critique of man's relationship with nature was associated by some environmentalists as emerging from a dominant science-based view of the world. As noted above, one view of the ecological crisis centered on the need for a new priesthood in which scientists would dominate the decision-making process to enable humanity to escape the problem.

However, these contrasting views of the role of science and scientists created problems for the development of political ecology with more authoritarian solutions being associated with the continued pre-eminence of a scientific or positivist analysis of the environment and the natural world. In contrast, the anti-rationalist arguments of writers such as Theodore Rozak were associated with the counter-culture and anarchistic trends within the movement, which rejected science based knowledge in favour of a more spiritual relationship with nature.

O'Neill has more recently argued for a middle way in which he contended that a rational scepticism in respect of claims made by scientists should not lead to a more dangerous general rejection of scientific knowledge (1993, p. 123). For O'Neill there was a basic problem in modern society arising out of the distribution and division of knowledge. Such a distribution of knowledge meant that individuals had to rely on the authority of others, who may have detailed knowledge of a particular area of expertise, including scientific ecology. As a result, each individual cannot rely on her own rational appraisal of that information but has to trust the judgement of others. However, he argued that while 'science is both a necessary and reliable condition for rational environmental policy. It is not however, sufficient' (*ibid.*, p. 147). It is this issue which provided a link between the various problems under consideration, for as O'Neill has noted members of the ecology movement often exhibit signs of conflict in their approach to science. On the one hand they are sceptical to the point of dismissiveness of traditional science while at times naive in their approach to 'new age' philosophies and so-called 'pseudo-sciences'.

For O'Neill there were two reasons for this apparent contradiction. The first was a belief that classical science 'separates' or 'alienates' us from nature, and that we need to overcome that separation to have proper concern for the natural world. The second was the belief that science was part of the ideology of industrial society (1993, p. 149). As a consequence the role of scientific knowledge and the implementation of technology needed to be controlled by democratic means. The role of 'discursive democracy' had a place here where scientific knowledge and decisions surrounding the application of new technologies are subjected to open democratic debate. In this way, it was contended, science will serve the needs of an ecologically sound society by rejecting instrumentalism and supporting open debate about the utilization of scientific knowledge. This would allow for collective decision making which would overcome the authoritarian nature of existing approaches to scientific debate and the associated administrative rationality of modern industrial society (Dryzek, 1997, pp. 84–101). John Barry supported such an arrangement as a way to control the self-interest of private decision making with an approach that would emphasize issues of the public good. If participants were debating problems within their communities they are more likely to subsume their self-interest under the peer group pressure of open debate (Barry, J., 1999, p. 217). However, Dobson raised the issue that Dryzek's original conception emphasized the importance of process as against ends which would present radical greens with the problem of subsuming their aims to the will of the majority where that majority may support ends which were less ecologically sound (Dobson, 1995, p. 135).

O'Neill (1993) appeared to favour a more traditional representative system where the older political institutions and forms of decision making are reinvigorated by new social movements and in turn defend these new movements from both the state and the market. What he rejected was the possibility of these new social movements redefining political culture. He argued that they were too weak as a social and political force and that their role was more evident in the way they have reshaped the mainstream political discourse.

This was reinforced by Goodin (1992) who argued in great detail the problems faced by ecologists in integrating the related concerns of decentralized political systems and the environmental theory of value. Goodin argued that the distinctive political system associated with the ecology movement was decentralization. However, he also noted that given the global nature of the environmental crisis there was a need to coordinate the activity of decentralized structures. Goodin noted the centrality of the green prescription to 'think globally, act locally' which had become increasingly important as environmental issues which go beyond state or local boundaries have taken centre stage, notably global warming and ozone depletion. According to Goodin the development of such global issues created the most significant problems for the ecology movement in trying to develop new political approaches to provide solutions. The phrase 'think globally, act locally' is therefore problematic in that the greens have yet to adequately develop some way to coordinate the decentralized systems they would like to see introduced. For Goodin the problem was linked to the classic 'prisoners dilemma' in which the outcome inevitably leads to a more authoritarian solution than radical greens would wish to see.

Goodin transferred the prisoners dilemma into a polluter's dilemma in which all would like to minimize costs and this would result in everyone polluting the environment. However, as a result of this behaviour everyone would be worse off than if everyone did not pollute and so each would be willing to accept some regulatory system to ensure that all would cooperate in reducing pollution:

> But since it would be in the narrow interest of each to defect from this regime if it could these regulations require enforcement. This enforcement might in principle come in any of a variety of forms; most commonly though, it must come in the form of sanctions imposed by some superior legal authority.
>
> (1992, pp. 158–9)

The polluter/prisoners dilemma was a strong reworking of the basic problem identified by Hardin as the Tragedy of the Commons, or in Goodin's terms, a beggar my neighbour approach. The basic prisoner's dilemma was at the heart of the difficulty of reconciling local, decentralized groups with the need to coordinate their activities to resolve global problems. Goodin proposed an Assurance Model of society in which all genuinely wish to act in an ecologically sound manner, but each actor cannot be certain that the other players do indeed think this way. In this model everyone may wish to behave environmentally but they do not wish 'to be played for a sucker'. There was therefore, the need for a superior authority to give each actor the assurance that everyone will behave in accordance with environmental principals:

> So long as that superior authority can threaten sufficiently severe sanctions against noncooperative behaviour, everyone will be thereby assured of others cooperative behaviour.
>
> (1992, p. 163)

For Goodin, therefore, there was this significant problem for the ecology movement that while decentralized political structures are at the heart of their present thinking and action, the global nature of the ecological threat presented them with the problem of coordination and cooperation between these structures.

At the local level such coordination may present limited difficulties, at the international level such difficulties are qualitatively different. For Goodin the most significant problem was the way greens arrive at a conception of decentralization and democracy as the agency for the delivery of a green theory of value:

> To advocate democracy is to advocate procedures, to advocate environmentalism is to advocate substantive outcomes: what guarantee can we have that the former procedures will yield the latter sorts of outcomes?
>
> (*Ibid.*, p. 168)

Consequently, while the basic assumptions about the processes involved in the end product of an ecologically sound society are largely agreed upon the period of transition and the method by which we arrive at that situation are still as far away as possible. For if we consider the list of opposing forces and the green agenda proposed by ecologists then the route to that society is a very long road indeed:

> What links together the various aspects of radical green political theory – decentralization, participatory democracy, egalitarianism, alternative technology, pacifism and internationalism – is the need to inhibit the environmentally hazardous dynamic that we are presently imprisoned within. Hence, the various elements of radical green political thought consists in the systematic negation of every element of this dynamic.
>
> (Carter, 1993, p. 53)

The range of political, commercial and individual interests ranged against such an agenda makes one pessimistic about the achievement of their aims within the context of a decentralist and participatory approach to oraganization and action.

While we may accept that a green society would be decentralized and convivial the problems associated with achieving this state are rarely considered by most authors outside of the need for local non-violent action to oppose the forces arranged against them. Even de Geus who has designed a series of principles for Ecological Restructuring does not take on board the consequences of direct opposition to such arrangements from existing interests (1996, ch. 10). While his proposals contain within them a range of limited forms of restructuring, with the idea that further reforms will emerge as society moves towards sustainability, most of his ideas would inevitably result in the need to confront specific interests in existing societies.

David Pepper (1993) identified the problems faced by eco-anarchists such as Bookchin in trying to elevate the role of small, decentralized social groups and rejecting the role of organized labour and the role of the state as a coordinating body. However, he also noted that the attempt to develop some form of detailed blueprint for the reform of society towards an ecologically sound society was 'on a hiding to nothing'. Critics can too easily find fault either with the route proposed, which was perhaps inevitably naive, or with the failure to confront the problem of transition. As a socialist Pepper argued for support for those actions by ecologists and others that emphasized the collective power amongst people as producers, involving members of the local community, with the emphasis being placed on economic issues (1993, p. 235).

However, Eckersley criticized eco-socialist thought on the basis that it still failed to reconcile the problem of breaking down the concentrated power of large corporations as one way of reducing opposition to an ecological society and also arguing for an increased planning role for the state:

> Eco-socialists have yet to resolve the tension between their quest for self-management and participatory democracy and their reliance on centralized institutions to carry out far-reaching economic and social reforms.
>
> (1992, p. 184)

Essentially, for Eckersley, the core stumbling block for eco-socialists was that they still operate within an anthropocentric worldview. For her there was the need to develop a political philosophy and structure which was truly eco-centric.

As a result, Eckersley rejected eco-socialist approaches as they inevitably resulted in the development of a highly contested arena surrounding a central plan. While the advantage of this approach may be that the purpose of the plan and its goals were highly visible the potential for a long-term agreement on these objectives was remote. Eckersley argued for the advantages of a highly regulated market system in which the 'impersonal, self-adjusting price signals of the market' provide a much more decentralized and depoliticized system of information flow and resource allocation than does any form of planned economy, no matter how ecologically sound (*ibid.*, pp. 138–9). The advantages of such a system were reinforced by the time factor involved in the transition to an effectively structured planned economy. Both the nature of the ecological crisis and the scepticism of the public and decision-makers towards planning as a result of post-war failures appeared to work against any such development (*ibid.*, pp. 139–40). The role for a market economy within a reformed system of pluralistic democracy was further reinforced by her discussion of eco-anarchism.

In this debate, Eckersley argued that eco-anarchism was over reliant on an optimistic conception of the cooperative nature of humanity and the apparently automatic identification of decentralization with ecological soundness. For Eckersley neither of these contentions was proved by the eco-anarchists such as Bookchin and Roszak. She argued that a multi-tiered democratic system of decision-making was more likely to be effective than a wholly decentralized non-state system:

> a democratically accountable nation State is much better placed than a large number of autonomous local governments when it comes to providing ecodiplomacy, interregional and international redistributive justice, and the protection of uniform human rights and freedoms via the rule of law. It is also more compatible with an ecocentric worldview than the simple web-like, horizontal structure of eco-anarchism, insofar as it recognizes the layered interrelationships between parts (social and ecological) of larger wholes.
>
> (*Ibid.*, p. 178)

Consequently, the view proposed by Goodin that decentralization was the defining feature of modern ecological thought on political structures was still open to interpretation. While the original authoritarian approach as a way of resolving an urgent environmental crisis has been largely superseded, the problems involved in both defining the content of an ecological society, and how that can be arrived at, still results in important debates about the role of the state. This sense of almost a wish-list arises from an attempt to put onto a future society the social cooperation exhibited by participants in some protest movements. However, such cooperation does not exclude the use of well-disciplined activists directing the work of volunteers.

The problems arising from the spiritual and essentialist nature of much deep ecological thought may also present a stumbling block for the establishment of a democratic society. John Barry has warned of the consequences of the religious nature of much deep green thought:

> While not wishing to claim that the views of deep ecology are inherently anti-democratic, there is a potential tension between its spiritual/metaphysical view of the ecological crisis and its commitment to democratic forms of decision-making.
>
> (1999, p. 201)

He contended that if the crisis was religious or metaphysical then the search for a solution was associated with questions of faith or belief in a 'true' solution whereas democratic debate was associated with the existence of a range of different value positions. B.P. Taylor (1996) who noted the idealist nature of much ecological thought also identified this problem. Essentially, a great deal of such writing tended towards the belief that a move towards an environmentally sound society was centered on a change in peoples attitudes and behaviour, where people will 'experience' an affinity with nature which will transform their modes of action.

Such a change was built on an altered sense of the self where we will identify our freedom through an appreciation of our relationship to each other and the rest of nature within an ecological system:

> Environmentalism is no longer a threat to human liberty or democracy. Rather it represents liberty's or democracy's completion.
>
> (1996, p. 92)

However, Taylor goes on to contend that such arguments are weak and have 'profoundly undemocratic overtones'. He centred his criticism around four main points of attack. First, he questioned whether the ideological change towards an environmentalist or even an eco/biocentric ethic would necessarily change peoples' behaviour and points to how Buddhist societies do not reveal any less destructive trends. A similar question arises in the case of Japan as a society where the Shinto religion is intensely animistic and yet is highly industrialized and modernist in its actions.

Secondly, Taylor raised the question of the extent to which such writers and activists are really convinced by their own arguments concerning an ecocentric approach to the planet. Too quickly they revert to propositions which assert that a move to an ecologically sound society will benefit humanity and, indeed, where the result is a reduction in material living standards, we are assured that 'this will actually make our lives happier, healthier and saner' (*ibid.*, p. 93). He contends that this may be so for some, but for the old and the poor such sacrifices may well be painful and ecologists need to be clear about this.

Thirdly, the belief by ecocentrics that ecological integrity provides the ultimate value upon which a moral imperative should be based was problematic. He gave the example of Westra for whom such an ultimate value must be considered before 'any other values or choices are considered' (quoted by Taylor, p. 94). This means, according to Taylor, a significant inhibition on all human activity as, by implication, any human action interferes with the healthy working of the rest of nature. While Westra's reasoning appeared to water down a strict interpretation of this imperative it still created a problem for the implementation of such a strict environmental ethic.

Taylor argued that the idealism associated with such an approach created problems for democratic societies. In considering Naess and Eckersley he contended that they both held the belief that democracy was only safe in the hands of those societies that were already converted to the belief in an environmental ethic (Eckersley, 1992, p. 173). For Taylor such questioning of democratic principles, where they potentially conflict with a new environmental ethic was:

> neither surprising nor incompatible with the views held by many biocentric theorists. By demanding a new philosophical world view as the precondition for principled, reasonable environmental policy, biocentric ethics wed itself to the process of a new 'philosophical founding': Westra writes, 'we are not "agreeing" to what might be right morally, but rather articulating what is already morally right, objectively'.
>
> (Taylor, 1996, p. 98)

It is to the problem associated with the attempt to establish an objective conception of value and a consequent objective, moral, ecological ethic to which we turn in the next chapters. However, what is argued here, in agreement with Taylor, is that the effort to redefine democracy in terms compatible with the primacy of ecocentrism is a doubtful project, which while potentially undermining democracy does not guarantee ecologically sound behaviour.

# 3
# Humanity and Nature: The Problem of Alienation

A basic question posed by the ecological crisis was, how did we get into this situation in the first place? Green theorists have seen humanity's relationship to nature and, in particular, the condition of alienation as central to the problems facing the whole of nature. Alienation has a long history which Meszaros traced (1970, p. 28) back to the Judeo-Christian conception of being alienated from God (or having 'fallen from Grace'). His study of Marx's theory of alienation centred on the discovery and study of Marx's early manuscripts of 1844. Dickens (1996, p. 56) also discussed Marx's theory contending that this was if anything an 'over-tight' conceptualeization while present day usage was now rather loose.

## Marx and alienation

Meszaros considered there to be four main aspects within the Marxian conception of alienation:

(a) man is alienated from *nature*;
(b) he is alienated from *himself* (from his own *activity*);
(c) from his *'Species-being'* (from his being as a member of the human species);
(d) man is alienated from *man* (from other men).

(1970, p. 14)

It may be argued that these four aspects were central to the ecological discussion of humanity's relationship with nature. By confronting the issue of alienation, Marxism and ecology can discover some appreciation of each other's position. However, there was a perceived limitation of Marx's perspective, which Mumford described:

> Karl Marx [was] in error in giving the material instruments of production the central place and directive function in human development.
>
> (Mumford, 1967, p. 4)

Mumford argued that Marx did not appreciate the full nature of humanity, a nature which cannot be considered solely from one aspect of his relationship with his/her environment, that of labour. Meszaros clearly brought out the pre-eminent position of labour in Marx:

> The converging point of the heterogeneous aspects of alienation is the notion of 'labour' (Arbeit). In the 'Manuscripts of 1844' Labour is considered both in general – as 'productive activity', the fundamental ontological determination of 'humanness' (*'menscliches* Dasian', i.e. really *human* mode of existence) – and in particular, as having the form of capitalistic 'division of labour'. It is in this latter form – capitalistically structured activity – that 'Labour' is the ground of all alienation.
>
> (Meszaros, 1970, p. 78)

For Marx, nature was without value until acted upon, and therefore he was at odds with the radical ecologists on this point. For many ecologists nature was seen as a value in itself, beyond mere utility, but in Marx 'labour' was the central human activity which 'mediates' between an individual and the world, both as s/he acts upon it and, in turn, as it acts upon the individual:

> Productive activity is hence the source of consciousness and 'alienated consciousness' is the reflection of alienated activity or of the alienation of activity, i.e. of labours self-alienation.
>
> (*Ibid.*, p. 81)

Further to this, the idea that man objectifies himself in the alienated labour process resulted in the conception of his values in material forms, as objects. Meszaros returned to earlier writers, notably Kant, to explore the foundation of this aspect of alienation, that of 'reification' (*ibid.*, p. 35).

It was for Marx particularly in this area of human relations that the problems of alienation and reification were most evident. In selling his labour to another, man alienated himself from his labour and confronted its products as objects, as commodities. This disguised the true nature of the social relations which take place within our society and these 'appear as relations between material objects', particularly when mediated through the 'finished form of the world of commodities – the money form' (Marx, 1976, pp. 168–9):

> the *divine* power of money lies in its *nature* as the estranged and alienating *species – essence* of man which alienates itself by selling itself.
>
> (Marx, 1975, p. 377)

So the properties of things are judged by the monetary value we place upon them rather than any inherent value. Nature has no inherent value in itself and people are even insensitive to its beauty (Dickens, 1996, p. 58).

These ideas helped to influence the development of the New Left of the 1960s, especially as they were interpreted by contemporary thinkers, particularly Marcuse, who attempted to integrate the ideas of Marx and Freud. For Marcuse this resulted in his concept of 'one-dimensionality' which was the limiting of the individuals ways of thinking and acting by the development of the consumer society. If, for Marx, capitalist society was to create the productive powers which were going to open the way for the new society, then Marcuse contended that capitalism, in order to survive, developed 'needs' in people which it fulfilled in order to tie individuals to their society and to give them a stake in it (1968, p. 22). Alienation was, therefore, seen to be pervasive and it was also perceived in the sexual sphere where Fromm noted that society had fought harder to suppress the expression of such desires more than any others. In this way Fromm saw the impulse to break sexual taboos as being an expression of an urge to rebel (1979, p. 85). Marcuse related how such rebellion against sexual taboos expressed itself in art as a form of sexual sublimation, that is, the sexual desires which were repressed by society were turned away from concrete expression and resulted in works of art which gave vent to desires and resulted in the development of an alternative mode of thought, a negation. But within modern society such works have become absorbed into the consumerist culture. Further, modern art itself has also become a commodity, but one within which sexuality is fully expressed in its '*de*sublimated' form and therefore essentially harmless

(Marcuse, 1968, p. 73). In this manner we have the 'negation of the negation', elements of rebellion are absorbed into the dominant culture.

For Fromm this tendency expressed itself in a change from what he termed the 'being mode' to the 'having mode' of existence. In this, humanity was seen to express itself through possessions, and once again we see people considering values as material objects rather than as active elements in a persons life. The possession of things was seen as a way of perpetuating one's existence and Fromm explored this further by an examination of the Freudian idea of the *anal character*, a childhood phase which can be carried over into adulthood as a neurotic symptom (1979, p. 88).

Bringing together the sociological and psychological aspects of man resulted in a more complete view of alienation, a view in which materialism, in the sense of possessiveness and hoarding, was seen as a neurotic element of arrested human development (Fromm, 1963). Therefore, the belief was that there is such a thing as 'human nature', a nature around which technology and science must be worked rather than humanity being moulded to fit in with those techniques.

Through this analysis, the idea that humans within a capitalist industrialized society are alienated from their true nature means that if humans reproduce themselves through the act of labour, transforming nature as a reflection of an alienated nature, a false image was created. Fromm stated that in the having-mode happiness is found 'in one's superiority over others, in one's power and in the last analysis, in one's capacity to conquer, rob, kill' (Fromm, 1979, p. 86). It was in this sense that Bookchin stated that,

> The notion that man must dominate nature emerges directly from the domination of man by man…Just as men are converted into commodities, so every aspect of nature is converted into a commodity, a resource to be manufactured and mechanised wantonly.
>
> (Bookchin, 1974, p. 63)

From a similar perspective Marcuse also noted a 'concrete link between the liberation of man and that of nature' (1972, p. 61). In addition, he argued that in a newly liberated society a new science might emerge which would be based on a holistic rather than a reductionist view of nature (Eckersley, 1992, p. 105). Bookchin, for example, stated that in order for the necessary balance and harmony to exist between humanity and nature, which was the demand made of us by ecology, we must realise our dependence upon 'the sovereignty of nature' (1974, pp. 57–9).

## Alienation and ecology

There are a number of threads running through the above, but one is the idea of a human nature from which we are alienated, an alienation reflected in our treatment of the environment and which resulted from the conception of both humanity and nature as commodities which is emphasized by capitalist social relations. This view, that humanity is alienated *from* something, was noted by Meszaros:

> 'Alienation' is an eminently historical concept. If man is 'alienated' he must be alienated *from* something, as a result of certain *causes* ... which manifest themselves in a *historical* framework.
>
> (Meszaros, 1970, p. 36)

Within the writings of the ecologists this led to two areas of thought, firstly that history is a continuing process where we can look into our past and search for that image of ourselves from which we believe we are now alienated. Secondly, we can investigate trends which existed in the past and the present and project them forward.

The search into the past to rediscover our true nature and the attempt to project a future in which we shall recapture this 'golden age' led to approaches such as Goldsmith's neo-feudalism. This contained the belief in the need for a new religious awareness which will act as a cohesive force, as did Heilbroner, although his religious base is 'statist' and 'nationalist' in order to breed a collectivist ethic (1977, pp. 94–6).

A less authoritarian position was held by authors such as Theodore Roszak and Henryk Skolimowski. The problem according to Skolimowski was

> one sided, one should even want to say, a crippled cosmology, in which science is one thing, the process of evolution another, and values yet another.
>
> (1976, pp. 13–14)

Roszak also considered that this was the root cause of, what he has termed, the 'failed experiment' of industrialism. For him the problems of the environment are,

> the outward mirror of our inner condition, for many the first discernible symptom of advanced disease within.
>
> (Roszak, 1974, p. xxiii)

Indeed even Ehrlich and Pirages (1974, pp. 279–80) considered the problem of materialism and rising expectations to be at present a universal religion and that the future will require new forms of religion to effect a true social transformation. Roszak and Skolimowski, however, were critical of the attitude which they saw behind Ehrlich and Pirages position, but more especially that of Heilbroner. They argued that such a new religion would be used as a manipulative tool for effecting a certain form of social ordering and the concern with ecology could become 'a form of disguised instrumentalism' (Skolimowski, 1976, p. 8).

This criticism is further developed by John Barry (1999) who had contended that the link often made between deep ecology and spiritual conversion, in which the ecological crisis can only be overcome by a complete healing of the alienation between humanity and nature, is fatally flawed:

> It seems that only a final solving of the problem between humanity and the world constitutes a solution. Solutions which prevent the destruction of the natural world but are not motivated by a reverence for nature fall short of the deep ecology standard.
>
> (p. 18)

Such an approach runs the risk of divorcing itself from the need to discover practical solutions to existing problems and failing to develop politically. It also supported a belief in the strength of ideas which can change and affect the individual's responses to the world. At a basic level this was seen in the adoption of the idea by Robertson, who saw it as the way in which conversion can take place:

> For example, human beings can see themselves as outside nature, whence they can observe it, dominate it and exploit it; or by contrast, they can feel themselves to be an integral part of nature.
>
> (1978, p. 79)

This paradigm shift would result in a change in the conceptions of the nature of wealth, growth, power, etc., and Robertson saw this paradigm already emerging, and the task was to convert the holders of the orthodox paradigm. By attacking the problem at this basic level the aim was to undermine the paradigm upon which the present system was based and prepare the ground for a new social system.

The major area for attack was that of the scientific worldview, in particular logical positivism. The scientific method was criticized as requiring the separation of 'values from cognitive knowledge, thus from knowledge about the world, thus from the world itself' (Skolimowski, 1976, p. 11). Marcuse was critical of the division between science and values which led to the use of scientific rationality to sanction social control. This was the result of an instrumental view of nature which had become dominant in which the enquiry centred upon the use and organization of nature for productive purposes:

> Science, *by virtue of its own methods* and concepts has projected and promoted a universe in which the domination of nature has remained linked to the domination of man.
>
> (1968, p. 136)

Consequently, Marcuse saw modern science as profoundly anti-democratic and providing a technology for domination of the natural world and the rest of humanity. This feature of science was also criticized as reductionist, in that the scientific method in itself, and when applied to activities such as agriculture, failed to recognize the connections between the different elements of nature (Thompson, 1995, pp. 129–36).

The effectiveness of technology in its application of science acted in a manner reminiscent of Marx's idea of the function of money; it disguised the social relations which were acting behind it. For Marcuse this was reification at its most mature and subtle:

> The social position of the individual and his relations to others appear not only to be determined by objective qualities and laws, but these qualities and laws … appear as calculable manifestations of (scientific) rationality.
>
> (1968, p. 138)

In this way scientific method, in its positivist sense, was an expression of alienated thought and the result was the continued domination of man by man, and of nature by man. Up to a point we have seen that there was agreement between Marcuse and Skolimowski, in that they both attack positivism on the grounds that it attempted to remove ethical values from scientific inquiry.

However, Marcuse was criticized by Illich for continuing the project to produce a totally artificial environment, for rather than attempting to define values in technical terms Illich suggests that,

> The re-establishment of an ecological balance depends on the ability of society to counteract the progressive materialisation of values.
>
> (Illich, 1973, p. 65)

Science and technology were considered to be an expression of alienated consciousness insofar as they existed in a world conceived in terms of instrumentalism, and therefore domination. Such an approach also encouraged an expert-based political structure which promoted anti-democratic forms of decision making. There was a need to reject the viewpoint that promoted the idea that the ecological crisis was purely a technical, scientific problem open to a technical fix (Barry, J., 1999, p. 200). The answer was seen to lie in replacing this positivist conception with ecologically correct values to guide the scientific enterprise, which Jagtenberg and McKie (1997, pp. 84–8) have identified as a post-modern science.

Skolimowski noted that although positivism *attempted* to exclude values from the picture, the fact that it was both alienated and instrumentalist in its approach did not make it value-less. Skolimowski wrote of the positivist world as being one where:

> *Values* are man-centred, or physical-universe-centred. In the former case, we arrive at *individualism* and its ultimate extension-selfishness. In the latter case, we arrive at *instrumentalism* and its ultimate extension-consumerism.
>
> (1976, p. 12)

In Marx's view the power of money lay in its ability to 'create' values and power for its possessor. So within the artificial environment, science and technology 'create' values:

> Even such imponderable values as creativity, dignity and heroism have become inseparably wedded in the popular imagination with our power to boss nature about and to surround ourselves with the products of advanced technology.
>
> (*Ibid.*, p. 21)

Roszak was equally critical of Marx's view of man's nature as he was of positivism because he considered that Marx, being a man of his time, allied to the distortion of Marxism–Leninism, created a 'caricature of nineteenth century bourgeois scientism (Roszak, 1974, p. 14). Fromm also contended that Marx adopted some of the authoritarian and patriarchal spirit of his time so that he could present a convincing picture to his audience. For this reason he was forced to project a 'scientific' socialism opposed to a 'utopian' socialism (1979, p. 156).

## Alienation as a spiritual problem

Now in order to examine more deeply the ideas of Roszak over the problem of the modern scientific world-view it is necessary to consider a further definition of positivism presented by Etienne Balibar:

> *Positivism is still a form of rationalism*, combining the heritages of empiricism (Hume) and formalism (Leibniz), tending to present all phenomena of nature and society as amenable to logic and observation, 'reasoning', 'calculation', or 'the experimental method' and proclaiming on those grounds the end of irrationalism, 'fetishism', mysticism and so on.
>
> (Balibar, 1978, p. 12)

Positivism was therefore a method of 'knowing' or 'investigation' which based itself upon the ability to examine phenomena under conditions which allow the observer to recreate or repeat the experience of those phenomena. It allowed the observer to judge them in order to promote 'the needs and advances of knowledge' against the 'residue of feeling, of pathology' (*ibid.*, p. 12). Roszak considered that this was a narrowing of the concept of what humanity and nature were and how we can come to know them.

To the feeling that this was an instrumentalist approach and tends to domination Roszak also believed that it was inadequate in its attempt to promote knowledge because of its restricted view of the procedures of investigation. Roszak proposed in its place the acceptance of what he termed the 'Old Gnosis', which promoted those aspects which Balibar contended that positivism rejected; of mysticism, irrationalism and emotion:

> It is a visionary style of knowledge, not a theological one; its proper language is myth and ritual; its foundation is rapture, not faith and doctrine; and its experience of nature is one of living communion.
>
> (Roszak, 1974, p. 118)

Within this, there are two important elements which relate to the rest of ecological thought. Firstly, the proposal was to counteract the scientific worldview of positivism with a religious, spiritual approach to relations with, and the investigation of, nature. Secondly, there was a rejection of the theological aspect of religion represented by the Judeo-Christian tradition, a tradition also criticized by Lynn White Jr. in its

Christian and western development. White stated that the problem arose from the belief that,

> God planned all this [creation] explicitly for man's benefit and rule; no item in the physical creation had any purpose save to serve man's purpose ... Especially in its Western form, Christianity is the most anthropocentric religion the world has seen.
>
> (1973, p. 25)

In this way White saw that Christianity left open the way to the domination and exploitation of nature by preparing the mental attitude for it. Roszak contended that this treatment of the world as an object resulted in the final conception of the earth as material which can only result in waste. Because it was without an element of the sacred it therefore had no other value than that which was man made and no other end than waste (Roszak, 1974, pp. 125–8).

The alternative sacred world-view was an element of past or 'primitive' cultures, and it was part of the historical aspect of alienation noted earlier, the search for the true nature of man which the world of capitalism and industrialism had removed us from. This led to a search for anthropological evidence of the religions of primitive man and a look towards third-world nations. This project came partly out of the increasing identification with Third World liberation movements and the spread of interest in Eastern philosophies.

This search was at the centre of the moral and philosophical ideas elaborated by E.F. Schumacher as an alternative approach to conventional economics. It had as its basis the Buddhist conception of the function of work as an important element in a man's moral growth (Schumacher, 1974, p. 45).

According to Schumacher, the idea of wealth pursued by Buddhism does not entail the concept of material wealth from growing material production but, rather, spiritual growth from dependence on fewer and fewer material possessions. This was similar to the idea of the paradigm shift in Robertson where, rather than a replacement of concepts such as wealth, growth and work, we should move to a new definition of what these mean. For Schumacher, this did not exclude Christianity from the picture altogether, for he saw such teachings as the Sermon on the Mount giving 'pretty precise instructions on how to construct an outlook that could lead to an Economics of Survival' (1974, p. 130).

This search for solutions in Eastern concepts of the natural world was criticized, particularly by John Passmore. To begin with Passmore considered the dominant tradition in the West which had come under fire and concluded that ecologists did indeed have a point. He saw the essential historical turning point as the radical interpretation of the place of nature in Christianity held by such writers as Bacon and Descartes:

> It found expression in a metaphysics, for which man is the sole finite agent and nature a vast system of machines for man to use and modify as he pleases. This is the metaphysics the ecologists are particularly and rightly, rejecting.
>
> (Passmore, 1974, p. 27)

Passmore argued that this was not the whole of the western tradition, which was one of remarkable diversity, and for this reason it was inappropriate to go searching elsewhere. The two traditions Passmore looked towards were those of Conservation and Stewardship. The first of these was, in essence, one of maintaining the fertility of the earth through the act of 'good management'. But stewardship was seen as rather more radical in its relationship to nature:

> it looks to the perfection of nature by man, but a perfection which always takes account of nature's resources and of what man has already achieved in his civilising of the world.
>
> (*Ibid.*, pp. 39–40)

This alternative tradition was also represented by Fitchte and Hegel, and therefore in elements of Marx's thought.

Passmore criticised the introduction of mystical elements into the attempt to solve ecological problems. He attacked the conception of nature as being perceived as sacred, for if this were so 'a nature that can heal men can surely heal itself' and can not be destroyed (*ibid.*, p. 176). The quality he found in ecology was its holistic nature and the major benefits were in the way it could lead to a greater degree of interdisciplinary study and teach that the 'doctrine that nature is infinitely malleable is not merely an illusion – but a dangerous delusion' (*ibid.*, p. 178).

Secondly, Passmore considered the East as having little to offer when confronted by Western culture which had been successful because of its dynamism (*ibid.*, p. 182). However, this underestimated the detrimental impact of Western capitalism and the resulting dominance of Western mass culture in particular. It was also blind to the possibilities of borrowing aspects of Eastern culture by the West in the form of art and science.

An ecological analysis also existed in the work of Dubos (1976) who looked at western alternatives and considered the two major monastic traditions, developing what he termed 'Franciscan Conservatism' and 'Benedictine Stewardship'. The difference he saw between the two was basically between a passive (Franciscan) and an active (Benedictine) philosophy. Franciscan conservatism was the worship of nature and an absolute identification with it. But this was abandoned by the followers of St Francis who recognized that humanity had never been purely passive towards the natural world. Benedictine Stewardship, however, was an active principle of management and improvement.

These traditions are seen as very important within the development of western culture, and the transmission of the ideas of stewardship had shaped the landscapes of Europe, which conservationists defended as if they had always existed instead of the result of an interplay between man and nature.

In contrast Skolimowski attempted to develop a secular philosophical foundation for ecology based upon adapting the western humanist tradition to the ideas of ecological science. Skolimowski looked back to Kant and saw a 'transcendent' view of humanity, but one separated from an orthodox religious concept. Kant's view acted as 'a buffer zone against the growing encroachment of instrumental values' (1976, p. 17). Hayward (1994, p. 18) also identified Kant as presenting an alternative to Descartes in that his dualism was based on the boundaries of knowledge and where nature cannot be understood in any mechanistic way.

Skolimowski argued that the mechanistic world-view of positivism reduced the idea and spirit of progress to a simple concept of material development. John Barry also noted that ecological thought meant that progress needed to be seen as more than a simple increase in material wealth. Rather, it meant the increasing 'democratization of people's lives' (1999, p. 254). For Skolimowski progress needed to be seen in an evolutionary and biological sense as signifying a 'process of perpetual transcendence' (1976, p. 19), that nature and all matter were constantly reassembling in an urge towards something superior, perhaps in humanity's case beyond matter into a spiritual realm. This entailed a new cosmology which saw the universe centred, not on humanity, but on a concept of evolution in which all matter was joined, with humanity the leading edge, in a 'moral adventure'.

## Deep ecology and alienation

The spiritual and metaphysical dimension of green thought and the sense of something lost was also central to the development of deep ecology. As John Barry noted,

> Re-enchantment of nature goes hand in hand with psychological reconnection and the overcoming of the self's alienated state. It is the metaphysical vision of deep ecology which furnishes the objective criteria by which ecological selves are to be judged … Deep ecology's general frame of reference is the restoration of something that has been lost, a return to the true path from which we have diverged.
>
> (1999, p. 23)

Consequently, the psychological sense of alienation as found in authors such as Marcuse and Fromm, was also a key element in deep green thought where the sense of self within modern Western society was seen as narrow and unhealthy. For Naess, the essence of deep ecology was the nature of the questioning of existing situations rather than any sense of the content of those questions. According to Fox, Naess considered that the formal concept of deep ecology rested on the idea of asking 'progressively deeper' questions about ecological relationships, a kind of 'green reductionism' (Fox, 1995, p. 92). As a result, the questioning went beyond the area of technical and scientific problem-solving:

> Consequently, the recommended policies also touched fundamentals such as man's attitude towards nature, industrial man's attitude towards non-industrial cultures, and the ecological aspect of widely different economic systems.
>
> (Quoted in Fox, 1995, pp. 93–4)

For authors such as Naess and Fox one of the central issues was that of anthropocentrism and its embodiment in the scientific and rational project. Eckersley (1992, pp. 26–31) was also identified the centrality of the distinction between anthropocentrism and ecocentrism across the whole spectrum of green thought. She noted that this distinction could be identified in such diverse writers as Naess and Bookchin. The anthropocentric approach tended to see the non-human world as 'a storehouse of resources' with only instrumental value, while an ecocentric approach valued nature for its own sake.

For Fox it was the assumption of 'human self-importance' which had placed humanity at the centre of the universe in a position of superiority to the rest of nature. The Judeo-Christian tradition had been central to the development of this assumption through the belief that man was created in the image of God, and the scientific revolution had done nothing to significantly alter this position. Garner (1996, p. 37) had also noted that while within the Judeo-Christian tradition there was a place for the concept of stewardship, in which humanity should show respect for nature as a creation of God, scientific rationality had divorced humanity from nature and undermined this spiritual concern. Equally, Fox had stated that,

> Francis Bacon, for example, saw science as 'enlarging the bounds of Human Empire'; Descartes likewise saw it as rendering us 'masters and possessors of Nature'.
>
> (1995, p. 10)

In this way, the concept of stewardship was replaced by that of domination and exploitation. The debate over the preservation of the non-human world was, therefore, too often couched in anthropocentric terms. In addition, the process of Cartesian thought and the philosophical tradition emerging from it, divorced humanity from the rest of nature as the process of reductionism questioned the existence of everything but the human engaged in the act of thinking. As a result, reductionism and the associated dualism in the conception of humanity and nature as separate and distinct entities, were fundamental aspects of our alienation and significantly contributed to the emergence of the environmental crisis (see Thompson, 1995, pp. 129–30).

Fox, therefore, contended that anthropocentrism was essentially self-serving in its assumptions. He presented five essential points against anthropocentrism as a way of thinking. Firstly, when examined empirically such assumptions were incorrect and tended to be 'disastrous for the development of our theoretical understanding of the world'. An example of this was the view that humans were unique within the natural world. Secondly, the consequences of anthropocentrism for the natural world were 'disastrous' in terms of ecological damage. Thirdly, the arguments in favour of an anthropocentric approach tended to be inconsistent as by identifying some unique characteristics, such as free will and rationality, these views excluded some people as not quite human, including infants and people with severe mental incapacity. Fourthly, a purely human centred perspective was increasingly seen as morally objectionable. Finally, anthropocentrism did not fit with genuine experience when confronted by the natural world, where the beauty of creation puts humanity's efforts into perspective (1995, pp. 14–19).

The all-pervasive nature of anthropocentrism also entailed an oppressive aspect of 'human chauvinism and human imperialism' (*ibid.*, p. 21). As such it contained within it authoritarian and exploitative patterns of behaviour in relation to the non-human world. This problem was also identified as being a consequence of the modernist project stemming from the Enlightenment in which 'it has become almost natural for social theorists to portray humanity as angst ridden, fractured, exploited, oppressed, and, in many other ways, off center' (Jagtenberg and McKie, 1997, p. 4).

For Jagtenberg and McKie, modernism and the associated concepts of scientific rationality, progress and economic growth, all contributed to an alienated and exploited humanity. In defining alienation they referred to Chesneaux whose concept of *off-ground* was a 'general category of modernity, the state of being radically dissociated from the natural, social, historical and cultural environment' (p. 13). As such, the alienation of humanity from nature was associated with exploitation, domination, control and repression, all deeply anti-democratic positions. Alternatively, deep ecology, and eco-feminism were ecocentric and went beyond alienation.

Anthropocentric thought was strongly linked to the development of Enlightenment thinking and humanism as the twin pillars underlying the movement towards a modern secular society. For Hayward, the issues centred on an ontological problem concerning the nature of science and our way of thinking. He argued that ecology presented a critique of Enlightenment thinking and the Cartesian method of scientific inquiry because,

> Its methods and epistemology are not reductionist, its ontology is not dualistic, and its ethics are not atomistic.
>
> (1994, p. 23)

For Hayward, the Enlightenment values which ecology counteracted centred on the idea of mastery of nature, with its subsequent association between the domination of nature and the alienation of humanity from nature. Deep ecology, therefore, arrived at a metaphysics which was built on a critical evaluation of modernity and the development of the Western rational tradition (Barry, J., 1999, p. 16).

However, Pepper was critical of the way in which deep ecologists perceived the alienation of humanity from nature. He argued that deep ecology also contained within it a dualism which it supposedly rejected. Pepper stated that for Marx alienation meant separation from an aspect of the self, and therefore alienation from nature was a 'failure to recognize nature *as* a social creation' (1993, p. 114). Wilderness existed only in an artificial sense because it was withdrawn from true nature by the human decision not to transform it through human action. Deep ecology saw alienation as humanity's separation from something out there, a dualism in which nature was something to be revered. However, Pepper contended that,

> Reverent mystification really *separates* us from nature…Gaia is an inhuman force we cannot change but to which we must adjust for our survival.
>
> > (*Ibid.*, p. 115)

An anthropocentric approach to alienation recognized the central role of humanity not just in the ecological threat to our survival but also in the solution. It was not through submission but rather through action that humanity can overcome the alienation brought about through social injustice, authoritarian and repressive structures.

Deep ecologists would argue that this was a misunderstanding of the relationship and one which would continue to maintain our sense of alienation. Alienation was the result of the arrogance of humanity and the attempt to recover our sense of self was a weak form of anthropocentric ecology based on 'enlightened self-interest' (Eckersley, 1992, pp. 53–7). Eckersley went on to note that some deep green writers have criticized humanism as a particular form of anthropocentrism, for establishing this sense of human arrogance, particularly because of its secular nature. However, she contended that humanism was a 'complex tapestry' and contained within it some concepts which are compatible with ecocentric positions while other strands needed to be rooted out.

This issue of the arrogance of humanity in our relationship with nature was also identified by John Barry and seen as part of the need to rethink the concept of progress as a central theme of modernist thought. Indeed, the existing and dominant Western concept of progress was embodied in the trend towards globalization which was the main cause of much environmental degradation (1999, pp. 254–5).

## Conclusions

These are the philosophical traditions which were initiated by early ecological writers throughout the 1970s. This tradition included a concept of humanity's relationship to nature which attempted to place a sacred link between them which is at once both spiritual and humanist. The task they set was an attempt to re-identify the interdependence between man and nature in order to heal the wound of alienation. This could lead in two directions, either that of stewardship as in Dubos, or the total surrender to nature which Goldsmith upheld and which was termed 'paraprimitivism' or 'tribal' ecology which contained many repressive elements:

> School leavers will be conscripted into a 'Restoration Corps' ... followed by conscription into a Defence Corps. Goldsmith's attitudes towards women are also repressive ... The theme of woman as childrearer and servant is strong in Goldsmith's references to the social position of women.
>
> (Bradshaw, 1978, pp. 336–53)

This was partly due to Goldsmith's acceptance of violence and competition in ordering the development of the hierarchy of a 'natural' system. The political result of stewardship on the other hand has a relationship to the utopian socialist's and anarchist's ideas of the 19th century, with Kropotkin particularly relevant:

> The anarchists were commonly ethical naturalists ... Usually they studied nature in the nineteenth century positivist style of science, hopeful that it would yield moral as well as empirical truth. Not one European anarchist felt he searched in vain ... It is no accident that Kropotkin wrote 'Mutual Aid' in answer to Huxley's portrayal of nature as 'red in tooth and claw'. Nature contained a standard which prescribed what was good.
>
> (Fowler, 1972, pp. 738–52)

Excluding the 'positive style' we can also see why the adoption of ecology as a source for a political philosophy by writers such as Bookchin and Roszak was not surprising. Positivistic science has been perceived as a reflection of alienated thought and a division of labour has built up to inhibit understanding between different branches of science as well as scientists and laymen. Ecology was felt to be the answer, the healer of wounds.

Passmore criticized Roszak for introducing a mystical element into the ecological sphere, but as we have seen, Roszak's desire was to broaden our approach to the world, our way of knowing the world, and to place science within a framework which would end its predominance (Roszak, 1976, ch. 7). Roszak developed the idea of 'Person/Planet' which was linked to the evolutionary idea he and Skolimowski proposed, the idea that man was the 'leading edge' of a single organic whole in the process of transcendence to a new spirituality. Roszak believed that,

> The scientific status of this connection between person and planet can only remain speculative in these pages; but I have little doubt that within the next generation there will emerge a well-developed body of ecological theory that illuminates this subtle interrelationship and gives enough political force to displace the inherited ideologies of industrial society.
>
> (*Ibid.*, p. xxx)

Ecology as a science, therefore, was an aid to understanding nature and humanity's place in it, in order to replace the instrumentalism which treated both humanity and nature as objects. By acting on and inquiring into the world from a standpoint of interdependence we can, it was hoped, end the confrontation with the world as something artificial or alien, and with others as strangers. With this analysis of the nature of alienation and the potential for ecology to overcome it, green thinkers turned their attention to redefining the relationship between humanity and nature.

For Eckersley this was particularly important as the critique of scientism and instrumentalism associated with critical theorists such as Marcuse, was too centred on questions of who exercised power. She also noted that as such it was too anthropocentric in that their 'objection to the domination of nature ultimately comes to rest on the human-centred argument that it leads to the domination of *people*' (1992, p. 11). While this was an inevitable cause of humanity's alienation from the non-human world as well as the social inequality and repression associated with modern industrial capitalism, ecologists sought to redefine this relationship through the establishment of a new ethical position.

# 4
# The Need for an Environmental Ethic

Out of this concern with alienation has emerged a concerted effort to develop an environmental ethic, an attempt to redress the balance between humanity and nature. As part of this development there has grown up a wide range of ethical positions reflecting the diversity of the present state of ecological thought. As Karen J. Warren (1996) pointed out:

> In many respects, contemporary environmental ethics reflects the range of positions in contemporary normative philosophical ethics... There are consequentialist (e.g., eco-utilitarian, utilitarian-based animal liberation) and nonconsequentialist (e.g., human rights-based, rights-based animal liberation, land stewardship) positions that extend traditional ethical considerations to animals and the non-human environment. There are also non-traditional approaches (e.g., holistic Leopoldian land ethics, social ecology, deep ecology, ecological feminism).
>
> (p. xvi)

This dual distinction between traditional and non-traditional forms of thinking about ethics was evident in a range of different approaches to the ethical problem of how humanity should relate to the rest of nature.

## The challenge of developing an ecological ethic

Dobson described how the development of an ecological ethic could be divided between the search for a code of conduct or alternatively the establishment of a state of being. Part of this distinction, he argued, was due to the problems encountered in the search for an objective value for nature or the identification of 'intrinsic value'. The attempt to establish value as something objectively defined, as intrinsic to nature, rather than something that belongs to humanity alone has created a series of challenges to green theorists. An associated approach has characterized the development of a radical Deep Ecology with the desire to move towards an 'ecocentric' position as against an anthropocentric position found more in so-called Shallow Ecology. The debate over the development of an ethic suggested a,

> latent distinction … between, first, the attempt to develop an ethics from within the current mode of discourse, and second, the idea that such an ethics could only be produced from a more profound and general shift in ecological consciousness.
>
> (Dobson, 1995, p. 51)

Such a distinction is essential to understanding the problems surrounding the whole ecological debate. While some writers attempted to utilize the science of ecology and engage in rational debate utilising physical evidence for environmental degradation, others rejected rational and scientific approaches on the grounds that it was this approach which was at the root of environmental problems. Instead, there was the need to change consciousness and essentially identify with the feelings or spirit of the natural world:

> The idea involves the cultivation of a sense of self that extends beyond the individual understood in terms of its isolated corporal identity. To this is added the notion that the enrichment of self depends upon the widest possible identification with the non-human world.
>
> (Dobson, 1995, p. 57)

Taking a position from Ayer and Emotivism as well as the longer British empiricist tradition stemming from Hume, it can be seen that Deep ecology recognized that morality is rooted in our sentiments. Consequently, the search for a rational, objective basis for ethical rules was in itself highly problematic. However, the position adopted by Deep Ecologists also had its critics and could in turn lead to difficulties in the establishment of guidance as to how we should approach the non-human world.

Critical social theorists in the late 1960s and 1970s including Marcuse, Horkheimer and Adorno saw the Enlightenment as a world view which conceived of nature only as an 'object of instrumental manipulation' (Vogel, 1997, p. 175). Dower (1989) also stated that there was a distinction between the development of an ethic with new prescriptions but based on an older philosophical tradition and an ethic which developed a whole new perspective, rejecting the older rationalist moral tradition:

> its newness, relative to typical modern thought, is brought out by the fact that a common assumption or prejudice in Western thought is that moral relations only exist between beings who are themselves moral agents.
>
> (p. 34)

This moral reciprocation was built on the concept of rational discourse enabling actors to enter into agreements with one another. Consequently, Dower suggested that an ecological ethic, whether this aimed to displace humans from the centre of our moral attention or simply broaden our concept of human responsibility beyond our relationship with other humans, faced the intellectual barrier of western rationalist traditions.

In addition, the development of alternative ways of seeing nature sometimes created significant difficulties due to an attempt to establish purpose in nature. For example, Holmes Rolston III attempted to introduce a pseudoscientific approach by seeing genetic development as purposive, and utilizing computer imagery. When speaking of the processes involved in DNA as a purposeful force he stated that,

> An organism is a spontaneous, self-maintaining system, sustaining and reproducing itself, executing its program, making a way through the world, checking against performance by means of responsive capacities with which to measure success... it gives the organism a telos, or end, a kind of (nonfelt) goal. This executive steering core (the DNA) is cybernetic – partly a special kind of cause-and-effect system and partly something more.
>
> (Rolston III, 1994, p. 70)

The problem with this approach was that it appeared to fall into two significant traps. Firstly, he awarded purpose and goals to non-sentient beings and nature as a whole, which may lead him towards a dubious ecological metaphysics. Secondly he used mechanistic metaphors for biological organisms, a trap identified by authors such as Roszak, as being linked with the scientific objectification of nature which green theorists have attempted to surmount.

These various examples reveal the difficulties entailed in the continued development of green thinking and how the establishment of an ecological ethic is subject to significant problems. A central problem in the development of an ecological ethic was the distinction between those who maintained an anthropocentric position and critics who considered such an approach to be inadequate. Hayward (1994, p. 58) has argued that there was a perceived need to move away from 'speciesism' or 'human chauvinism' in which the rest of nature was seen in instrumental terms, having no value except that which related to its usefulness to humanity. Such anthropocentrism was equated with a conception of the rest of nature solely from the point of view of the human species. His argument was that this approach was doubly flawed in that it not only allowed for the abuse of other species but also it was cognitively flawed in that it failed to understand the relationship between humanity and the non-human world. Such an approach was narrow in the sense that it failed to recognize the way in which humanity was created and defined by its place in nature, rather than humanity defining nature.

Equally, Paul Taylor (1994, pp. 85–6) argued that unless we can understand the world from the perspective of non-human nature we can not establish any respect for nature, 'we cannot see the point of taking the attitude of respect'. Consequently, he argued for a four-point definition of an ecocentric or biocentric approach involving:

1. recognizing that humanity is part of nature on equal terms with the rest;
2. that all species are interdependent;
3. that all creatures are 'teleological' and pursuing their own good; and
4. that humans are not superior beings.

The difficulty with this approach again centred on the idea of purpose, and the idea that each individual aspect of nature was pursuing its own good. However, can the good of one creature outweigh that of another and what are the deciding factors in any particular situation?

This problem was raised as an issue by Brian Barry (1995, p. 21) where he noted that the development of an ecocentric ethic (and also a zoo-centric or animal rights ethic) was 'indeterminate' in the sense that it would not guide our actions in all cases. While nature may be accepted as having a moral worth of its own, with the idea that the good of the ecological community or 'biotic community' is the measure of moral worth or value, significant issues of disagreement can still arise:

> It is easy to imagine that even a society all of whose members adhered to this objective might well disagree a good deal about exactly what is called for in a given situation.
>
> (p. 21)

Consequently, such an ethic may be a guide in respect of areas of arbitrary decisions or discrimination and rule out such actions, but would find it difficult to guide action where the beings or aspects of nature in question are significantly diverse. An example that was often used was that between sentient mammals and the hookworm or tsetse fly.

However, Eckersley noted that there was a range of different perspectives that were all compatible with an ecocentric position rather than any one particular form. These included an intrinsic value concept of nature, deep ecology's psychological/cosmological approach, and ecofeminist essentialism. In addition, she pointed to,

> certain Eastern philosophies such as Taoism and Buddhism that emphasize the interconnectedness of all phenomena and the importance of humility and compassion; and the animistic cosmologies of many indigenous peoples who see and respect the nonhuman world as alive and espirited.
>
> (Eckersley, 1992, p. 60)

Approaches such as the Gaia hypothesis could be seen to involve a spiritual perspective, while others tried to avoid this kind of speculation because of the suspicion that modern society often has for spiritual and moral concepts in political activity. Consequently, Steven Yearley (1992, pp. 144–5) argued that the development of scientific knowledge resulted in the idea of the Earth as a regulated system and therefore the Gaia hypothesis had a basis in science:

> To talk in this way about 'regulation' might seem suspect and anthropomorphic. After all, there was no one there to do the regulating … But the Gaia hypothesis proposes that it is not just a metaphor; according to it, the earth really is regulated. Life on the planet is somehow co-ordinated in a way that worked to keep the planet habitable.
>
> (p. 145)

According to this perspective humanity has a moral obligation to humans, animals and Gaia born out of this relationship. However others, such as Dryzek, have spoken of the need for an eco-theology where the problems associated with the ecological crisis were essentially spiritual and consequently the solutions were also spiritual.

## Goodin and the objective value of nature

The problem facing some anthropocentrics in developing an adequate practical ethics was contained in the aim of establishing the objective value of non-human beings. In many ways the attribution of values was bound up with a belief that a recognition of such value was the result of enlightened self-interest. For example, Norton (1984, pp. 133–48) noted that religious taboos on the killing of animals was the result of a concern with the moral and spiritual well-being of the believer rather than a concern with the life of the non-human being *per se*. He went on to argue that such beliefs were difficult to disprove or prove because of their nature as beliefs or expressions of faith. However, the maintenance of an ethic, which was anthropocentric, did not mean that human actions towards the non-human world should inevitably be exploitative. From an instrumental point of view the continuation of species and the maintenance of a healthy planet was essential to the preservation of human life (see Brian Barry, 1995, p. 21).

However, an objective concept of value can also be developed from an ecocentric position and in order to explore this issue Goodin's 'Green Theory of Value' may be seen as a point of reference. Goodin contended that nature had a value independent of humanity. Essentially, that value was contained in its 'naturalness' and its history apart from humanity, but including humanity. Goodin contended that a green theory of value contained three component parts: people want a sense of purpose and pattern; this can only be achieved within a wider setting; natural products provide that setting. For Goodin, therefore, the independence of natural products from human action signified something beyond us, something larger than our petty human actions. Only by providing such a context did nature establish a higher purpose beyond the merely human:

> we value the products of natural processes precisely because they are the products of something larger than ourselves ... for my purposes, it would do equally well to say that the processes in question are things 'outside' of ourselves. The point is merely that such natural

processes, and our relation to them, serve to fix our place in the external world.

(Goodin, 1992, p. 39)

While Goodin tried to distance himself from the metaphysical or spiritual implications of such an approach this was certainly not the case with others. However, he did acknowledge that this placed him in a weak anthropocentric point, along a continuum from anthropocentrism to eco-centrism, in that although the value of nature lay apart from humanity the idea that this therefore gave meaning to the activities of humanity maintained an anthropocentric quality. It should also be added that there was a difficulty inherent in trying to establish a concept of value based on the idea of the separateness of nature from humanity while humanity remained a part of nature.

Regan (1983) also raised questions from his position as a supporter of animal rights rather that being an ecologist. He noted that there were severe difficulties in developing an environmental ethic because it lacked the issue of reciprocity. For Regan it was difficult to identify natural objects as having rights because they were not subjects-of-a-life. Consequently natural objects can be seen as 'good of their kind', and this would include not just an oak tree as a good example of an oak tree but also cancer cells may be good examples of their kind but not necessarily 'good' as such.

Goodin confronted this problem by acknowledging that humanity was part of nature and yet what we did was not necessarily equally natural. Goodin essentially argued that there are social actions which harmonise with nature and others which attempt to dominate nature. He used as an example the contrast between an English landscape garden and the French formal garden of the same period, in which, he contended, one tried to work with nature while the other aimed to shape nature to the designer's own ends:

> People who live more in harmony with nature … are living more in a context which is outside themselves, individually or even collectively.
>
> (p. 51)

While this is a fairly well-founded rationale for establishing a clear distinction between the setting of an English village and the modern artifice embodied by life in Los Angeles, there is still the problem of establishing at what point does the activity of humanity change from natural to artificial? Is a town of 30 000 more artificial or less than one of 35 000?

Is Rome more artificial than New York simply because of its history? It is easy to make such distinctions when the contrasts are stark, but much more difficult to establish where the boundary between something of value and something to be opposed is small. In the end many ecologists appear to rely on the idea that 'we know' when something is unnatural.

For some eco-feminists such an approach is also open to question on the basis that it was trying to establish an environmental ethic from the perspective of a rationalist tradition which in itself is part of the problem. Val Plumwood (1994, pp. 142–59) has argued that the rationalist tradition is too centred on a dualism between man and nature and between man and woman. In this tradition, rationalism attempted to establish objective and universalist ethical concepts which help our understanding, while emotional contact with nature was identified as subjective, particular and therefore unreliable. This dualism relegated nature and 'feminine' concepts of the relationship with nature, to an inferior status. The effort of writers on environmental ethics to work within the rationalist tradition undermined the project. However, this critique while having some value in relation to approaches which try to establish an objective value for nature, such as that engaged in by Goodin and to some extent by Eckersley, in itself is problematic in trying to overthrow rational thought altogether.

Dobson noted that because of these difficulties some ecologists have dropped the attempt to develop an objective value for nature on the basis that this was related to the rationalist approach which they rejected. The approach should be one which was linked to an essentialist perspective and a more metaphysical concept of the humanity/ nature relationship. Such a questioning of rationalism was also at the heart of one of the most influential positions, that of deep ecology.

## Deep ecologists and ecocentric ethics

Arne Naess was the first author to make the distinction between deep and shallow ecology (1973, pp. 95–100). Various authors (Dryzek, Devall and Sessions) have identified two core characteristics of deep ecological or deep green thought. Firstly, that human self-realization can only truly come about through going beyond the self towards an identification with the whole of the natural world. Secondly, through this process there was a realization of a 'biotic equality' in which all species are equal with no hierarchy between species, including humanity. Eckersley argued strongly for this position to counter the idea that an ecocentric position was misanthropic. She argued that ecocentrics see each individual human and their culture as of value, provided their activity does not hinder the development of other non-human lives:

> Moreover, many critics of ecocentrism fail to realise that a perspective that seeks emancipation writ large is one that *necessarily* supports social justice in the human community.
>
> (1992, p. 56)

Consequently, the idea was that through the establishment of such a consciousness there would be an end to speciesism and humanity would act in a way which was more naturally ecologically sound. For example, Fox has contended that through such a 'transpersonal' ecology where the self is absorbed into the wider natural world,

> ethics (conceived as being concerned with moral 'oughts') is rendered superfluous! The reason for this is that if one has a wide, expansive or field-like sense of self then (assuming that one is not self-destructive) one will naturally (i.e. spontaneously) protect the natural (spontaneous) unfolding of the expansive self (the ecosphere, the cosmos) in all its aspects.
>
> (1995, p. 217)

For Dobson, such a position does not escape logical problems leading him to criticize Fox on three main counts. Firstly, the core of Fox's approach was centred on self-realization by humans and so opened itself up to the charge of a weak form of anthropocentrism. Secondly, in situations where there was a conflict of interest could humans who have integrated their interests with those of the natural world actually come down in favour of the human choice because all is now whole and so human interests are identical with the interests of the earth? Finally, a problem which confronted all those who centred their beliefs on a transformation of human consciousness, how do deep ecologists go about convincing the wider population that such a changed consciousness is ethically correct? (Dobson, 1995, pp. 58–60) The danger was also present, although Dobson did not go this far, that anyone who does not develop such a consciousness was seen as ethically wrong and so in the transformation to an ecologically sound society may they need 're-educating'?

Fox did not recognize such a difficulty and indeed believed Naess's views meant that he did not have to reject anthropocentric viewpoints. Rather, he could 'simply claim that ecocentric views go "deeper" than anthropocentric views' (1995, p. 141) and that if their analysis were to deepen then anthropocentrics would come round to a deep ecology view. Fox's support for Naess led him to a contradictory view where he argued that Naess may well believe that the deep ecological position was superior this actually allowed him to accept other approaches as part of a philosophical and moral diversity. However, it can be argued that the use of the terms 'deep' and 'shallow' are in themselves morally loaded, with 'shallow' seen as a pejorative term.

Other authors have taken Naess's (1989) lead and gone on to try and develop further an ecocentric ethic as a way of escaping the anthropocentric nature of traditional ethical thinking. Aldo Leopold was frequently cited as an influential figure in the development of an environmental ethic, due to his association with the concept of a 'land ethic':

> All ethics so far evolved rest upon a single premise: that the individual is a member of a community of interdependent parts. His instincts prompt him to compete for his place in that community, but his ethics prompt him to co-operate (perhaps in order that there be a place to compete for).
>
> (Leopold, 1949, p. 204)

This approach entailed the inclusion of both non-human and non-sentient creation, including the land, in the community. For Regan as an animal rights supporter this could lead to the sacrifice of individual beings for a perceived greater good of the species. This led him to accuse Leopold and his supporters of a form of eco-fascism (Regan, 1983, p. 362) where individual rights are sacrificed to this greater good. However, an ecocentric position could also be seen as more all inclusive of all living beings and the earth itself than the more narrowly defined interests and boundaries of animal rights supporters.

Eckersley (1992) tried to develop a detailed definition of ecocentric thought in which,

> Ecocentrism is based on an ecologically informed philosophy of *internal relatedness*, according to which all organisms are not simply interrelated with their environment but also *constituted* by those very environmental interrelationships.
>
> (p. 49)

Through this conceptualization of the interelatedness of all nature, including humanity, the idea is to abolish boundaries. Eckersley argued that the world was made up of events rather than substances and therefore this made it more difficult to establish boundaries between individuals or species. Through such an approach any faculty that we may choose to support our claim to superiority would be undermined because individual humans may not possess such an attribute or a non-human may exhibit evidence of such a faculty.

Such interrelatedness was not just something that informed our thinking about the relationship between humans and non-humans but also about relations between humans and the cultural, political and economic framework within which these are played out (*ibid.*, p. 53). Such an approach undermined the individualistic and atomistic conceptualization of the human condition dominant in the western capitalist tradition. Rather, it promoted the idea that we have a mutual interest and interrelatedness with all the rest of humanity:

> we do not exist as separate entities and *then* enter into these relations. From the moment we are born, we are constituted by, and coevolve within the context of, such relations.
>
> (Eckersley, p. 53)

She quoted Zimmerman who contended that the humanistic belief that humanity was the summit or goal of evolution or history, and the source of all value, justified the 'plundering' of nature because it was valueless. Clearly if one took on board the writings of political philosophers such as Locke, who argued that nature was only given value through the action of labour in its transformation, then such a view was logical. Indeed, it could be argued that Marx's labour theory of value also promoted the exploitation of the natural world. However, it may be argued that by seeing humanity as the summit of evolution this linked mankind to nature and gave all nature a share in a common evolutionary history.

## The alternative western tradition

However, the idea frequently argued by greens that western ethical traditions were 'inadequate when the problems at hand include non-human entities' (Cuomo, 1996, p. 47) as with Leopold, were unsubstantiated. While it may be said that the dominant tradition was rationalist, particularly since the Enlightenment and the advent of modern scientific method, this should not ignore the significance of an alternative tradition of critical and sometimes anti-rationalist thought. The work of

Isiah Berlin has been a notable exploration of this alternative tradition. As he pointed out,

> Opposition to the central ideas of the French Enlightenment and of its allies and disciples in other European countries is as old as the movement itself. The proclamation of the autonomy of reason and the methods of the natural sciences, based on observation as the sole reliable method of knowledge, and the consequent rejection of the authority of revelation, sacred writings and their accepted inter-preters, tradition, prescription, and every form of non-rational and transcendent source of knowledge, was naturally opposed by the Churches and religious thinkers of many persuasions ... More formi-dable was the relativist and sceptical tradition that went back to the ancient world.
>
> (1998, p. 243)

Writers such as Schelling viewed humanity's relationship with nature as beyond the analytical capacity of the natural sciences. For him, the universe was a 'self-developmental' force, which could only be understood in a non-rational way by poets and philosophers. Nature, however, was

> a living organism, responds to questions put by the man of genius, while the man of genius responds to the questions put by nature, for they conspire with each other ...
>
> (*Ibid.*, pp. 260–1)

This relationship was evident in the development of the Romantic movement and was, according to Berlin, 'commonplace' in the works of authors such as Wordsworth, Goethe and Carlyle. Such scepti-cism, and indeed downright opposition, was contained in the anti-rationalist works of writers such as Vico, Herder and Joseph de Maistre. However, Berlin pointed out that frequently the anti-rationalist tradi-tion was fearful of nature and often felt most alienated from it. For example,

> Maistre ... accepted the ancient view that men before the flood were wise; but they sinned and were destroyed; and now their degenerate descendants can find truth not by the harmonious development of their faculties, not in philosophy and physics, but in revelation

vouchsafed to the saints and doctors of the Church of Rome, supported only too clearly by observation.

(1990, p. 110)

This observation did not reveal harmony, rather it saw nature 'red in tooth and claw'. In contrast, it was the figures of the Enlightenment who were more often the ones who identified nature, and humanities place in it, as harmonious with 'civilization' undermining that relationship:

> Holbach and Rousseau were complete adversaries, but both spoke of nature with piety, as being in not too metaphorical a sense harmonious benevolent and liberating.
>
> (*Ibid.*, p. 110)

While Rousseau saw the revelation of natural harmony as being given to 'the untutored heart' of native peoples, Holbach believed that it was truly revealed through rational thought and enquiry.

Other aspects of this alternative tradition of western thought were also evident in modern ecological writers. The belief in the diversity of cultures and their value was not a new post-modern development. It was evident from the period of the Enlightenment and has been of particular importance in the development of Nationalism. For Berlin it was evident that,

> Vico is the true father of the modern concept of culture and of what one might call cultural pluralism, according to which each authentic culture has its own unique vision, its own scale of values, which, in the course of development, is superseded by other visions and values but never wholly so.
>
> (*Ibid.*, pp. 59–60)

It was in the Romantic movement that Roszak also identified an important strand of thought that could supply an alternative to the mainstream tradition. Consequently, in searching for an ethic which recognized the importance of nature, the idea of working within the western tradition of rationalist (and, indeed, anti-rationalist) discourse should not be excluded. The potential danger that may be seen as evident within a great deal of ecological or environmentalist writing is that it unthinkingly rejects western concepts and culture by attaching blame to it for environmental damage, while embracing non-western cultures in a half-digested way, simply because they are non-western.

Indeed, such an acceptance of non-western traditions and the search for an environmental ethic to heal the alienation felt by modern humanity can lead to difficult areas of debate between ecologists. Pepper (1993) has shown how the urge to identify with 'primitive' or 'traditional' societies can lead into problem areas or indeed political cul de sacs. While ecological anarchists such as Roszak saw small scale traditional societies as possessing a health and spiritual understanding in their relationship with nature, these societies have significant drawbacks, although some authors see these as virtues:

> Young is at pains to stress that millions in poor countries have that spiritual confidence which deep ecologists seek, yet have very different priorities. Particular people (families) come first, then dead and future kin, then other species, and, lastly, ecosystems.
>
> (Pepper, 1993, p. 167)

In addition, Young rejected the social ecology of writers such as Bookchin in areas such as patriarchy. While Bookchin rejected patriarchy, supporting equality and social liberation, Young argued that patriarchy

> has been part of many cultures which have for a long time achieved a high degree of 'harmony' with nature.
>
> (*Ibid.*, p. 167)

For Young, therefore, experiments with equality and open families are not to be undertaken, as there was no evidence that they would be ecologically sound. The priorities were tradition and harmony with nature even if this resulted in strong, hierarchical and patriarchal societies and within the families of those societies. For Peppper, the problem associated with the deep ecology perspective was that it romanticized traditional societies and was consequently profoundly conservative in its social message:

> It is hard to see how it differs from Goldsmith's constant appeals for a return to 'traditional' societies, by which he once held up the oppressive Indian caste system as ecologically desirable, or from deep ecology's call to the 'minority tradition' – a confusing conflation of native American cultures, Taoism, and 'some Buddhist communities' with the 1930s Spanish anarchists and the 1871 Paris commune.
>
> (Pepper, 1993, pp. 168–9)

Such an approach could significantly conflict with more socially radical concepts such as Pepper's own social ecology or indeed the ecocentric approach propounded at times in Eckersley.

## Intergenerational responsibility

A further area of concern for an ecological ethic was that of intergenerational responsibility. This issue centred on the problem of the responsibility we may owe towards future generations. In particular, the environmental movement asked right from the beginning, what condition should we leave the earth in for future generations to enjoy? Much of the early literature, including *Blueprint for Survival* (Goldsmith, 1972) and *Limits to Growth* (Meadows, 1972), centred on the consequences of using finite, non-renewable resources for both our own immediate future and that of future generations.

Cameron argued that such a concern was so central that without it 'much of the steam would go out of the environmental movement':

> One of the toughest moral issues which confronts us is how we should balance our responsibility to posterity against our responsibility to our own generation – how we should weigh the moral imperative to alleviate poverty and starvation today against the obligation to conserve the environment for the sake of those who will come after us.
>
> (1989, p. 57)

However, authors such as Passmore have argued that we have no direct responsibility for future generations, as we cannot know with certainty the consequences of some of our actions. Our responsibility only relates to those consequences that are foreseeable and there are significant problems is forecasting even a decade ahead. Again, the predictions concerning resource depletion contained within both Blueprint for Survival and the Limits to Growth were so far out that for a time it led to a decline in support for the environmental perspective.

One approach to intergenerational problems has been that undertaken by the group of economists associated with the *Blueprint for a Green Economy* and *Blueprint 2* (Pearce, 1989 and 1991). They noted a range of different possible approaches to environmental resource management as a solution to the intergenerational issue. Firstly, a traditional cost–benefit analysis (CBA) in which environmental damage as well as benefits are discounted over time so that the costs and benefits associated with a project are given a greater value if they affect the present generation rather than future generations. Investment in the present will encourage the development of new technologies and solutions to environmental problems which future generations will be able to resolve. Such an approach was generally associated with a technical fix attitude to ecological problems. The second approach argued for in *Blueprint 2* was a 'stewardship ethic' aimed at considering the interests of future generations who are deemed to lack the ability to participate in decisions taken in the present which will affect them:

> Sustainable development is seen to involve compensating the future for environmental damage being done now, and damage done in the past. Compensation requires the passing-on to future generations of a stock of natural assets no smaller than the stock in the possession of current generations.
>
> (Pearce, 1991, p. 214)

This was not to say that these 'natural' assets are the same physical resources but rather that where such resources have been depleted then there have been investments or technological developments which can compensate for the loss of the original resource, a replacability thesis. A modified CBA can include such replaceable value in its calculations of costs and benefits for future generations.

The third approach was that of a more 'preservationist' ethos in which Environmental Impact Assessment as a technique took priority over the more economic concepts embodied in CBA. The EIA approach involved giving priority to non-economic values, such as cultural and ethical criteria. For the authors this signified a more ecocentric approach and one centred on Leopold's Land Ethic (p. 219). Finally, there was the more radical deep green approach in which intrinsic or inherent value was assigned to the natural world and consequently CBA had to be abandoned. Intrinsic value may be identified as the dominant value and so the exploitation of natural resources was minimal:

> Such minimum intrinsic depletion rules risk wholly inequitable 'trades', such as conserving intrinsic values now at the expense of social justice – and even survival, if the context is that of poor developing countries.
>
> (p. 221)

For the authors of the *Blueprint* the choice rested between the two middle concepts, with the mainstream CBA approach and the deep green approach both being ruled out.

Perhaps the most comprehensive statement on the relationship between ecology and future generations was that provided by Avner de-Shalit (1995). De-Shalit aimed to establish a theory of intergenerational justice as the 'moral basis' for environmental decision making and one in which there was a form of distributive justice between the generations. He challenged other concepts of ethics which tended towards an individualistic approach to justice and could neglect responsibility towards future generations.

De-Shalit argued that the development of an adequate intergenerational ethic needed to be based on a communitarian concept in which the individual was conceived within the context of a community. In addition, that community was not restricted to the present generation or indeed to the next one. Rather, its identity was not time limited as we cannot be sure that any future generation will find solutions to the problems we leave them with, consequently we have an obligation not to do anything which could damage future members of the community. In addition, by acting to conserve resources and the natural world for future generations we also benefit ourselves. This was not because, as with utilitarians, we would be imposing our present conception of the good onto future generations, rather we are benefiting present generations as well:

> according to the communitarian theory, the obligations that we have to future people and the policies adopted for their sake do not necessarily contradict obligations to contemporaries in all respects. Indeed, if we think about environmental policies, they are for the sake of posterity, but also for the sake of our contemporaries.
>
> (p. 127)

De-Shalit contended that such an approach to the environment recognized that we are not simply concerned with resources but also with the quality of life. In addition, by rejecting an individualistic approach, such as that contained in utilitarian, contractarian and rights based approaches, the communitarian approach did not speculate on the potential life of some future individual but started from the idea that any obligation to conserve resources and the environment rested with us. This was because we are part of the same community as are future generations so our efforts are centred on the obligations we have to that community. It was not a question of hypothetical future lives but the life of the community, a community with shared values.

For de-Shalit the problems that confront other ethical theorists concerning what we should be leaving future generations was not at issue. For others there was a problem with the possibility of leaving behind a world that future generations may not actually value. De-Shalit for example considered the idea of a future generation that favoured industry over picturesque villages. While this may be a problem for other ethical approaches, de-Shalit argued that from a communitarian perspective a change in values amongst future generations removed them from 'our transgenerational community' (p. 130) and therefore this reduced our obligation to them.

This appeared rather problematic because rather than solving the problem identified by other theorists about what we should leave, he seemed to be saying that if future generations have different values then we can disown them, they are not part of our community! This significantly side-stepped the issue by determining that our ecological values are the important ones which link us into this wider community and any other was irrelevant. However, not only did it therefore exclude future generations from this value community if they did not accept these values, logically it also excluded members of the present day human society from this community if they also rejected these values.

## Metaphysical or spiritual ecology

Much of the debate on how we can overcome the alienation of humanity from nature has so far been centred around the tradition of ethical debate and efforts to try and overcome its limitations by including the rest of the natural world. However, some would argue that such a debate is irrelevant even when it rejected the Western rationalist tradition. Rather a metaphysical or spiritual awareness of nature was required, one which goes beyond such rational debate. Dobson noted how this affected the movement and how it encouraged a belief in the relationship between ecology and lifestyle. It was the rejection of the idea that change should be limited to the formal political arena that was central to this perspective.

However, Dobson (1995) also pointed out that this approach was the result of problems associated with change through conventional means, given the size of the crisis:

> The general point behind the religious approach is that the changes
> that need to take place are too profound to be dealt with in the

political arena, and that the proper territory for action is the psyche rather than the parliamentary chamber. This approach takes seriously the point...that political opposition to radical green change would be massive – and side steps it.

(p. 136)

He referred to the work of Bahro, Porritt and Winner where Bahro argued that the situation required a much greater change than the points of debate preoccupying Green parties and committees. Porritt and Winner (1988, pp. 246–9) argued in favour of a 'metaphysical reconstruction' which perceived the need to recognize the spiritual nature of the earth and our relationship to it.

For Bahro, therefore, the spiritual side of the equation was much more significant than the economic and political when considering appropriate levels of change. This was also reflected in Roszak and Schumacher where they both referred directly to the spiritual needs of humanity to relocate themselves within nature. The Buddhist economics of Schumacher was of significance for the development of a new approach to the environment.

For Wallace the spiritual dimension was also the most appropriate approach towards overcoming differences within the environmental movement itself. Wallace (1997, p. 304) discussed the differences between groups that he terms 'antitoxics' and 'preservationists'. Wallace noted that these two extremes disassociated themselves from the idea of environmentalism. On the one hand the antitoxics were concerned with the environmental health of human communities by opposing dumping and pollution, arguing that they were for protecting humans not 'birds and bees'. Preservationists on the other hand were frequently associated with a misanthropic disregard for human wellbeing, associating themselves with wilderness as the 'only reality'. Wallace argued that by developing an ecological spirituality these two groups could be mediated:

> To uphold, therefore, the integrity of the *whole* is to experience the *holy* or sacred through living a life of communal *healing* and *well being*. My suggestion is that sustainable religion enables a mediation between antitoxics and conservationists by explicating the common spiritual-holistic philosophy that is implied by the beliefs and actions characteristic of both movements.
>
> (Wallace, 1997, p. 304)

However, Wallace was arguing from an evangelical position in which he saw his role and others as what he termed a 'priestly' function, whereby activists within both movements come to accept this common spiritual perspective to enable them to maintain a struggle which may well have significant setbacks (p. 307).

The role of spirituality was also significant for the ecological attitude towards cultural diversity. The appreciation of the lifestyles and beliefs of traditional cultures was based on the idea that such societies had a closer relationship with the environment and their spiritual beliefs helped to explain the world to the society, but also to identify a place within the world for the society in question. While this belief was subjected to detailed criticism (e.g., see Milton, 1996) the attachment to such a view was held by a significant number of writers and activists.

However, there was also a strong belief that as alienated beings we need to re-establish a close relationship to the soil. Leopold's Land Ethic was one example of this as was Goldsmith's view that small communities were more natural. However, as Garner (1996, p. 35) and Dobson (1995, pp. 124–34) noted, a large number of people found the pursuit of material comfort satisfying while ecologists often spoke disparagingly of such a lifestyle.

This also created a problem for developing strategies for change towards an ecologically sound society. While some people may become 'converted' to the ideas contained in such a set of beliefs the problem was, what should be done to those who are not convinced and may adopt opposition tactics to the implementation of ecological regulation? For the movement as a whole the adoption of direct action tactics, often in an effort to overturn the decisions that have been adopted through the existing democratic processes, may in fact open the way for opponents to adopt similar tactics when their interests are affected by the decisions of a green government.

## Conclusion

The problems associated with the development of an ecological ethic are numerous. In the first instance the aim of developing such an ethic from within the tradition of western ethical thought was open to criticism because that tradition was dominated by an approach which centred on humanity's responsibilities, rights and duties with little reference to the wider natural world. Secondly, much ecological thinking began from a fundamental critique of the traditions of rational thought emerging from the enlightenment, and as a consequence a number of theorists tended to reject the use of rationalist debate over ethics as a valid process.

This presented a particular difficulty for those who have tried to develop an objective theory of value for nature or a concept of intrinsic value. This was questioned on the grounds that it failed by being essentially an anthropocentric perspective which even writers such as Goodin, who had invested a lot in the development of such approaches, admitted to. However, the development of an ecocentric position was equally problematic and too frequently led to a rejection of rational thinking and the adoption of a more spiritual, and essentialist approach that can become morally exclusive.

# 5
## Eco-feminism and Post-modernism

Political ecology is one of the most significant developments in modern thought and social action. The development of feminist thought is of equal if not more importance in challenging traditional social and political thought. Feminist authors have brought to the analysis of environmental issues possibly the most significant new insights into the debate. This is not surprising given that women provide the majority of activists in the environmental movement, as well as in the animal rights movement, although still finding themselves under-represented in the most senior full-time positions in the new green bureaucracies.

The combination of mainstream feminist thought and their consideration of environmental issues gave rise to the concept of eco-feminism. While this has been subject to criticism by deep ecologists, feminist approaches may well be the most fruitful area for the future development of environmental thought and action. Mary Mellor (1997) has provided the clearest exposition of eco-feminist ideas that, as with mainstream environmental thought, provide a range of positions rather than a single dominant view. Mellor placed these ideas under two major categories, affinity eco-feminism centred on the natural relationship of women with nature, and radical approaches based on social constructivist approaches.

However, within Mellor's writing these two main categories may be separated out further: feminist spirituality and an affinity eco-feminism related to the biological essence of women; social/ist eco-feminism and development eco-feminism or what she terms 'the view from the South'. Each of these raised important issues which challenged not just critics of the ecology movement but important voices in the movement itself. Indeed, while Mellor herself recognized that eco-feminism had within it an 'essentialist' strand which she was critical of, the existence of such a position was useful in questioning some of the ideas within ecology, particularly from the right of the political spectrum.

For Mellor, the problem with essentialist ideas was the way in which they opened up the possibility of women being identified with a biological nature that hid the differences in material experience between women. Critics of essentialism saw it as 'reactionary because it essentializes and naturalizes both women and nature' (1997, p. 2) thus universalizing the female experience and hiding inequalities. The spiritual feminism evident within much eco-feminist writing from an affinity standpoint also included writings which emphasized the biological bases of social difference where the experience of men and women are different because of their bodily existence. This resulted in the 'embeddedness' of women in nature where they were reminded of their position as part of the natural order through the ebb and flow of their bodies and its link to the 'cycle of life and death'. The concept of embeddedness was also central to the eco-feminist critique of rationalist approaches to environmental ethics (see Plumwood, 1994) where emotional contact with nature was subordinated to the rational project of establishing an objective value for nature. Affinity-based eco-feminism reinvested such emotional contact with meaning and raised it to a higher level of importance.

This in turn was reflected in the way in which authors such as Luce Irigary attempted to replace the concepts of separateness and alienation through the use of myths in which 'mother and daughter lived attuned to a fertile, benevolent nature'. It was the break with nature that was comparable to the treatment of women by men and was associated by Irigary and Helene Cixous with a historical period now reaching an end. As part of this process they identified the creation of an affirmative relationship between humanity and nature as one '*between subjects* and not of a subject/object dualism' (Conley, 1997, p. 137).

Such a concern with how we relate emotionally as well as intellectually with nature was also reflected in the way we speak of the Earth in western traditions, and in many other cultures, as She or Mother Earth. For some eco-feminists it was our use of such concepts which revealed the link between how humanity treated the Earth and how women were treated (see for example C. Roach, 1996, pp. 52–65).

Mellor identified socialist eco-feminism as being at the centre of the relationship between the peace movement, 1960s direct action, and the Left in the USA. She noted particularly the position of Ynestra King as the leading writer and activist who established this link through actions such as the Women's Pentagon Action between 1980 and 1981.

However, the materialist basis and left-wing nature of social constructivist approaches to eco-feminism have found some difficulty in becoming established as the mainstream due to the historical antagonism to socialist thought within America. Consequently, Mellor noted that such approaches were more common in Europe while spiritual eco-feminism, with its discussion of the role of native American and other aboriginal cultures, was much more at home in the USA.

## View from the South

The 'view from the South' was centred on the position of women in developing countries who were subjected to 'maldevelopment'. The exemplar of this approach was Vandana Shiva who made the connection between a concern with women in the developed world; the introduction of modernity as the only model for development. The role of western scientific knowledge in the establishment of a 'mono-culture' where non-Western cultures were increasingly marginalized reinforced this model of development (Mellor, 1997, pp. 64–7).

Shiva made a connection between the critique of modernism in post-modernist thought and the concern expressed by ecological writers over the way in which positivist science attempted to establish the scientific method as the only approach to knowledge. The approach to eco-feminism developed by Mies and Shiva (1993) aimed to establish a link between the situation faced by women in the developing world and the productive process. This combination of ecology, Marxism and feminism resulted in a complex analysis of the relationship between woman's position in the productive process and an analysis of the relationship between grassroots movements in the developed world and subsistence in the developing world.

They argued the need for a different approach to economic activity, which they termed the 'subsistence perspective'. Essentially this approach was based on the idea that women were still the main economic actors in the most basic areas of economic activity, such as housework, child rearing, caring and food production and preparation. This was the case within both developed and developing worlds where men tended to lose sight of the essential requirements for subsistence:

Women are more concerned about a survival subsistence perspective than are men, most of whom continue to believe that more growth, technology, science and 'progress' will simultaneously solve the ecological and economic crisis; they place money and power above life.

(Mies and Shiva, 1993, p. 304)

For Mies and Shiva the subsistence perspective was based upon a number of core characteristics:

1. Economic activity to be needs-based and not centred on production growth.
2. Economic activity therefore required a new, non-exploitative relationship both with nature and with other individuals. This would involve a change in the existing division of labour between men and women and would replace a money-based economy with one centred on community.
3. Decision-making would be based upon participatory and grassroots democracy which would reflect the feminist concern that the personal is political.
4. A recognition of the interconnectedness of social and ecological problems.
5. A re-evaluation of the scientific project which would reject a positivist and reductionist position.
6. A reintegration of culture and work.
7. A rejection of private ownership of common resources, such as land and water.
8. The inclusion of man through a redefined identity.

They argued strongly that such a set of principles could overcome the alienation of humanity, including men, from nature, and overcome 'established dualisms and false dichotomies' (*ibid.*, pp. 319–21).

   The link with the problems facing the non-western world was particularly acute when considering the attitudes towards population growth. For eco-feminists the issue of population was associated more with the need to empower women in patriarchal societies, providing them with the opportunity to take control over their own bodies. The population issue was not about the limits to the earth's carrying capacity, but the economic control of the land, which lay in the hands of men and their organizations (Mellor, 1997, p. 32). Mellor also pointed out that in many cases, where ecological writers have taken on board some of the issues raised by eco-feminists, it was with the aim of seeing a happy coincidence between increased access to education and employment with a reduction in family sizes. However, there was also an attachment to a more conservative view that ecological societies and the more traditional extended families required women to take a more home-based role. Mellor noted the view of Goldsmith who contended that the,

> communities that he sees as emerging 'naturally' are ecologically benign, part of an evolutionary process, whereas human attempts to make conscious progress (science, the state) are ecologically destructive. Women's position is ordained within the family. For Goldsmith, hierarchy is part of nature – 'the Way' – and must not be challenged.
>
> (Mellor, 1997, p. 129)

Consequently, the eco-feminist position challenged some of the assumptions of more mainstream ecological thinking, in that it reinterpreted the concern with population and the relationship between the developed and the developing world. The important aspects contained within some eco-feminist thought was that it challenged some of the assumptions about the nature of development, but also in some areas raised the problem of over-romanticising the nature of traditional societies. The assumption that all women in the developing world have the same problems, and were not part of the problem of environmental degradation but champions of an ecologically sound future, failed to identify the differences between women (Braidotti *et al.* quoted in Mellor, 1997, p. 35). This position echoed the criticism of essentialist eco-feminism, but also identified some of the contradictions within ecological, eco-feminist, and indeed post-modernist thinking.

The radical deep ecology position early in the development of environmental thinking identified population growth as a core issue in the ecological crisis. Both Hardin's 'Tragedy of the Commons' and Ehrlich's 'Population Bomb' were part of this trend. For example, Ehrlich advocated aggressive and coercive approaches to population control in the USA and abroad. Indeed, as Hayward (1994, pp. 147–8) argued, the neo-Malthusian position of authors such as these led to a criticism of human rights at the most basic level. Efforts to maintain subsistence amongst existing populations were simply delaying a period of inevitable, and much worse, mass-starvation:

> The claiming of a universal human right to subsistence is therefore self-defeating, hence unrealisable, and so cannot be spoken of without wilful disingenuousness as a *right*.
>
> (*Ibid.*, p. 147)

Hardin's position resulted in the development of the so-called 'life-boat ethic' where the rich nations had to make the decision to reject pleas for aid from the poorest as this would only store up trouble for the future. Deep ecology's dismissal of the anthropocentric approach resulted in the rejection of the rights of individuals in support of the wider needs of the species, with humanity as one species amongst many, and of the planet as a whole. However, as such the result was the allocation of the ability to choose to individual men in power who would be able to enforce their choices in the apparent belief that they were supporting the planet's needs and not their own privilege.

## Affinity eco-feminism and deep ecology

Some would argue that women have a particular relationship with nature and this places them closer than men to resolving the problem of alienation. Jagtenberg and McKie (1997) stated that,

> For many environmentalists, their location as women has influenced their environmental views. Women's identification of patriarchy as a dominant institution of oppression has enabled environmentalism to develop a more thoroughly pluralist movement.
>
> (pp. 118–19)

This relationship has been the subject of some tensions with deep ecology as some eco-feminists see the ecological crisis as a result of the oppressive nature of a world based on patriarchy. Their identification with nature was part of their identity as women. For deep ecologists this presented a problem in that eco-feminism was still tainted by an anthropocentric world-view (*ibid.*, pp. 32–3). The authors did not reconcile this difference as they accepted it as part of the pluralism of ecological thought and indeed of post-modernity.

It may be argued that this position left eco-feminism open to challenge by its opponents. With eco-feminists failing to develop a more rigorous conclusion, and maintaining a pluralistic stance, opponents, utilizing their own interpretation of the feminist position, presented a flawed image. An example of this was shown by J.B. Callicott (1993, pp. 331–2) in his critiques of Fox and deep ecology. Fox presented an extreme position for eco-feminism by stating that if feminists argued that patriarchy was responsible for men dominating nature as well as dominating women, then if women are liberated from such domination this will 'automatically liberate nature' (p. 331). Not only does Fox contend that such a position was humanistic, and therefore anthropocentric, but it was also a diversion for activists away from the main challenge of the environmental crisis.

Callicott criticized the view presented by Fox as a misreading of the eco-feminist position, arguing that it was 'self-serving and facile':

> Other movements…can make (and indeed have made) the same claim: If we only abolish the ideology of racism, capitalism, imperialism, etc. then we will usher in the millennium and all will be right with the world, natural as well as social.

> (p. 332)

According to Callicott, Fox argued that by trying to identify patriarchy as the root problem of oppression and domination eco-feminism opened up the possibility of a society in which the domination of one part of humanity by another was eradicated but nature was exploited for the communal benefit of humanity. Callicott noted that it would be unlikely that any society in which all other forms of oppression had been eradicated would continue to dominate nature. In addition, Plumwood had cogently argued that to assert that eco-feminists are stating that the liberation of women from domination by men would be the complete answer was a 'straw woman'. For Plumwood the role of eco-feminism was 'not to absorb or sacrifice the critique of anthropocentrism, but to deepen and enrich it' (Plumwood, 1994, p. 158).

For eco-feminists it was the dualism contained within the scientific method and the positivism of the modernist agenda, which was central to domination. While Fox may be able to assert that a liberated, humanist society could still exploit nature, deep ecology was subject to similar criticisms. The identification of a critical debate between centralist and decentralist approaches to political action and structures was evidence that human rights and liberty could be suppressed in order to resolve environmental issues. An ecologically sound society with sustainable resource use may be one dominated by a 'new priesthood' determining the family and social activity of individuals. In addition, green thought often centred on the maintenance of species and their habitats, involving culling or at least control of individual members of the species for the benefit of the whole.

The problem identified in relation to deep ecology was that it may be raising the environment to the point where it becomes a moral absolute in which all natural entities should 'unfold in their own way unhindered by the various forms of human domination' (Fox, quoted in Milton, 1996, p. 207). Such a position at its extreme runs counter to the post-modernist framework which, it can be argued, contains within it ecological thought. For example, in respect of the pluralism identified as central to eco-feminism, Gare contended that post-modernism supported

> the efforts of eco-feminists and other environmentalists to revive the suppressed discourses of women and non-Europeans in opposition to patriarchal Western discourse (provided these are not in turn raised as absolutes).
>
> (1995, p. 93)

Because of these issues, deep ecology and eco-feminism have found themselves at odds, with both accusing the other of shallowness. As Sessions (1996) argued, each tended to emphasize the others weaknesses without recognizing their areas of similarity. For eco-feminists, deep ecologists responded to the problem of duality in the same way as conventional western thought by considering nature as an alternative duality. Nature was the 'other' 'with which one becomes unified in some kind of self-transcending love' (King, 1996, p. 86). King also argued that there was a similar criticism that could be levelled by eco-feminists against the animal rights writings of Singer and Regan. The aim of trying to include animals in the 'moral domain' occupied by humans resulted in the effort to 'construct a moral community on the basis of sameness rather than leaving space for a community of difference' (*ibid.*, p. 85).

Plumwood was equally critical of the way in which some deep ecological thought developed a metaphysics aimed at eradicating differences between humans and the rest of nature. What she called the 'indistinquishability account' asserted that there were no boundaries between the human self and nature, that the dualism that formed the core of modernist or positivist thinking was wrong. However, according to Plumwood there was no real effort to understand the development of this dualism and the resulting concept was both too general and too powerful a tool for the reconciliation of these issues:

> ...the view of humans as metaphysically unified with the cosmic whole will be equally true whatever the relation humans stand in with nature...the human self is just as indistinquishable from the bulldozer and Coca-Cola bottle as the rocks or the rain forest.'
>
> (Plumwood, 1994, p. 149)

Those who argued in favour of such an approach believed that it would lead to the identification of human needs with those of the natural world, and so lead to an eco-centric viewpoint. Plumwood argued that one could just as easily come to identify the needs of the natural world with the self-interested needs of humanity. Consequently, she contended that we needed to reject the Cartesian dualism of modernist science and recognize our animal nature, while also identifying the existence of mind within the natural world. Indeed, her criticism of dualism extended to the idea of essentialist eco-feminist positions as she asserted that the identification of a specifically feminine culture was to adopt the dualism of previous thinking:

> To celebrate womanhood is to celebrate something that has been created by inequality. Making the same point as Ynestra King, Plumwood argues that the challenge must be to the dualism itself, i.e. to the master's story.
>
> (Mellor, 1997, p. 115)

However, deep ecologists argued that eco-feminism's central concern with patriarchal domination was too shallow and anthropocentric, neglecting the wider natural world (Sessions, 1996, pp. 148–50). Sessions believed that both strands underestimated each other. Deep ecology placed an emphasis on the diversity contained within nature and at its heart there was the recognition of bio-diversity within a global unity. Eco-feminism on the other hand needed to clarify its position concerning the human relationship with the non-human world. However, eco-feminism was clear in identifying the role of domination within species, particularly humanity, as well as between species. Sessions concluded by stating that the question for both groups was,

> How are we to comprehend our relationships with the elements and the inhabitants of the non-human world such that they are equal but different.
>
> (p. 150)

Plumwood also argued that while deep ecology, like eco-feminism, considered the need to establish a connection with a universal Self, she also contended that deep ecology failed to fully embrace a wholesale critique of reason. Her criticism centred on the way in which deep ecology saw the need for humans to sacrifice the self for a greater Self associated with a wider cosmology. But in doing so she argued that deep ecologists rejected the emotional embrace of kinship with nature at a personal level:

> This treatment of particularity, the devaluation of an identity tied to particular parts of the natural world as opposed to an abstractly conceived whole, the cosmos, reflects the rationalistic preoccupation with the universal and its account of ethical life as oppositional to the particular.
>
> (Plumwood, 1994, p. 151)

The concern of deep ecology with the universal, the species, as opposed to the particular, or the individual animal, presented a problem in relation to their natural allies including eco-feminists and animal rights supporters.

## Eco-feminism, post-modernity and ecology

Some eco-feminist writers in their critique of rational thought and their rejection of the universal, placed them squarely within the post-modernist realm. In addition, the desire of many ecological writers to develop a new environmental ethic to move forward from the earlier critique of humanity's relationship with nature as an expression of alienation, also revealed significant, although flawed, connections with post-modernism. Postmodernism raised questions not just central to the way in which environmental thinking was critical of the modernist project but also explored the nature of eco-activism as an example of new social movements. The problem of identifying ecological thought with post-modernism was, however, a further example of the contradictions inherent within some of the writings on environmental thought.

In defining post-modernism, Jagtenberg and McKie argued that it went beyond the alienated and angst-ridden conception of humanity which was associated with modernity:

> ... in the recent history of social theory in the humanities and the arts, alienation and humanism have been more dominant concerns than the radically decentering processes of postmodernism, deep ecology and eco-feminism. Their former concerns are predominantly centred around the imperatives of science, technology, progress and economic growth and are significantly pre-ecological.
>
> (1997, p. 4)

As with post-modernity, they argued that green theory went beyond the modernists agenda of trying to identify a single cause thesis. Rather, green theory was 'politically and theoretically diverse', but was also in the process of developing a new paradigm which could incorporate such diversity. Consequently, they were critical of social theorist who neglected eco-feminism, arguing that this was the result of the dominance of Enlightenment, modernist values with late-Marxist elements (*ibid.*, p. 190).

While the work of eco-feminists was valuable in moving away from the patriarchal concerns reflected in some mainstream ecological thinking, it created other problems. By centring on patriarchal domination and affinity with nature as the solution to environmental problems, and indeed to the problems faced by women themselves, the perspective was too narrowly focused. In addition, the linkages identified with the problems facing women in the developing world as the embodiment of the worst aspects of the ecological crisis appeared to romanticize the position of such traditional societies. Too often in eco-feminist and mainstream ecological writing, 'traditional' societies were seen as environmentally sound while modern western societies were seen as ecologically devastating and embodiments of patriarchal domination. Some eco-feminist literature pointed to the need to challenge the patriarchal nature of many traditional societies, but failed to identify their damage to the environment. The issue facing post-modernist thought, as well as ecological and eco-feminist writers, concerned the way that in challenging the universalism of western rationalist/scientific thinking, it frequently accepted everything non-western and rejected only the very western tradition out of which such positions had themselves evolved.

At the heart of this problem was the attempt by post-modernism to reveal the failure of the modernist project to create a unity of thought, while at the same time trying to establish itself as part of an epochal change. An example was the work of Jagtenberg and McKie where they stated that the modernist project had led to the problem of the identity of a positivist science with the possibility of nuclear destruction or ecological night-time:

> Our own hopes lie with the environmental movements, with enlarging our own eco-culturalist area, and with creating the consciousness for a genuinely global movement with common goals – despite conflicting politics, asymmetrical North-South power axes, and differing sets of eco-problems…To be 'post-man' scientists

though, they must be capable of steering clear of any residual modernist trajectories insensible to knowledges that are not exclusively Western, modern, male and middle-class.

(1997, p. 85)

Consequently, the critique of the modernist project was associated with a critical assessment of progress as an illusion in which positivist science was identified as a key symbol. The possibility that the scientific/modernist project was leading towards the destruction of the planet was seen as a negation of the hopes contained in those c19th beliefs in progress.

Other post-modernist authors also developed a definition of modernism in which progress played a central part. For Gergen (1992, pp. 211–12), modernism was associated with Enlightenment beliefs in reason and observation; the search for core concepts or essentials; a belief in progress towards a better future and finally, a systemic/mechanistic approach to the world rather than organic. Cook, Pakulski and Waters (1992) also noted the importance of a 'central organizing principle' for society in the modernist project. They argued that the main identifying features of modernist society included industrialization, resulting in a social structure determined by the means of production which were essentially Fordist in nature. A second feature was an increasingly centralized form of organization in which family, community and culture, the 'life-world', were 'subsumed completely within a centralized steering system' (*ibid.*, p. 33).

At its heart, was rationality based on science or more particularly the scientific method? The entry of science into the social sphere was especially characterized by the development of the social sciences and the efforts embodied in the development of scientific management and the concept of the 'one best way'.

However, Jagtenberg and McKie presented a problem for the identification of ecology as part of post-modernism. They noted the importance of ecology in moving away from an anthropocentric approach to the world and its association with alternative world-views provided by aboriginal cultures (1997, p. 70). They also argued in favour of the universal development of ecological concepts. They looked approvingly at the ideas contained in the establishment of a 'post-modern science with ecological implications', or the way in which

Lovelock's (1979) Gaia hypothesis generates congruent reconceptualisations, including global systems theory. Because, as Paul Davies

(1992) further reminds us, the whole planet shares a common origin as 'animated stardust', perhaps we humans should adopt a less exclusive and superior attitude to the subsequent shape shifting of all life on earth.

(Ibid., p. 72)

It was a situation in which post-modernism was the new universal and the science of ecology revealed an organic whole where everything was connected, for example the new cosmology and eastern theology. It was the idea that the reality of the world was found in its multiplicity within an integrating holism, where authors such as Capra and Roszak searched for the evidence of a relationship between new scientific understanding, traditional cultures and religious conceptualizations of the universe. This was the divided heart of both ecology and post-modernism. Both rejected the universalism of modernist and positivist conceptions of science and society, with their objectification of nature, the feminine and a consequent rejection of other, non-western, modes of thought. Post-modernism and ecology speak in terms of the interconnectedness of nature and humanity, a world of variety, difference and moral relativism, but within an holistic scientific ecology and an all encompassing concept of the post-modern.

Science in particular was the connecting feature of the modern world, which linked the post-modern critique and radical ecology. As Cook *et al.* (1992) noted, science and technology can be seen as an institutionalization of the enlightenment and modernist aim to control nature. With the commodification of science through technology, progression in science resulted in the production of new knowledge. However, in the period of post-modernization these features were subjected to pressures, both economic pressures and changing perceptions of failure, which resulted in a period of 'change control' (1992, p. 223). They contended that a 'post-science' would aim to break down barriers between different 'knowledges' and practices removing it from reliance on Western traditions.

It rejected the 'big science' identified as characteristic of modernist society, including its position within institutionalized academic settings and its relationship to the industrialization and militarization of society. The creation of an exponential development of scientific knowledge was also associated with the industrialization of science through the increasing division of scientific knowledge and the professionalization of science (*ibid.*, p. 200).

They also contended that more recently the *dis*organization of post-modern science was due to an increasing view that 'science is too important to be left to the scientists'. However, this was a misreading of the history of the scientific endeavour in which the development of 'big science' was intertwined with the history of an increasingly interventionist state. In the work of Easlea and Junk for example, the development of the 'nuclear state' and the spectacular aspects of modern science could only be the result of massive state intervention.

Indeed, as Commoner stated in the late 1960s, scientists have become concerned with public issues because they feel some responsibility for the problems that have arisen, notably the development of nuclear fission (1970, p. 123). However, the involvement of scientists in the public realm also opened them to criticism and the later post-modern critique because 'the citizen has begun to doubt what he used to take for granted that science is closely connected to truth' (*ibid.*, p. 127).

Another view was put forward by Pepper, who asserted bluntly that green politics were indeed post-modern politics. He, too, argued that modernism was associated with grand visions and, particularly in the academic world, a search for a unifying or grand theory to explain the world. However, the failure of this endeavour resulted in the development of a post-modernist position which asserted that we can only believe what we see, the surface appearance of things:

> …post-modernism holds that the surface appearance of a world increasingly experienced via sound reproduction and images, where the main value of many consumables is in creating or enlarging our individual or our group status, *is* reality for most. So post-modernism celebrates surface and superficiality, style, phenomena and consumerism.
>
> (1993, p. 57)

This concern with appearance resulted in media, art and architectural studies being particularly associated with post-modernism. Green politics was closely associated with image and presentation as part of its methods of direct action. Pepper also noted that Green politics was close to post-modernity because it lacked 'structure and coherence, reject(ed) authority and embrace(ed) cultural relativism – paradoxically despite their desire to see *all* societies conforming to universal meta-theories of ecology: i.e. the laws of nature like carrying capacity' (*ibid.*, p. 57).

It was the rejection of universals and the associated belief in progress which placed green politics so close to post-modernism and, like post-modernism, the rejection was all inclusive with the exception of itself, that is the universal, scientific truths of ecology and/or the globalization of the post-modernist world. The link with eco-feminism was also clear and Pepper alluded to the work of Cosgrove, arguing that postmodernism was concerned with feeling and the *experience* of unity with nature. Such subjectivist, emotional links with the rest of the natural world were clearly evident in the identification of women as close to nature in the affinity strand of eco-feminism, but where this relationship could only be experienced and not 'reasoned' through. While this approach may be the dominant concern of ecological thinkers the tendencies towards universalism within deep ecology, warned of by some eco-feminists, provided a countervailing trend.

In addition, the position adopted by ecologists in their aim to develop a new environmental ethic, ran counter to significant aspects of the post-modernist stance. In particular, post-modernism was subjected to critical assault because of its rejection of a single moral worldview, which by its nature would condemn alternative forms of thought. Instead what it provided was a 'nihilistic, cynical' position lacking any moral purpose:

> It poses a problem for many Greens who, despite the postmodernity of their politics, affirm the need for a clear moral meta-theory emanating from the 'natural order'.
>
> (Pepper, 1993, p. 137)

Pepper quoted from a Green Party member who asserted that the only things that will be banned are those activities that infringe the 'ecological imperative'. The problem for Green politics was, therefore, that there existed such an 'imperative', which acted as a determining universal while often asserting a moral, or value neutral, relativism which sought to raise the status of non-western worldviews.

Andre Gorz was also critical from a neo-Marxist perspective of the way in which 'new social movements' developed an inadequate analysis of the post-modern world. Their critique centred on the cultural framework of post-modernism and the cultural hegemony asserted by science and technology over non-western cultures:

> These movements are certainly anti-technocratic – that is, directed against the cultural hegemony of the leading stratum of the ruling class – but they strike only at the cultural assumptions and social consequences of the relations of domination, not at their economic material core.
>
> (1994, p. 72)

The green movement, as a central player amongst new social movements, needed to assess this problem and was closest to doing so in its criticisms of economic rationality and growth. Pepper recognized this when he contended that the transformation to an ecologically sound society required that economic investment should seek to reduce growth and 'the sphere governed by economic rationality' (*ibid.*, pp. 33–4).

Jagtenberg and McKie argued that efforts to link ecological thought to more traditional Marxist and neo-Marxist traditions had failed because of the perception that the adoption of green concepts was superficial. They asserted that green ideas were a classic example of cultural diversity, because of the variety of sources for their ideas from across the political spectrum, while Marxists still aimed for the dominant ideological position. Jagtenberg and McKie, however, revealed the problem that the deconstruction of existing world-views was based on an ecological imperative which itself may be seen as hegemonic. Green theorists rejected traditional, dominant positions in favour of a new system of ethics, and while they absorbed all existing political positions there was the creation of a new 'moral imperative' which was equally, if not more, universalist, essentialist and dominant:

> Green theory is politically and theoretically diverse, containing many fault lines, tensions and conflicts. Within this diversity and difference, there is, however, an emergent worldview or new paradigm that is able to contain the radical differences of eco-feminism, deep ecology, scientific ecology, and all other stakeholders in green and environmental institutional locations.
>
> (1997, p. 118)

This may also be seen as a definition of the post-modernist agenda, which also tried to provide a universal container for all traditions of thought and action which are outside the western modernist/enlightenment paradigm.

Perhaps here was the greatest dilemma facing post-modernism and ecology, in that their shared goal was a rejection of dominant western, rationalist paradigms, but the end result was the development of a critique whose aim was equally universalist. While post-modernism was inherently critical with no apparent intention of devising a new moral or ethical framework, political ecology was clearly identified with trying to establish a new ethical imperative. Indeed Gare identified this as a weakness in eco-feminism as well as the wider ecological debate. She asserted that some eco-feminist thought tended to be 'logocentric' and,

> affirms the deepest values of the structure it purports to oppose. It reinforces the idea that there is some absolute truth, and this gives some privileged group the authority to rule the rest of society.
>
> (Gare, 1995, p. 92)

It is here that my central point re-emerges, in that Gare asserted that activists have too readily adopted the approaches of their opponents. By identifying a moral absolute or a universal truth they have developed a belief in the identity of all within a holistic concept which subsumes difference. It was in line with Plumwood's critique of deep ecology and Mellor's analysis of some essentialist eco-feminist writing which rejected or at least tried to overcome difference and develop a concept of unity and holism. Gare refers to Cheney's concern that an attempt to establish that 'knowers' are all the same refuses to recognize that each individual brings to their experience of the world their own unique history and so their perspectives are,

> incommensurable with all others. The thesis of the sameness of all knowers can only be an ideological tool designed to coerce agreement, to socialize people to a particular conception of reality.
>
> (Gare, 1995, pp. 92–3)

Consequently, at this level of thinking and action there was, within the development of some ecological and eco-feminist thought, the potential for dictatorship. However, there was also here a failure to recognize that post-modernist concerns also created a tendency to reject all positions but the post-modernist approach, which may also have authoritarian aspects. But the situation embodied in post-modernism was less threatening because its position did not have at its centre an attempt to establish a new ethic, rather its potential problem was contained in its rejection of all such moral or ethical considerations as purely relative.

Gare also identified the way in which both approaches emphasized the need to look to local action, local and limited because they were facing an attempt at universalism through globalization and the modernist project. Consequently, Gare identified the relationship between postmodernist writers such as Deleuze and Guattari with their concept of a 'nomadic' politics, with deep ecologists such as Naess who

emphasized thinking globally but acting locally. While Naess supported a non-violent approach to political action, post-modernist ideas
and deep ecology did not rule out violence:

> ... the sabotage of environmentally destructive enterprises, 'monkey-
> wrenching', a strategy vigorously promoted by Dave Foreman of
> *Earth First!* also accords with the new kind of politics called for by
> Deleuze and Guattari.
>
> (Gare, 1995, p. 96)

Consequently Gare concluded that in translating post-modernist ideas
and ecological needs into political action there was an increasing need
for environmentalists to become more effective through combining ecological thinking with nationalism. Gare developed a worrying conclusion in which she contended that nationalism was the most appropriate
political form to counter international capital and globalization:

> ... environmentalists should spearhead the attack on the policies
> and the institutional changes effected by the champions of greed as
> a nationalist struggle against global capitalism and its quislings...
> Environmentalists should attack not only the ideological despotism
> of economists and pedants, but should also strive to counteract the
> nihilistic decadence which is now undermining civilization.
>
> (pp. 162–3)

It is hardly surprising that when such language is used in an academic
study, opponents of deep ecology can accuse it of fostering a form of
eco-fascism.

## Conclusion

Consequently, while postmodernism makes a claim to encompass feminism, environmentalist groups and therefore, eco-feminism (Cook,
Pakulski and Waters, 1992, pp. 138–57), there is potentially a conflict
between ecology, feminist approaches to the environment and post-
modernism. The search for a moral framework evident in much ecological thought posed a problem for those who saw a need to maintain a
moral relativism, through the recognition of a variety of cultures and
approaches. Equally, while feminism often asserted the importance of
multiculturalism and the relevance of different cultures within the
developing world, to understanding the experience of women, they

sometimes struggled with the need to recognize the patriarchal within many traditional societies. While ecologists frequently argued for the preservation of, and non-intervention in, other cultures in the belief that they can often teach us a great deal about the relationship between humanity and nature, they often found that traditional social structures were hierarchical and patriarchal. This situation was identified at times as leading some eco-feminist writers to overlook the patriarchal nature of pre-industrial societies (see Agarwhal, 1992). More conservative ecologists, such as Goldsmith, utilize traditional societies as a means of shifting back the position of women in society to a traditional and frequently more disempowered position.

For postmodernism, the important aspect of new social movements which needed further consideration was the blurring of the boundaries between the traditional realm of politics and those areas seen as the private sphere. Whether it be the claims of feminists that the personal is the political, or the essentialist position of eco-feminists that it was the physical relationship between women and nature that made the difference, such positions were considerably removed from mainstream political debate. Indeed, for traditional conservative thinkers, the very idea that there was such a connection was problematic. Traditionally the state should not be involved in the private lives of its citizens, and yet one of the dangers involved in moving towards a different political perspective, involving such personal transformation, intimately involved the private life.

Indeed, postmodernism identified the role of new lifestyles and in particular their transmission via the media and representation through images and symbols as being at the heart of new social movements. This led to the modern ecological movement being particularly good at utilizing the media to transmit its messages and images:

> Movement events are often planned by activists in a way that maximises media access and facilitates coverage. For movement activists this is an effort aimed at informing, educating, converting and mobilizing. Mass media serve this purpose and they fit a form of protest which inhabits public space and leisure time.
>
> (Cook *et al.*, 1992, p. 156)

Such an attachment to image and the associated concern with the perception that all approaches to ethics, culture and morality were relative, led to the criticism that postmodernism was superficial. As Pepper noted, postmodernism 'celebrates surface and superficiality, style, ephemera and consumerism' (1993, p. 57). Consequently, I would argue, against Pepper's position, that while postmodernism may have some valid things to say about the nature of ecology as a social movement and the way it is organized, it cannot be argued that as a philosophy or political idea ecology embodied a postmodernist position. While ecology may identify the potential value of traditional societies and act as an important critique of rationalism and the dualism of Cartesian science, its promise was the establishment of a new political and cultural morality based on the appeal of a specific branch of science. Although frequently there is an assertion of the emotional and spiritual renewal of our relationship with nature this is tied to an attachment to the lessons of science.

It may be that the science it appeals to is very different in reality to the way in which it is utilized by activists and writers on the subject of the environment. However, the use of scientific evidence and the problem of our limited scientific understanding of the interrelationship between species and their ecology was fallen back on in much of the debate. Indeed, it may be argued that the most successful areas of environmental action are those where the proponents of ecological thinking have utilized scientific evidence to back up their positions, such as on the issue of global warming and the depletion of the ozone layer. Whether such a science is post-modern is highly debatable as the methodologies utilized are still those of the traditional form of positivist science. While the lesson may be that 'everything connects' the evidence for these connections are made through a particular branch of science, albeit a multi-disciplinary branch.

# 6
# Animal Rights: An Ecological Problem?

Supporters of animal rights represent an area of significant development towards a reassessment of our relations with the non-human world. The transformation of wildlife conservation, from a concern with the protection of wilderness areas through the national parks movements, to the radical defence of animals through anti-hunting and anti-vivisectionist lobbies, was central to the more general change in radical thought. However, while there have been notable areas of overlap between the activities of animal rights supporters and environmentalists in protests and direct action over issues affecting hunting, factory farming and medical research, there have also been significant areas of disagreement.

In assessing the nature of animal rights as an environmental issue I wish to explore the reasons for such areas of divergence. What this suggests is that when we consider the work of ecologists and animal liberationists differences of approach are frequent and occasionally extremely hostile. In order to explore why this is the case the work of Peter Singer, the author most frequently cited in the serious literature on animal rights and animal liberation, will be considered.

## Peter Singer: from animal liberation to animal rights

In 'Animals and the Value of Life' Singer (1993) argued that there were three central questions to be asked after we have accepted the premise that we should not permit animals to suffer. Firstly, whether it was wrong to slaughter animals painlessly for food after they have had a happy life? Secondly, why was a mammal such as a dog different from a human being? More particularly, should we put to sleep animals whose lives were miserable when we don't do it to humans whose lives were equally miserable? Thirdly, should we stop animal experiments because they involve the needless death of animals or should we continue on the grounds that the lives of these animals in themselves are without worth, even if the experiment may not result in benefit to humans?

In addition, these questions need to be seen within the context of a wider philosophical question, that of the value of human life, the extent of that value and why it has value (*ibid.*, pp. 281–2). By considering a range of different approaches to this issue Singer arrived at a conclusion which rejected humanity's uniqueness. He argued against the idea that consciousness was unique to humans by centering a definition of consciousness or sentience on the ability to feel pleasure and pain. Extending his position from that of earlier traditions, notably the Utilitarianism of Bentham, Singer placed the ability to feel pleasure and pain at the centre of the debate over liberation. However, this could be contested and was problematic as it provided a very narrow definition of consciousness, albeit one which served Singer's central aim, the rejection of actions by humans which cause animals to suffer. Therefore, if we accepted that animals suffer, and we see consciousness in terms of pain and pleasure, then animals by definition are conscious. He contended that Descartes' dismissal of animals as mechanisms was to be rejected as it was against the 'common sense' view that animals feel pain and therefore suffer, unlike clocks:

> Descartes' attempt to show that animals are machines therefore fails; and with it fails the attempt to show that human life has unique value because human life is unique in possessing consciousness. Consciousness is something that we share with other animals, and if human lives possess unique value, it cannot be in virtue of our possession of consciousness alone.
>
> (*Ibid.*, p. 287)

However, can this conclusion be wholly secure? It may certainly be the case that all animals experience pain and pleasure, and remember the sources of such pain and pleasure, but was this the nature of consciousness we associate with humans when we speak of our self-awareness?

Singer's second argument concerned the theological question of the possession of a soul. Once again he reflected on the writings of Descartes and those of Aristotle. Singer stated that the Christian belief that only humans have souls was based, via Saint Augustine, on Aristotle's views. Singer failed to adequately explore this issue and his own position, and simply wrote off centuries of belief. He contended that Christians may be wrong in assigning greater value to the life of a human when that life was merely a small part of their greater, immortal life. Christians dismissed the life of a mortal animal, even though that life could be seen as the entirety of the existence of the creature. Singer stated that early Christians were fearful of killing other humans as the individual who was killed may have been condemned to an eternity in hell as an unrepentant sinner:

> … this attitude is not entirely logical either, since for every murder that sends to hell an unrepentant sinner who would otherwise have repented and gone to heaven, there is presumably another murder that is responsible for adding one member to the heavenly choir who, while innocent at the time of death, would have sinned mortally had he or she lived to have the chance … This last failure exhausts the lie of argument that seeks to defend the idea of the unique value of human life by reference to immortal souls.
>
> (*Ibid.*, p. 289)

However, this argument of Singer's was not just poor theology, it was poor logic. Even in his own terms the murder of a 'sinner' did not simply condemn the sinner to hell it condemned the murderer, having committed a mortal sin. Even if the murdered individual now rejoices in heaven having lived a blameless life the murderer was still condemned. In addition, if he was asserting that the more murders the merrier because more would be rapidly despatched to heaven then this was obviously nonsense. More importantly, if mankind was created in the image of God the killing of a human, rather than any other animal was an attack on the image of God.

This was connected to his next point where he discussed the idea that humanity, as the creation of God, could only be disposed of by God. God, however, had given man 'dominion' over animals and the rest of His creation. In this debate Singer again appeared to create some confusion over the relationship between God and His creation. He argued that the Dominion Theory was about rights and not about value, in that while God gave humanity the right to take the lives of animals it does not necessarily reduce their value. However, he went on to argue that as God was omniscient and a loving God He would not give humanity the right to destroy something of value:

> God would not have given humans the right to kill animals without good reason, and yet He must have known that humans do not

need to kill animals for food to survive. It would therefore appear to be an implication of the Dominion Theory, in the Judeo-Christian context, that animal life is of little or no value – for why else would God have given humans dominion over the other animals and told us that we may kill them for food.

(*Ibid*., p. 291)

Here Singer hit a problem that all animal rights supporters appear to dodge. Even if we rejected the scientific evidence about our biological and nutritional needs in respect of the use of animals for food, it was not simply about humanity's dominion. In other aspects of creation there are ecological relationships in which one species appeared to hold sway over another, for example because the lion holds dominion over the wildebeest does that mean that God values the wildebeest less than the lion? As with a number of Singer's arguments, the debate only included the relationship between humanity and other species with little in the way of an evaluation of how they affected the relationship between other species without reference to humanity. It was here that we see the emerging differences between animal rightists and ecologists. In particular it was the question of species relationships as opposed to the needs of individuals that have given evidence of strains in the relationship.

Singer's approach to the question of species centred principally on the issues of Speciesism. The idea he developed was centred on an analogy of humanity's relationship with animals with other social relations where domination or preference existed, notably those of racism and sexism. He acknowledged the criticism of this approach from those who would argue that differences between species are of a different order to those between races and gender within the same species. But he dismissed these on the grounds that the use of reason, complex language, planning for the future *et cetera*, were not present in some humans, notably young infants and those he termed 'the intellectually disabled'. Singer equated the ability of some adult primates with the abilities of infant children, and often asserted their superiority. He contended that if we selected a special capacity, such as problem solving or language skills, then these skills were not limited to human beings and, indeed, some humans did not possess these skills. Because of this more than one class of beings with these skills overlaps with the human rather than humans being a uniquely skilled class:

Thus, if we select any mental capacities on the basis of special worth the class of specially worthy beings will diverge considerably from the class of human beings. Those who attempt to eliminate this divergence by forging some logical link between these two classes will make themselves liable to the charge of Speciesism. The alternative is to abandon the belief that human life has unique value.

(*Ibid.*, p. 294)

In order to redefine this cross-species category, Singer developed a definition of the person, which was not equivalent to the class of 'human being'. In this way he hoped to extend the class of person beyond biological categories to incorporate human and non-human species (Singer, 1994, pp. 172–83).

However, the effort to redefine such a commonly accepted term as 'person' presented Singer with significant problems, particularly because in his own terms such a category had to be made from criteria which were only 'roughly' adequate. These criteria included self-consciousness or self-awareness, rationality and the ability to feel pleasure or pain (1993, pp. 295–6). Utilizing these criteria, Singer identified boundaries beyond which there was a legitimate denial of rights, although where these boundaries lay was difficult to establish. He also faced a significant problem in that in order to deny the uniqueness of humanity he asserted that infants and people with learning disabilities or other intellectual disabilities of a particular severity are not persons. His aim in doing this was to contend that other creatures, notably chimpanzees involved in language experiments in his example, were persons because they appeared to have the necessary traits.

This left him open to a further problem, in considering that personhood only came with maturity and that young infants do not have the traits of a person. Does this therefore mean that the young of other species also fail this test and so are denied personhood? If this was so, when do other species as well as humans actually gain such a status? Was it therefore more legitimate to kill lambs than sheep or calves than cows?

Singer used the arguments of the American philosopher, Tooley, who contended that an individual had a right to life if they 'at some time have been capable of seeing themselves as existing over time'. This capacity to understand the concept of a continuing self ensured that they would have an *interest* in its continuation and that interest expressed itself in the desire to continue to live (*ibid.*, p. 299). Singer therefore stated that,

> the capacity to have an interest in continued existence is relevant to the possession of a right to life in a way that mere species membership cannot be relevant.

(*Ibid.*, p. 300)

Regan took the debate a step further in that he considered this problem through the concept of a 'subject of life'. For Regan, beings must have beliefs and desires, a perception of their past and future, feelings of pleasure and pain, and an ability to act in pursuit of their desires:

> Like a rights based view and unlike a utilitarianism, Regan's view would not allow subjects of a life to be killed even if a greater good – perhaps the saving of a greater number of lives – could thereby be achieved. For those unhappy with both utilitarianism and Tooley's view of interests, Regan's position may therefore be an attractive third possibility.
>
> (*Ibid.*, p. 300)

However, Singer then made a leap in his reasoning which was not justified by Regan's position, and appeared to make the kind of assertion for which he condemned others. In order to fully support his position he must downgrade human beings and this was done not just by the attempt to dismiss uniqueness. After considering the evidence for personality in chimpanzees from observation he stated, quite legitimately, that until we have carried out close examination of other species in the same way, we could not say that chimpanzees are the only non-humans with a right to life because of their personhood. However, he then appeared to do just this when he considered the rights of children and people with severe learning disabilities:

> My own view is that the mere potential to possess a capacity does not necessarily carry with it the rights that arise from actual possession of the capacity … Even readers who do not accept [this argument] have to recognise that there are still some humans – those with irreparable severe mental retardation – who are not persons and who do not have the same right to life that persons, including non-human persons, have if it is true that all and only persons have this right.
>
> (*Ibid.*, p. 303)

However, if Singer accepted Tooley's position on self-consciousness and the need for close examination, his conclusion here was wrong. Tooley contended that an 'individual does not … have desires at other times unless there is *at least one time* at which the individual possesses the concept of the continuing self' (*ibid.*, p. 299). What Tooley did not say was when that time might be, for in the infant child it will be in the future and for the victim of a traffic accident it was in the past and may yet be in the future as well. Singer had to reject potential as, no matter how well developed a chimpanzee may be in intellectual capacity it does not have the potential of either of these human individuals.

## Regan and subjects in a life

A similar position was found in Regan where he needed to accept an age or maturity factor in recognizing the sentience of beings. Regan, in advancing animal rights, considered the age of 'one or more' for normal mammals as appropriate for the existence of sentience (Kleining, 1991, p. 107). Regan's position was based on an effort to establish the existence of inherent value in 'subjects of a life' rather than see value as being a relational attribution, 'in which the valuer considers something to be worth choosing for its own sake'.

Leahy (1991) noted that Regan found himself in difficulties with the concept of a 'subject of a life' because he wanted to ensure that the rest of nature potentially had rights:

> Regan's unease about his sentience criteria is underlined by its only being a *sufficient* condition for IV [Inherent Value]. Thus those that *fail* to satisfy it, for example 'permanently comatose human beings', can nonetheless possess IV. Even plants and 'cancer cells' are not debarred from IV …
>
> (p. 74)

Consequently, Leahy questioned whether Regan need bother with the subject of a life proposition if he deemed it unnecessary in the case of non-sentient creatures. This was further weakened as a central part of Regan's argument because the concept of inherent value was a postulate, a foundational assumption, on which all his other arguments were based. What he seemed to be arguing, in Leahy's view, was that inherent value was a response to a 'gut feeling' or intuition. Consequently, Regan

> … has simply *invented* a quality and invested it with significance. Such creations can be powerful weapons of rhetoric and persuasion in the hands of the converted; witness the charisma of Original Sin, a notion with which inherent value has many, if reverse, affinities.
>
> (*Ibid.*, p. 74)

However, the efforts of Regan and more especially Singer to establish that sentience, the ability to feel pain and pleasure, and even the ability to reason, are not unique to human beings can also be argued as anthropocentric. Milton noted (1996, p. 207) the concern of animal rights supporters for sentient beings as anthropocentric because it was based 'on the understanding that non-human animals are worthy of consideration insofar as they are *like us*'. For Milton this contrasted with deep ecology or eco-centric views in which all natural entities have inherent value, and should be free from human interference in their development. However, it may be argued that humanity's interaction with the rest of nature is so all-pervasive that the very effort to draw back and allow nature to develop 'naturally' is the result of a conscious human decision, an expression of choice, and simply reinforces our understanding of humanity's dominant position. We choose to give a value to certain species or eco-systems and as a consequence of such a choice we act to sustain that valued entity. But the option to exploit it in an instrumental fashion at a later date is still there.

Benton (1996) raised the problem of a rights approach based on the idea that animals and humans share important aspects of consciousness. He noted the work of both R.G. Frey and M.P.T. Leahy who contended that consciousness was linked to issues such as the ability to express beliefs about ones desires or the psychological capacity to engage in language games which only humans have. In addition, the work of Carruthers was cited in arguing that the existence of non-conscious states may lead one to contend that the similarity between humans and non-humans was not sufficient to grant non-humans equal rights.

While Benton noted these points of dispute he still accepted the issue of continuance between human and non-human species while also raising the issue of whether we can fully know that this was the case. His argument was based on our lack of knowledge of the nature of the well-being of other species. While there were occasions where close bonds existed between animals and their carers we were still denied full access to 'the "phenomenology" of their mode of being in the world' which acted as a barrier to understanding (1996, p. 41). Consequently, Benton's argument centred on this lack of knowledge meaning that we could not know in what ways we may damage their well-being. This position, while also open to use by critics of the animal rights movement, was in line with some deep ecology supporters who argue for a cautionary approach to human action. If we do not have full knowledge of the impact of our actions then it was better not to act. In the case of animal rights from an ecological perspective this was also important because it was linked to the idea that authors such as Singer and Regan were looking to value animals by denying the uniqueness of humans and identifying human characteristics in animals. Benton on the other hand, contended that humans and animals were not the same and so we could not really understand whether we were infringing their rights and therefore should adopt a cautionary instinct.

This debate was also clear within the work of Stephen Clark (1997) on the self-awareness of animals. He contended that animals in social groups clearly had an awareness of self in order that they might respond to the actions of their fellow group members. This self-awareness was particularly important in the relationship that existed between dominant and sub-dominant members within a social hierarchy. There was an obvious appreciation by individual members of their position within that hierarchy, without which individuals would be attacked and suffer at the hands of a dominant member. However, as with Regan and Singer there were problems in relation to animals existing outside any social setting and therefore lacking such self-awareness.

Singer was aware of this problem and asked questions concerning the value of life for those animals and other entities which fail to attain his own definition of personhood. In debating a rights approach, which he rejected, Singer attempted to include those humans who he charaterized as not being 'persons', notably the 'severely mentally disabled'. His discussion of a rights approach concluded that they would have desires as long as they were conscious and that they had a right to life because any other action would frustrate their pursuit of those desires. If this approach was adopted it would be the consciousness of beings which gave them a right to life 'wherever the boundary of consciousness is to be found, there too is the boundary to the right to life' (1993, p. 305).

He rejected this approach as it would resurrect the idea that all human life was of equal value simply by being conscious and he had already rejected this position. Singer cannot accept any approach which would give intellectually disabled humans an equal footing to 'normal' human beings. For his position to be sustained he had to reject any approach which failed to accept inequalities in humans and gave a higher standing to some non-human persons over those of human 'non-persons'.

Additionally, while Leahy (1991) contended that Singer was essentially a utilitarian in his use of pleasure and pain as the defining principal for establishing personhood, Singer rejected classical utilitarianism. His major point of disagreement with utilitarianism was that it was built on a concept of 'replaceability', that is, that an action was wrong only if it reduced the overall level of pleasure or happiness:

> Essentially, the problem is that classical utilitarianism makes lives replaceable. Killing is wrong if it deprives the world of a happy life, but this wrong can be righted if another equally happy life can be created without any extra cost.

> (1993, p. 305)

Singer accepted the earlier position of Salt that the replaceability argument was problematic because it was based on assumptions about a future yet-to-be creature in comparison with an existing life. We can not really base our actions on the assumption, or indeed hope, that the replacement being will be happy or happier than the one it was to replace.

Finally, Singer turned to feminist and post-modernist doubters of the whole ethical agenda, who had argued that it 'may be a mistake to base ethics on universal principles, rationally derived ... these (feminist) works link the prevailing emphasis on abstract reasoning in ethics to the dominance of male philosophers' (*ibid.*, p. 309). However, he also rejected this approach and contended that it substituted emotional links between species for the development of universal principles. Such 'mild-speciesism' allowed for a turning away from the ethical dilemmas involved in factory farming for example, and that such an emotional relativism led to a fragmented and varied response to issues. The result was to undermine the development of a solution to the problem of whether eating animals was wrong. This also presented a problem in relation to aspects of deep ecology where there was a strong critique of rational thought as a product of the modernist project and the scientific method.

## Animal rights versus deep ecology

Singer was also critical of deep ecological thinking in which the maintenance of species carried more weight than the suffering of an individual unit of that species. Singer's position reflected the existence of a division between animal rights supporters and ecologists which centred on the 'intractable conflict between the individualism of animal liberation and the holism of some environmentalisms' (Luke,

1997, p. 333). Evidence for this division was also found in the accusation levelled at Aldo Leopold of 'environmental fascism' by Regan (1983, pp. 361–2) and Callicott's attack on Animal Liberation as anti-natural and life-loathing!

Callicott contended that the animal welfare ethic was inadequate to the task because it excluded most of the environment and nature from moral consideration and set up a hierarchy of sentient beings:

> No theoretical means is provided for ethically distinguishing between wild and domestic animals. Worse, when the welfare of an ethically franchised … animal comes into conflict with a specimen of a rare or endangered species of plant or ethically disenfranchised animal, the rights or interests of the former prevail over the latter.
>
> (1993, p. 374)

He further contended that the logic of such an animal welfare ethic could lead to a policy of 'predator eradication'. However, the problems encountered by Regan noted earlier aimed to overcome this kind of hierarchy by including all nature within the compass of inherent value.

Luke responded to this problem by rejecting the idea that systemic health was always more important than individual well-being and that both animal rights and ecology aimed at accepting 'diverse values as those values are threatened by structures of human domination backed by a common anthropocentric ideology' (1997, p. 354). For Luke deep ecology and animal liberation could come together through the project of ending the ideology that human life was sacred and non-human was not. Indeed, this was where the differences between deep ecologists and animal rights supporters were more apparent amongst writers on these issues than amongst grassroots activists.

Luke evaluated the work of Sperling who, in studying the ideas of animal rights activists, found that they made a direct connection between the development of nuclear weapons, environmental pollution and factory farming. Luke pointed out, this sensibility was strongly linked to a questioning of an anthropocentric world-view, or an attitude of mind which supported domination and exploitation. However, Sperling wrote in terms of metaphor and symbol where 'animal experimentation is the key metaphor for the abuses by technological society of living organisms and the ecology' (quoted in Luke, 1997, p. 352). Sperling suggested that animal liberationists were not concerned with the wellbeing of individual animals, but rather with identifying an accessible symbol of the environmental crisis. One of the most vitriolic critics of animal liberation from an ecological perspective was J. Baird Callicott. He contended that it was the contrast between the organic aspects of animals caught within the non-organic world of research laboratories which affronted the liberationists rather than the 'quality of pain' suffered or inflicted (Callicott, 1992, pp. 37–69). Luke argued that this was a wilful misunderstanding of the views of activists who identified closely with the welfare of individual animals and saw vivisection and factory farming as real suffering. Rather than seeing it as a metaphor for the environmental crisis they placed it at the centre of a real ecological problem. While there was real substance to Luke's criticism of Sperling there was also a valid point to the view that the behaviour of some animal liberationists appeared to give little thought to the future of animals released from laboratories once the political act was over.

Luke argued that the divisions between Sperling and Callicott on the one side and Regan and Singer on the other, was a false debate. Where the real debate lay was over the extent to which consciousness may be seen as the defining principle for action. Deep ecology objected to this approach in that by making reference to consciousness one was leaving out of the equation the rest of the natural world.

The criticism of the animal rights position and that of animal liberationists from an ecological perspective was, therefore, that it was too narrowly based and too limited in its approach to organic and non-organic entities. Eckersley and Brian Barry considered this problem both from an ecological perspective and a more general debate on rights and justice. If it is true, as Barry contended (and Sperling above), that the contrast between 'zoocentric' and 'ecocentric' approaches was that animal rights supporters were concerned with individuals while ecologists were species based, the zoocentric approach met with a significant problem. Ecocentrics see the management of a species as being important and this may require culling or allowing some individuals to starve, while for zoocentrics individuals should be saved by intervention:

> From an ecological perspective the survival of the last members of a species would be valued far above the survival of an equal number of some closely related, but common species. But this judgement would be incomprehensible on an animal welfare ethic.
>
> (Barry, B., 1995, p. 22)

This problem was also noted by Tester (1991, pp. 190–2), where he contrasted the ideas of Porritt, an ecologist, with Ronnie Lee, a radical animal-rights activist. According to Tester, Porritt saw animals as just one aspect of the natural 'web of life' which went beyond 'the 1000 or so familiar and appealing mammals which are now threatened' (quoted in Tester, p. 191). Lee, on the other hand, stated that 'an individual animal doesn't care if its species is facing extinction – it cares if it is feeling pain' (quoted in Tester, 1984, p. 191).

However, both positions created problems whether we are considering the well-being of a species or of an individual animal. If humanity should intervene to defend individual non-humans or species does this not require a hierarchy of species? If one species was subject to attack and possible extermination by another, for example due to competition over habitat or evolutionary development, efforts by greens to save that species would require the possible destruction of individual members of the predator. In addition, if Singer's position was taken then when and how should humans intervene to defend an individual from suffering at the hands of a predator? The problem for animal rights supporters was that they tended to perceive the situation from a perspective which identified humanity as the only oppressor or predator. As Foreman noted, the contrast between animal rights and deep ecology centred on the recognition by the latter that pain, suffering and death are an essential part of nature (Milton, 1996, p. 207).

An additional criticism emerging from deep ecology was that the concentration on sentient beings failed to acknowledge the importance of the rest of nature except insofar as they have instrumental value by providing the habitats of an 'elite of sentient beings'. This resulted in what Rodman termed a 'zoocentric scientism' (quoted in Eckersley, 1992, p. 44). Eckersley further pointed to the logical absurdities which can emerge from the moral niceties of the animal rights/liberation movement:

> Critics have pointed to the tension between Singerian justice and an ecological perspective by noting that animal liberation when pressed to its logical conclusion, would be obliged to convert all non-human carnivores to vegetarians, or at the very least, replace predation in the food chain with some kind of 'humane' alternative that protects, or at least minimises the suffering of, sentient prey ... Singer has in fact admitted that the existence of nonhuman carnivores poses a problem for the ethics of animal liberation. Despite this concession, he nonetheless counsels a modification of the dietary habits of at least some domestic animals in referring his readers to recipes for a vegetarian menu for their pets!
>
> (*Ibid.*, p. 45)

While Eckersley accepted that Singer, Regan and other animal liberationists were on the same side as ecologists in rejecting an anthropocentric position, the logic of a belief that a world without carnivorous
activity would be morally superior was intensely anthropocentric. It is
imposing a human moral stance on the non-human world. Simply
because it would involve humans changing their attitudes to non-
human, sentient beings in eradicating vivisection, factory farming and
hunting does not change the character of the thought processes. The
choice either to intervene in animal activity or leave well alone, for
example keeping away from areas of wilderness, was still a human
choice.

## Ecological animal rights?

Given this critique of animal rights as an ethical problem were there
areas where ecologists or greens provide their own perspective on animal
rights? To a large extent there was an acceptance that animals should be
free from suffering and cruelty, but that right was not individualist in a
pure sense but part of a belief that species should be maintained and
protected from extinction. In addition, the aim was to maintain biodiversity and the sustainability of ecological habitats. Consequently their
opposition to the development of factory farming and agribusiness was
more centred on the way in which these approaches tended to develop
and exploit the most productive species and encouraged the manipulation of species to increase productivity and profitability.

Goodin argued that such a position was centred on the idea that the
whole was more valuable than the sum of its part:

> The green response is, I think, best seen as being rooted in their
> respect for nature as such – combined with the fact that destroying a
> whole 'type' (a whole species) constitutes so much more of a viola-
> tion of the natural order than does destroying a mere 'token' (a par-
> ticular animal of that species).

> (Goodin, 1992, p. 188)

Consequently, their concern with the development of agri-business
was linked to their critique of the scientific/technological programme.
The use of chemical pesticides and fertilizers was destructive of water-
courses and wild species, notably songbirds, while the development of
monocultures not only reduced habitats for other species and the
diversity of species but made them more susceptible to disease.

Midgley also appeared to associate the development of industrialization as a major problem for the development of animal welfare. She argued that while one might assume that we treat animals more humanely than our parents or grandparents did because of the way the debate had developed and with the increase in vegetarianism and support for animal rights, the reality was very different. It was the industrialization of the food industry as well as the fur trade, well away from the public gaze, that led to the increase in the exploitation of animals:

> The steady growth of callous exploitation is occurring at a time when our response both to individual animals and to nature as a whole is becoming ever more active and sensitive.
>
> (1992, p. 29)

This was reminiscent of the position adopted by Roszak who contended that there was a knowledge gap between the experience of the majority of modern Americans and their parents and grandparents in the way they perceived food. The pre-packed meat in the super-market bore little resemblance to the carcasses that used to hang in the butcher's window.

Indeed, it was important to recognize that the genesis of much ecological thinking emerged out of the earlier conservationist approach which was particularly concerned with animal conservation. The existence of animal protection organizations in various countries revealed the existence of a long-standing concern with the way in which animals were treated by humans. As Thompson (1995, pp. 126–9) noted, even strong deep green critics of the animal rights movement, such as Callicott, began their work in the areas of wildlife and conservation.

An interesting discussion of some of the major issues affecting the relationship between humanity and animals was that discussed by Peter Dickens, from a green Marxist position rather than mainstream ecologist. For Dickens the problem of alienation between humans and animals was associated with the development and treatment of animals as commodities and the establishment of a division of labour, even within the same species, amongst domestic livestock. In addition, there was increasing specialization and division of labour within the agricultural community so that the relationship between the stockman and his cattle had been broken. In the case of factory farming this,

> leads to a number of forms of alienation amongst animals, paralleling those outlined by Marx for humans. They are even being

alienated from their own products. They are, for example, made to have the maximum number of offspring and are then removed from their young as soon as possible. They are then 'de-skilled' in the sense that they are made to perform one or two basic tasks.

(1996, pp. 63–4)

For Dickens this process not only damaged the relationship between animals and the rest of their species, but also affected humans and could be a focus for political action and mobilization. He contended that, unlike animal liberationists such as Singer and Regan this situation could not be reduced to the concept of speciesism. Rather, it was a combination of 'capitalism, modernity and speciesism' (*ibid.*, p. 65).

Dickens not only developed a link with the New Left and neo-Marxism of the late 1960s, but also placed the debate within the context of the post-modernist critique of the modernist project. However, he also displayed some of the contradictions that are inherent in much ecological writing in the sense that he was arguing from a neo-Marxist and therefore materialist perspective while at the same time making reference to the need to enhance the spiritual. More particularly, he was still strongly committed to the role of the natural sciences in resolving some of our most problematic ecological difficulties:

> ... it is still true to say that the sciences such as physics and biology have the most to offer in terms of the most general understandings of the structural relations and mechanisms affecting or 'underwriting' all aspects of life.

(*Ibid.*, pp. 68–9)

Consequently, this placed him at one extreme of the ecological debate. He even went so far as to assert that the social sciences may one day be able to emulate the natural sciences in their development of methods of analysis, a position which for some time now has been held highly suspect.

However, at the other end of the spectrum ecologists from a deep green persuasion, have followed the lead taken by Aldo Leopold in developing a 'level of sympathy' for the non-human world which may be taken to an extreme level of idealization. While it may be possible to establish some degree of sympathy for non-human nature, critics of Leopold have argued that this was anthropomorphising. Ecologists were not just concerned with the efforts to achieve a sympathetic understanding with Leopold's wolf, but also with Leopold's mountain.

For di Zerega at the heart of this experience of the non-human, and indeed non-sentient, world was the concept of beauty:

> We have moved from a biocentric to an ecocentric position. The natural world is beautiful. Its beauty can only be experienced to the extent that we open ourselves to it in a noncalculative way.
>
> (1997, p. 70)

It was the expansion of the sense of affinity beyond not just the human, but beyond the sentient that was important. In addition, the view expressed by di Zerega also had within it an implicit criticism of positivist and reductionist approaches to the natural world. He stated that our understanding of beauty was non-analytical as in cases of such aesthetic appreciation we neither compare the object to other things, nor do we try to analyse the different components of the object to identify the reasons for our appreciation (p. 69). In addition, he argued that we lost our selves in the act of contemplation and identified with the subject of that contemplation.

## Conclusion

The problem facing animal rights which ecologists to some extent are able to overcome was the issue of hierarchy between individual animals and the various species. If animal rights was concerned with pain and pleasure as the identifying concept for recognizing the sentience of animals and therefore the extension of rights to those animals, they faced a problem over how to reduce the suffering experienced by animals which was not induced by humans. Either suffering was only caused by humans and therefore we have a moral burden to reduce the suffering we cause, or suffering was part of all experience and therefore we either tried to end all suffering or we recognized its role in life. If the former was the case then animal rights supporters had to make a choice about the rights of carnivores and whether they should be permitted to continue causing suffering to other species, or the rights belong to carnivores and we should leave well alone.

Holland quoted an animal rights activist as stating that 'when the last great whale is killed to feed man's greed … never again will one of the most intelligent non-human animals in the world be subjected to such an obscene lingering death' (quoted in Tester, 1991, p. 192). Was it possible to reply to this belief that the death of the last killer whale would mean that never again would a seal have to suffer an obscene death in the jaws of such an animal? For some ecologists there was a recognition that pain, suffering and death were part of life and that there may be times when, for the sake of the survival of rare species more common species have to be culled back. Such an approach was in line with that earlier tradition associated with conservation, but did not sit easily with some deep ecologists for whom such decisions are not for humans to make. As with animal rights supporters, there was a tendency for deep ecologists to place all the blame for suffering onto humans. Consequently, while there were some significant areas of disagreement between these two groups as discussed above, the core belief stemmed from a desire to move away from an anthropocentric approach to nature and towards a reduction in the centrality of humanity in the development of the earth.

As Luke made clear in his attempt to build a bridge between the two approaches,

> The key to a rapprochement between deep environmentalism and animal liberation is understanding that (1) potentially conflicting values such as systemic health and individual well-being need not be subordinated one to the other, and (2) the two movements are advocating for diverse values as those values are threatened by structures of human domination backed by a common anthropocentric ideology.
>
> (1997, p. 354)

The relationship between humanity and animals was intimately linked with anti-democratic, authoritarian structures of domination that existed in the modern industrialized world. Consequently, in some areas the conflict was not necessarily between animal rightists and deep ecology but rather between their more radical, and potentially more absolutists, approach to the environment and the reformist approaches of 'shallow' greens with their more anthropocentric understanding of nature and humanity's place in it.

# 7
# Ecology and International Summitry

The processes by which the environmental crisis is debated at the international level between governments, state actors and non-governmental organizations is now an extremely complex one. The range and diversity of organizations involved is only matched by the range and complexity of the issues under discussion. As a consequence this chapter can only scratch at the surface of the issues and does not propose to be a comprehensive analysis of all the activities that can be placed under the heading of international summits and conferences on the environment.

By its very nature the ecological crisis is a global issue involving as its does the potential for pollution crossing international boundaries. But more particularly within the context of a global market place and the issue of globalization the problems of resource depletion and competition between states for access to scarce resources provides the potential for conflict and the need for international coordination. While the concern with 'acting locally and thinking globally' is at the centre of radical activist thought there has been a growing identification of a need for international governmental action. The rate at which inter-governmental and United Nations conferences have been organized provides evidence of the increasing realization of the need to act. More regionally based agreements have also been established particularly through the various supra-state organizations such as the European Union. In addition to state actors there is an important role for non-governmental organizations (NGOs), and the internationally active pressure groups, such as the World-Wide Fund for Nature (WWF), Friends of the Earth (FoE) and Greenpeace. This chapter will review some of the major conferences and examine some of the criticisms that ecologists have targeted at their resolutions.

## 1972 UN conference on the human environment

The first major UN conference was held in Stockholm in 1972 after four years of preparation. Its aim was primarily to raise the 'level of consciousness' concerning a range of environmental problems that had emerged since the publication of Rachel Carson's 'Silent Spring'. In many ways the establishment of the conference and the years of preparation acted as a spur to the development of ideas on environmental problems and inspired the publication of Limits to Growth and the Blueprint for Survival. Maurice Strong, director general of the Canadian External Aid Office, was appointed as secretary general to the Conference and headed the preparatory committee. Apart from all the national papers presented to the preparatory committee Strong commissioned Barabara Ward and Rene Dubos to produce 'an unofficial report that would provide Stockholm delegates with the intellectual and philosophical foundation for their deliberations' (McCormick, 1995, p. 117). This was published as *Only One Earth* in 1972 and contended that international cooperation was essential and that there should be a greater loyalty to the planet than to individual nation-states. However, the greater loyalty that was to emerge from the conference was to the sovereignty of the nation state rather than to the planet.

The main issues arising from the conference were largely associated with the publicity generated by the preparations and proceedings rather than necessarily the detailed proposals:

> Virtually ignored by diplomats in 1969, the environmental crisis had by 1972 rocketed right up alongside nuclear weapons and economic development as one of the big issues of international politics. The second major achievement of the Stockholm Conference was the establishment of the United Nations Environment Program (UNEP) to monitor the state of the world environment and to provide liaison and coordination between nation states and among the multitude of governmental and non-governmental organizations concerned with environmental matters.
>
> (Ophuls, 1977, p. 216)

The Conference faced problems that were to remain with the UN and its efforts to develop international action throughout the next decades. In particular, the Soviet Union and its supporting states had withdrawn from the preparatory meetings because of their largely ideological standpoint that pollution and misuse of resources were the result of the workings of the capitalist system. Some radical socialist environmentalists also expressed this view within the West, with the additional belief being that such misuse of the environment and overuse of resources would not take place under a fully socialist society.

The second problem was the suspicion amongst some southern hemisphere countries that the agenda was one which was set by the wealthy North, a conspiracy aimed at preventing development of the poor economies and targeting population growth in Asia and Africa. The need to examine the relationship between economic development and the concerns of environmentalists appeared to the developing world to be unbalanced. The idea that economic growth and industrialization in poor countries should be subsumed to the less tangible concerns of future generations was anathema to some representatives from the developing world (L. Elliott, 1998, pp. 11–13).

Ophuls noted that environmental activists were unhappy with the way the conference was conducted in relation to the issue of development and the environment as well as its outcome. Given the problems identified by ecologists concerning development and environmental damage, they felt that the original ecological purity of the agenda was 'watered down' by the developing countries insistence that underdevelopment should be seen as a form of pollution. Ophuls contended that this debate was linked to what he termed 'ideological posturing' by supporters of development on issues such as colonialism. Certainly, Ophuls might have made reference to some of the announcements by the Chinese delegates who initially argued that,

> the preamble should state that the environment was, in some places, endangered by 'plunder, aggression and war by the colonialists, imperialists and neocolonialists', that overpopulation was caused by 'plunder, aggression and war', and that 'the notorious Malthusian theory is absurd in theory and groundless in fact'.
>
> (McCormick, 1995, p. 122)

This kind of declaration obviously placed the United States in a particularly difficult position as one of the main supporters of the Stockholm conference. They found that the detailed proposals emerging from the developing world were unacceptable to their own state interests.

However, Konrad Von Moltke and Atiq Rahman stated that,

> The linkages between poverty and environmental stress have been highlighted ever since the Stockholm Conference on the Human

Environment in 1972. The point was picked up in the Brundtland Report (1987) which decried a 'downward spiral of poverty and degradation', whereby the poor are forced to draw unsustainably on available natural resources to satisfy immediate survival needs.

(1996, p. 342)

This position was much more central to the environmental debate at the subsequent Rio summit on the environment and development rather than at Stockholm. However, McCormick noted that it was the presence of the LDCs (less-developed countries) which forced the MDCs (more-developed countries) to recognize the need to reconcile the problems of ecological damage with the issue of economic development (1995, p. 128).

The establishment of a range of 26 principles and 109 recommendations for action fell foul of these competing problems. In particular, the problem of how to reconcile international cooperation with national interests was inherent in all efforts to resolve problems of an international nature. No one state can establish and enforce international resolutions, and enforcement action by the international community was made more difficult by the often intangible and certainly contentious areas of debate at the heart of environmental problems. Within such a context the apparent contradiction that Elliott noted between the maintenance of state sovereignty over resources within national borders and the competing interests between individual states, in this case between developed and developing countries, were inevitable. McCormick described this problem when he noted that the 26 principles included the idea that,

Each state should establish its own standards of environmental management and exploit resources as it wished, but should not endanger other states.

(1995, p. 126)

Ophuls considered that this outcome entrenched an attitude concerning the existing world order which was 'most objectionable from an ecological point of view' (1977, p. 217). He spoke in terms which condemned such sovereignty as permitting states to exploit resources without consideration for the rest of the world community and also attacked the maintenance of the 'unrestricted freedom to breed' contained in the Universal Declaration of Human Rights. Ophuls also contended that the apparent lack of cooperation from associated agencies, such the the World Health Organization (WHO) and the Food and Agriculture Organization (FAO), was due to bureaucratic politics. There was a potential threat to the major policies of these agencies, such as the Green Revolution, from the adoption of an ecological approach.

Given the centrality of the problems associated with resource depletion identified by ecologists at the time it was not surprising that some organizations, such as the International Union for Conservation of Nature and Natural Resource (IUCN), were dissatisfied with the outcome of the conference. What was not certain was that developed and developing countries need necessarily have competing interests if development could be maintained at a sustainable level without impinging on the levels of economic well being in already developed countries. The issues of development and population growth could easily be perceived as a conflict of interests in which the developed world saw the urge towards development as a threat. Either the view was that resources were scarce and so the demand for development threatened the living standards of those in the West, or preventing economic development could lead to an increasing problem of economic migration. The West increasingly insisted that economic hardship was not an appropriate reason for population migration as opposed to political refugee status.

Such views were evident in the writings of ecologists such as Paul Ehrlich (1971) in 'The Population Bomb' and Garrett Hardin (1977) in 'The Tragedy of the Commons', and could only have set warning bells ringing in the capital cities of the southern hemisphere. The concern amongst developing countries must therefore have been that the aim of ending the 'Commons', either to breed or to develop their industrial potential, was aimed at constraining the poor and secure the existing position of the rich countries. Other radicals from the peace movement also considered that the conference failed to get to grips with issues such as biological warfare and 'the "ecocidal" activities of the United States in Indochina' (McCormick, 1995, p. 123). Such a position was inevitably associated with the fact that the conference was as much a product of the times as it was the result of the real emerging ecological crisis.

The legacy of Stockholm was mixed and McCormick (1995, pp. 127–9) identified four major features. These included, firstly, the introduction of the human or built environment into the debate, challenging the idea that the environment was something 'out there'. Secondly, the needs of the developing world were also placed on the agenda rather than seeing environmental issues as purely a problem facing the industrialized world. Third, the central importance of environmental interest groups or NGOs was recognized, and finally, the conference established of the UN Environment Programme (UNEP).

Elliot (1998, p. 13) also identified the achievements of the conference as political rather than environmental in that it brought political actors together on the theme of the environment for the first time. Also, the range of international environmental law that was to follow in its wake was partly a response to its existence. Indeed, Stockholm was the essential precursor to all the later UN and other international agreements on the environment. While not all UN countries accepted the findings of the conference they had to take note of its existence and the catalytic effect it had on the development of ecological pressure groups and the education of a wider public (Bryner, 1997, pp. 15–16). Much of the mainstream literature from green theorists and the rapid expansion of the environmental movement emerged after Stockholm. Subsequent meetings of the UNEP and a range of other international and bilateral meetings all helped in the development of the environment as an issue facing the international community.

## 1992 Rio UN conference on environment and development

Prior to the Rio conference one of the most significant publications was that of the Brundtland Report, by the World Commission on Environment and Development, published as *Our Common Future* in 1987. This report was the first to try and reconcile the differences that had emerged between the environmental movement and the development movement with the aim of creating,

> A vision of the simultaneous and mutually reinforcing pursuit of economic growth, environmental improvement, population stabilization, peace and global equity, all of which could be maintained in the long-term.

> (Dryzek, 1997, p. 126)

However, Dryzek noted that Brundtland did not propose a way of achieving this vision and the inclusion of economic growth in the equation would certainly set off some alarm bells amongst ecologists.

While there was certainly a belief amongst some commentators that the Bruntland Commission had 'seen the most radical departure yet from previous approaches to sustainable development' (McCormick,

1995, p. 253), there were doubts that nation states could adopt its proposals without significant structural reform. Such reforms would challenge powerful economic and political interests whose survival depended on the maintenance of the existing economic system. However, the publication of Bruntland and the ideas being developed within the UNEP, ensured that there was a momentum for the establishment of a new summit on the relationship between the environment and economic development.

The resulting Rio Conference on Environment and Development was seen to be the main successor to Stockholm. Between the proposals emerging from Stockholm and the run up to the Rio conference a wide-ranging literature had been established on the whole question of sustainable development. More particularly, the International Union for the Conservation of Nature and Natural Resources (IUCN) had prepared the World Conservation Strategy (WCS) at the request of UNEP. This strategy aimed at identifying the ways in which conservation and environmental protection could be promoted within a development framework. In this way three main strategies were identified which could guide the process. These included the need to safeguard ecological systems for the maintenance of foodstuffs, health and 'other aspects of human survival and sustainable development'. Secondly, the preservation of genetic diversity both as an insurance against disease to crops and also because of the potential for pharmaceutical developments. Thirdly, the sustainable development of 'species and ecosystems' particularly those which are farmed or cropped for human use. Obviously, the whole WCS can be seen to have a strong development perspective, which placed it in an anthropocentric position as against a purer ecocentric ideology. However, this strategy was a significant development in the transition from Stockholm to Rio and the evolution of thinking at UN and governmental level on the environment.

The link between environmental problems and the needs of development, which were initially recognized at Stockholm, were now to take centre stage. In particular, the development of Agenda 21 was seen as a significant achievement. Of particular interest was the way in which Agenda 21 sought to integrate the activity of states at both national and international level, but also within states at the local level. In some ways the ideas of thinking globally and acting locally are contained within Agenda 21. Chip Lindner (1997) pointed out that:

A new form of governance is emerging – that of 'stakeholders'. Local stakeholders in communities are linking together, whether they are local businesses or local authorities, non-governmental organizations or community-based organizations, women's groups or residents associations. Groups that have an identifiable stake in the future of the community are making these links to create a vision for the future which has a set of goals and measurable criteria or indicators.

(p. 13)

Such an initiative while optimistic was also problematic in that the establishment of specific targets led to disputes about the relative level of sacrifice that should be undertaken by each state and how those sacrifices might be shared. These problems were to become especially evident at the follow-up Kyoto summit (or Rio 2).

Out of the Conference a series of core principles were established which were in response to the growing awareness of the global nature of some environmental challenges and the new scientific understanding of the impact of environmental change. Consequently, the main proposals emerging from the conference included: the Framework Convention on Climate Change; the Convention on Biological Diversity; Agenda 21 targeted at helping local community actions; the Declaration on Environment and Development; and the Forest Principles on the exploitation of forest resources (McCormick, 1995, pp. 255–7). Through these proposals it was hoped that the development of the principles established at Stockholm would now find detailed development into practical action. However, as with Stockholm the response of the ecology movement was mixed in its judgement. Some have seen it as bringing the issue back into the mainstream political agenda and raising public awareness. In particular, the various statements from the conference on the rights of, and traditional knowledge possessed by, indigenous peoples were seen as particularly significant.

However, others have seen Rio as once again an opportunity for empty political gestures with the central concern to maintain the sovereign rights of nation states over their own resources being the main stumbling block to anything significant:

The declaration reaffirmed that states have 'the sovereign right to exploit their own resources pursuant to their own environmental and development policies', although they also have the 'responsibility to ensure that activities within their jurisdiction or control do not cause damage to the environment of other States or of areas beyond the limits of national jurisdiction'.

(Bryner, 1997, p. 16)

This qualification revealed little real development on the international law front from the Stockholm conference. The history of the post-Rio period, including negotiations in New York and Kyoto, and the position of the US on the issue of climate change revealed the problems encountered in trying to deal with the global environmental challenge while still operating in the era of the nation state.

This was also evident in the area of policies adopted by developing countries as well as the US. The Forest Principle, for example, was criticized because of the way it identified the 'sovereign right' of states to exploit their forests while paying lip-service to the concept of management and conservation of forests and woodlands (McCormick, 1995, p. 257). However, the belief by some critics that the UN's reliance on compromise resulted in a policy of accepting the 'lowest common denominator' was difficult to overcome without supporting some form of world government to enforce a policy which might be seen to run counter to the needs of particular geographical areas. In order to develop a more radical policy it was unclear how to overcome the problem of national sovereignty without establishing a more autocratic global regime, or at least at the level of coping with such global problems as climate change and deforestation.

The issues of poverty and development faced by the developing world were such that an appeal to the idea of the population accepting, at a local level, the need to tackle such global problems was difficult to imagine. Certainly environmental issues do play a part in the political thinking of parties and individuals in the developing world. However, many of these issues are associated with the more immediate problems of environmental destruction and the dumping of toxic waste created by the developed world. There have only been limited areas within the Stockholm and Rio declarations to convince developing countries that they are not too readily seen by the West as part of the problem.

The development of the UNCED also led to criticisms from the environmental movement and in particular from those NGOs involved in the process surrounding Rio. Finger (1994) noted how the UNCED process required environmental NGOs to coordinate their actions in order to gain influence in the process. Efforts by mainstream environmental NGOs to coordinate such work through the Environmental Facilitating Committee (EFC), established in 1990 to gain access to the UNCED process, led to the development of an alternative summit. The Environmental Liaison Committee International (ELCI) which aimed to involve people in a form of 'citizens summit' (p. 203) established this alternative meeting of NGOs.

Such action and reaction by the various strands of the ecology movement was also reflected in Lipietz's criticisms concerning the dispute between various environment groups in France:

> a year before the Rio conference, all over the world and particularly in France, NGOs in the development and environment field were at each others throats ... Was it a case of suspicions, groups not used to working together, inferiority complex on the part of 'young and penniless' French environment NGOs when faced with the 'big' development NGOs?
>
> (Lipietz, 1995, p. 99)

This problem of the contrasting perspectives between those NGOs concerned with the environment and those for whom development was of prime importance reflected the difficulties involved in achieving agreement on such issues. This was also emphasized by the size and diversity of states involved in the conference. Consequently, while the Rio conference aimed to overcome the problems encountered at Stockholm, the NGOs involved often continued the conflict outside the main conference.

McCormick pointed out that for environmentalists the size of the Rio summit, with representatives from so many states and organizations, created a series of questions. While it brought together the largest gathering of states ever to discuss the environmental situation and agree on significant issues of environmental management, the need to reach a consensus was seen as a weakness. However, supporters of the process and particularly the UNCED approach, argued that there were important achievements. As Jonathan Porritt stated, the Earth Summit did place a 'deal on the table':

> G77 and emerging countries *implicitly* agreed to sign up to a variety of action plans for addressing some of the big environmental issues (global warming, deforestation, loss of biodiversity etc), whilst OECD countries *implicitly* signed up to the idea of increased aid flows and other forms of development assistance as the quid pro quo for their buy-in to the environmental agenda.
>
> (1997, p. xvii)

However, such implicit agreements were subject to further negotiation, with the aim of establishing firm targets at the follow up summit in Kyoto.

A particular area of concern at the Rio summit was the issue surrounding climate change. Although ecological writings on the subject had been available from the early 1970s there was some uncertainty as to the direction of the change of climate and its possible impact (for example see Ophuls, 1977, pp. 107–11). The establishment of the Framework Convention on Climate Change (FCCC) was an important development but was one of the declarations that was most affected over the following years by political manoeuvring. (For the full text of the FCC see Appendix 1 in T. O'Riordan and J. Jäger, 1997.)

The convention itself had been the result of negotiations over the preceding 18 months and was signed by 154 countries at Rio. Its aim was,

> the prevention of dangerous interference with the climate system … Although no legally binding commitments to reduce emissions of greenhouse gases are included, parties are obliged to *aim* to reduce their emissions of $CO_2$ by the year 2000 set against emission levels as they stood in 1990.
>
> (Newell, 1997, p. 39)

The problems of the debate over climate change were central to the conflict between the developed and the developing world over the relative responsibility for ecological damage and the directions that should be taken. The desire to establish clear targets for the reduction in greenhouse gas emissions was central to the 1997 Kyoto conference and its aftermath.

## 1997 Kyoto UN conference on environment and development (Rio 2)

Following on from the Rio summit, arrangements were made to meet in New York to prepare the agenda for the follow-up in Kyoto. The purpose of the Kyoto conference was to translate the implicit agreements emerging from the Rio conference into specific areas of agreement. However, a number of high hopes emerging out of the Rio summit were frustrated, while the cynicism of some radical ecologists concerning the value of Rio was partly satisfied. In particular, the apparent changes in attitude by the Clinton administration over issues of global warming and the associated emission of green house gases, biodiversity, and the relative share in sacrifice faced by the developing world appeared to be the result of pressure from important corporate interests within the USA.

The Clinton administration was insistent that action taken by the United States on the level of emissions had to take into account the need to maintain economic growth and should not damage the prospects for jobs and industry. In addition, any reductions in emissions by the US should only be carried out if the developing world also showed a commitment to emission reductions. This approach conflicted with the views of representatives from the developing world, as their impact on levels of pollution and, most significantly, use of scarce resources was extremely small when compared to the developed world. The argument proposed by the Clinton administration in the US that they would only engage in actions to reduce climate changing gasses if the developing world also adopted a radical strategy was seen as patronizing when the US used so much of the earth's resources.

Even before the Kyoto conference the developing world was demanding that,

> until the industrialised nations show real progress in reducing their greenhouse gas emissions, the UN FCCC process is invalid.
> (Von Moltke and Rahman, 1997, p. 341)

As a result, it was not surprising that this conflict of interests and interpretation of the relative contribution to global warming of the northern and southern hemispheres was a central issue at Kyoto. Indeed, the limited targets for action agreed on at Kyoto did not fulfil the hopes of Rio and was a significant example of the problems of international cooperation in a world dominated by a market ideology.

An example of this problem, which came to the public's attention at Kyoto but has been causing concern since Rio, was that of Joint Implementation (JI). Under this arrangement countries could arrive at more of a bilateral agreement to share the burden of achieving the Rio targets by 'pooling' their overall emissions. In this way a country with a fairly high level of emissions could achieve their target by linking with a neighbour who had a significantly lower level, and indeed may not have a major problem in reaching their own target:

> Developing countries and some NGOs saw JI as an effort by the rich countries to avoid making substantive commitments and undergo necessary structural changes.
> (J. Jäger and T. O'Riordan, 1997, p. 21)

These difficulties were not to be surmounted during the run up to the Kyoto conference and indeed they are still the subjects of debate as to how they will be implemented.

This debate was centred on a collision of perspectives and fears for the future. One perspective saw the demands for development coming from the third world as the threat, while the other contended that it was over consumption and affluence on the part of the developed world that was the problem. The outcome of the Kyoto summit left this conflict unresolved, and while the issue of the sovereignty of individual nation states and the ideology of the market were the dominant foundation of any debates at international level then such a conflict appeared unresolvable.

## Cairo conference on population and development 1994

While this book largely avoids the debates over the population issue, the concerns expressed at the Cairo conference on population are of interest because they reinforced some of the divisions that existed between the northern and southern hemispheres found at Stockholm and Rio. In particular, the conflict of interest centred on the relationship between population density and economic well-being was much debated. In addition, the disparate interests evident throughout various ecological debates came to something of a head. Concern over population growth led to a range of different perspectives being expressed by, amongst others, feminists, Catholic and Islamic religious groups, and mainstream environmentalists, as well as those divided by North/South interests. While seemingly settling around the morality of abortion, the question of the causes of population growth were of special interest. Gita Sen had noted the way in which these issues were also present in Rio, and how the literature from those arguing for controls over population were based on an overly crude analysis of the problem:

> Unfortunately, the populist and activist literature has tended to ignore some of the important anthropological debates about carrying capacity, as well as to disregard the inconclusiveness of empirical evidence linking environmental change to population growth ... But the arguments of both developmentalists in the population field and women's health and rights advocates has been precisely that population is not just an issue of numbers, but of complex social relationships which govern birth, death and migration.
>
> (Sen, 1995, pp. 294–5)

Indeed, in the writings of eco-feminists there was a major criticism of the relationship between population and environmental degradation, centering in particular on the empowerment of women. The Rio Conference had involved NGOs representing women's interests, as well as those of indigenous peoples. However, as with the discussion concerning aspects of eco-feminism above, the attempt to develop a unified voice led a Brazilian delegate to note that the inequalities and differences between women had been overlooked, along with the lack of representation of women of colour (Mellor, 1997, p. 36). According to one critic, the desire to develop this unity of view led to women delegates being 'coopted' into the mainstream UN system. This allowed the conference to produce a 'business as usual' policy statement through the tactic of simply recognizing the role of women in the debate while failing to act on the issue (Hausler, quoted in Mellor, 1997, *ibid.*).

A similar situation had occurred at Cairo where there was a strongly expressed belief amongst some critics that,

> ...the emphasis on international family planning programs was a continuation of policies aimed at reducing the number of children of color born into the world. Underlying the Cairo conference, its critics argued, was racism.
>
> (Bryner, 1997, p. 68)

There were still significant problems identified in the development of a policy of population control. The use of family planning concepts, including that of abortion, was seen by many in the developing world as a policy of the developed world for the developed world with little reference to the real needs of development. This was made even more complex by the range of religious traditions and their formal objection to the use of contraceptives as well as abortion. In addition, while there was more general agreement on the need to empower women there were major cultural differences and significant ideological conflicts about what this entailed. Consequently, the provisions emerging out of Cairo are not binding and certainly have to take second place to both national and religious traditions.

As with the Stockholm and Rio conferences, Cairo was always confronted by the stumbling block of the sovereignty of the nation state. In addition, more established philosophies and religious world-views confronted the fledgling ecological perspective. These proved to have an equal, if not greater, capacity to develop an alternative view on the issue of population growth.

## Obstacles for international agreements

This chapter has been concerned with a limited number of international conferences on the major environmental issues. As the Table 7.1 shows, there were a whole range of agreements both globally and regionally which have attempted to tackle the huge variety of issues under the heading of the environmental crisis. These have spawned an equally large number of international organizations and programs established by the UN with often fairly specific remits, for example the Office of Ocean Affairs and the Law of the Sea (OALOS) and the International Board for Plant Genetic Resources (IBPGR). Bryner (1997, pp. 181–5) provided a comprehensive list of UN bodies, some of which were related to specific areas of concern while others, such as the World Food Programme (WFP) covered a range of issues such as agriculture and forestry.

Bryner argued, however, that there were some significant problems with the range and diversity of such arrangements:

> The large number of environment-oriented organizations and programs reflects the widespread recognition of the importance of international environmental issues. There is, however, little coordination among these sometimes competing organizations, nor is there an overarching body to ensure that environmental concerns are given priority at the highest levels of policy making.
>
> (1997, p. 193)

Critics of the process, and indeed of the United Nations as an organization, tend to be critical of its inability to enforce its authority on

*Table 7.1*   Selected international agreements and conferences

| | |
|---|---|
| 1972 | UN Conference on the Human Environment (Stockholm) |
| 1972 | London Dumping Convention |
| 1973 | International Convention for the Prevention of Pollution from Ships |
| 1973 | International Convention on International Trade in Endangered Species |
| 1979 | Geneva Convention on Long-Range Transboundary Air Pollution |
| 1979 | First World Climate Conference |
| 1985 | Vienna Convention for the Protection of the Ozone Layer |
| 1992 | Rio UN Conference on Environment and Development (Rio) |
| 1994 | UN Conference on Population and Development (Cairo) |
| 1997 | Kyoto (Rio 2) |

*Note*: For a fuller list, see Hurrell and Kingsbury (1992), pp. xi–xiv; and Bryner, 1997, ch. 1.

signatories. Bryner saw the UN as too confined to governments and lacking membership from multinational corporations, financial organizations and NGOs. However, if these organizations were fully involved in the UN it would be even more of a 'bloated, clumsy organisation' (*ibid.*, p. 193). As it is, the UN does contain within it governmental representatives and it is the existence of these forces, which are both its advantage and its downfall.

The need to carry with it the backing of the major powers, particularly the USA, was built on the fact that the UN is not, nor was it ever intended to be, a world government. Rather, the basis of its decision-making was consensus and the apparent desire to see its decisions enforced, and to be critical over its apparent inability to do so appeared to go against the ecological belief in diversity and local, community decision-making. Gare's view noted that nationalism should be endorsed as a way of opposing the globalization trends promoted by multinationals, may well work in opposition to the desire to see UN resolutions fully enforced. It is difficult to see how the UN can be blamed for some problems when global developments are towards the creation of regional economic groupings and the richest nations meeting on a regular basis separate from the UN in organizations such as the G7 summits.

This is not to deny that there are very serious problems with the ways in which the UN operated and this was not surprizing in such a large bureaucracy where the main aim of each national representative was to look out for their own national interest. Again, Bryner pointed out that the duplication, overlap and bureaucracy of the UN had led to increased demands for reform, with the US withholding finance from the UN and the replacement of Boutros Boutros-Ghali as secretary-general by a candidate with their backing. However, some have argued that the criticisms of the UN emanating from the US have been the result of the loss of some important votes to a coalition from the developing world.

There was, therefore, at the heart of the criticism of the UN an apparent desire to see some kind of world government to enforce environmentally sound developments. This created a problem as the level of intervention in the behaviour of states would have to be increased significantly while the potential for opposition from powerful state and non-state actors would be increased. For example, the proposals emanating from the Stockholm Initiative on Global Security and Governance in 1991 referred to in Bryner (pp. 196–7) were generally modest, but they do represent an important increase in the environmental role of a form of world government:

> The creation of a supranational environmental agency with powers to direct nations' behaviour is not likely, at least in the short run. Much more realistic is the expectation that international organizations can encourage and facilitate political change in national and sub-national governments rather than imposing it externally.
>
> (p. 199)

As such, there are conflicting tendencies within the environmental critique of the process of international summitry. The desire was to see global action on issues of resource use, global warming and ozone depletion, while at the same time promoting a philosophy which emphasized local diversity.

## Conclusions

The Earth Summit was seen as relatively successful in the development of its various protocols and resolutions. However, critics have argued that while this resulted in a significant increase in global public attention, the position of environmental issues in international relations is still marginal:

> There have been few successful attempts to integrate environmental protection and development; development activities are themselves often plagued by competing and conflicting institutions, overlapping efforts, lack of co-ordination, and failure to integrate the less-developed nations into the world economy.
>
> (Bryner, 1997, p. 193)

As a result, the main environmental conferences have reflected this problem by identifying the differential nature of pollution and environmental degradation in the developed and the developing world. Indeed, with the transfer of some major industrial processes to the developing world by multinational companies and the continued expansion of the tertiary sector in the developed world much of the worst kind of environmental pollution is being transferred from the developed to the developing world. In addition, multinational corporations have been accused of trying to circumvent or undermine the implementation of international environmental agreements:

> They have sought both to influence international rules and standards setting and to limit the impact on them of any domestic legislation enacted to give effect to international commitments...Portet and Brown argue that corporations have worked 'to weaken several global regimes'.
>
> (L. Elliott, 1998, p. 124)

Where international agreements have been forthcoming these have tended to be in areas where the scientific evidence was strong and the economic consequences very specific, as in the case of agreements on CFC gases. Climate change was more contentious, with a wide range of possible sources of climate warming gases, and the perceived threat to economic growth such that national interest took priority over loyalty to the planet (Jäger and O'Riordan, 1996, p. 29). The more successful developments have tended to be more bilateral and centred on particular environmental problems, or those areas where existing arrangements begin to develop a more environmental focus, for example in the negotiations over the Laws of the Sea.

According to Bryner, the issues confronting the development of international environmental organizations centred on two major issues. Firstly, the process of institution building was a 'dynamic process' where the institutions were established in order to develop the norms and principles for environmental controls rather than the other way round. Waiting for the development of international rules before establishing the institutions would take too long. Once established they can respond to issues and then develop further regulatory systems. Secondly,

> the development of non-partisan, widely accepted and acknowledged scientific assessments is critical.
>
> (p. 195)

However, due to the way in which our knowledge of environmental conditions change, these institutions should not make such rules and regulations too difficult to amend.

This reliance on scientific knowledge was sometimes problematic for radical ecologists as it operated within the rational, positivist paradigm that they openly criticized. However, the scientific establishment led the development of our knowledge on a range of environmental issues and the search for their solution. Indeed, some critics have argued that there was now a significant degree of vested interests amongst these scientists in maintaining a concern with still contentious issues such as ozone layer depletion, and more particularly global warming.

Bryner analysed the development and implementation of international environmental agreements from an international relations and policy process perspective. In this he found that there were a series of problems associated with the development of an adequate international regulatory framework. These problems included, the need to develop incentives to encourage states to participate, the complex nature of institutional interaction surrounding environmental problems, and a lack of clarity in the regulatory framework that resulted from such conventions (1997, pp. 109–23).

As early as 1977, William Ophuls identified the problems facing governments on environmental issues, and in particular the problems associated with international conferences and agreements. While the challenge at each individual meeting may be to try and reconcile national and ideological differences and perceptions, a more central problem was the way in which each meeting dealt with a discreet issue with no apparent link with other areas of the global problem (p. 218). For Ophuls, given the logic of his own centralizing tendencies and his Hobbesian approach to the ecological crisis, such a problem proved the case for the development of a world government. Such a government would have 'enough coercive power over fractious nation states to achieve what reasonable men would regard as the planetary common interest' (p. 219). However, the reality facing green activists is the fragmented and highly politicized process of international summits and the, often tortuous, implementation of consensus-led agreements. This is made even more problematic in the developing world where fragile regimes have difficulties in enforcing regulation (Hurrell and Kingsbury, 1992, pp. 36–47). The concern is not simply that such a process is frustrating, but what may be the resulting actions of radical greens who would like to force the pace of change through more direct action.

# 8
# The International Green Movement

Ecological pressure groups have become amongst the most numerous political organizations in the world. As with green theoretical ideas and concepts they are varied both in their approaches to environmental issues and to political action. As with the ideal of 'thinking globally, acting locally' these groups vary in their range of action and focus of attention. Some organizations are a response to immediate local environmental threats, such as a new road or dam, while others are international organizations which tackle a wide range of threats, pressuring governments, multinational corporations and multinational agencies. This makes an assessment of their activity extremely difficult and so this chapter will attempt to bring together a number of points to reflect that diversity while attempting to assess some general trends.

At the start of this book I tried to make a distinction between the concepts of conservation, environmentalism and ecology. While there is obviously a significant degree of overlap between these terms in their areas of interest they may be seen as a potentially useful typology for pressure groups in the area, although it may be seen as only one amongst a number of valid approaches. It is not the intention here to develop a rigorous definition that would need more detailed research into groups' structures, methods and ideologies. Through the use of this approach we can see, for example, that in the case of both the United States and the United Kingdom the earliest forms of activity were concerned with the conservation of wildlife and wilderness. The various animal protection groups, such as the Royal Society for the Prevention of Cruelty to Animals (RSPCA) and the American Society for the Prevention of Cruelty to Animals (SPCA), along with the development of the National Parks movement and organizations such as the Council for the Protection of Rural England (CPRE), can be seen as representatives of the conservation ethic. Environmentalism was seen as a having a wider interpretation of what comprises the natural environment with organizations such as the Sierra Club, the Conservation Society and the World-Wide Fund for Nature (WWF) taking an interest in the relationship between all the component parts of the natural world. Finally, particularly since the 1970s, new ecological groups with a wider critique of the role of humanity in nature's fortunes and a focus on direct action were established, including Friends of the Earth (FoE), Greenpeace and Earth First! Other definitions include the contrast between 'shallow' and 'deep' ecology in which the ecological groups listed above would be seen as 'deep' green while the conservationist and environmentalist groups would be characterized as 'shallow' green.

There are a number of ways of examining the activities of such groups including the existing work on the roles and organization of pressure groups. More particularly, the development of a range of such groups also revealed a trend away from conventional work in the areas of expertise building and lobbying. These groups also worked to present alternatives to existing industrial and commercial interests in fields such as agriculture, power generation, transport and industrial development. The new groups of the late 1980s and 1990s often portrayed a marked alienation from the traditional process of mainstream political lobbying activity. For example, in the area of direct action some radical groups have formed out of even the ecological or deep green organizations:

> The Sea Shepherd Conservation Society, for instance, was formed in 1977 by Paul Watson, who was expelled from Greenpeace for his willingness to pursue a more rigorous and aggressive form of direct action … Earth First! has … advocated, and carried out, attacks (known as ecotage) on equipment used on construction sites. Even more controversially, activists have driven long nails into trees with the intention of, at best, deterring loggers and, at worst, seriously injuring them.
>
> (Garner, 1996, p. 84)

Such a movement towards more radical direct action has also been seen in the area of Animal Rights where, in the United Kingdom, the radical offshoot from the RSPCA, the Animal Liberation Front has also given rise to even more aggressive groups.

An alternative typology or conceptualization of the green movement was developed by Mark Dowie (1995) in his study of the US green movement. He considered the changing fortunes and development of the movement in chronological terms in four waves. These comprised the following:

> The First Wave: 'came in the early twentieth century during the presidency of Theodore Roosevelt, ushered in the era of land and wildlife conservation'.
>
> The Second Wave: 'sparked by Rachel Carson's *Silent Spring*, was marked by a decade of landmark environmental legislation banning or limiting the pollution of land, air and water'.
>
> The Third Wave: an era of backlash associated with the Reagan administration '*market-based incentive, demand-side management technological optimism, non-adversarial dialogue,* and *regulatory flexibility*' (p. 106). These reformist approaches, based on a belief that the market operated more efficiently than regulation as a way of introducing environmentally sound practices, were seen by Dowie as the present mainstream.
>
> The Fourth wave: 'Democratic in origin, populist in style, untrammelled by bureaucracy, and inspired by a host of new ideologies – the fourth wave should crest sometime early in the twenty-first century.'
>
> (pp. 206–7)

Dowie also argued that the fourth wave would be '*very* American' in that it will be multiethnic, multicultural, multiclass and multiracial. However, this was characteristic of ecological thinking internationally with its increased emphasis on the role of traditional cultures and decentralized politics. Dowie noted that the way in which this movement towards a deeper ecological view developed meant that there were debates about terminology within the US:

> Some conservationists are so frustrated by the multiplicity of terms and ideologies that they prefer to consider their movement totally separate from the environmental movement: Dave Foreman is among them.
>
> (p. 222)

Dave Foreman was one of the founders of Earth First! and for him the mainstream movement was concerned with human health rather than an ecocentric perspective. Consequently, there were grounds for trying to establish a typology that would disentangle these different perspectives.

This was important because a number of authors have made a range of distinctions between various groups but in a way that is only partly enlightening. The reason for this was because they have considered the environment as largely a single-issue policy area rather than one that provided a holistic guide to other areas of politics. McCormick (1995) noted the range of possible typologies that were available:

> Sandbach, for example, identifies two different kinds of environmentalism: the ecological/scientific kind (which uses a scientific argument based on ecology and systems analysis), and the anti-establishment variety (concerned more with human alienation from society and nature, influenced by the New Left, anarchism and the counterculture). Cotgrove also identifies two kinds: traditional conservation (taking up in many ways the 19th century liberal revolt against economic individualism) and radical libertarianism (opposed to the present industrial system and in favour of new lifestyles). To Cotgrove's classification, Porritt adds a third group: reformists (political centrists nervous of fundamental change). Porritt further argues that not all environmentalists are greens, and believes that most greens would fit into Cotgrove's second class.
>
> (McCormick, 1995, p. 216)

This rather long quotation revealed the problems that have been identified in establishing a clear classification. An early effort to identify the range of environmental groups in the UK, and link this to when they were established, was made by Philip Lowe and Jane Goyder (1983, pp. 16–17). They identified three periods of growth, from the 1880s to the turn of the century, from the interwar years, and finally from the late 1950s and 1960s. However, they neither tried to establish a typology within these chronological periods, nor did they really identify the rise of more radical groups in the 1970s as an exceptional period of change.

McCormick also contended that green values were difficult to disentangle from other areas of social concern, finding that many environmentalists were also actively engaged, for example, in the peace movement. While McCormick appeared to see this as a complication I would contend that this actually tends to clarify the issue. What was clear for ecologists was the relationship between the belief in the need to overcome the alienation of humanity from nature with the ideas emerging out of the New Left, the peace movement and the counter-culture of the 1960s and 1970s. Indeed, for ecologists, as opposed to conservationists and some environmentalism, the holistic approach based on the revelations of the science of ecology demanded a perspective which involved the peace movement, alternative technologies, a concern with the problems facing the developing world and the need to overcome inequalities between cultures.

The work of Muller-Rommel, Inglehart, Capra and Spretnak referred to by McCormick (1995, pp. 217–8) also tended towards the identification of a typology based on foundational values and a chronological understanding of organizations. Muller-Rommel's (1982) study of party foundations in Western Europe identified three main routes to the establishment of an ecology party. Firstly, existing socialist parties, which adopted wholesale environmental priorities and so changed in the eyes of their public. Secondly, liberal and agrarian parties with a traditional concern for conservation and the environment. Thirdly, new parties founded explicitly on ecological principles. While he argued that the first two categories were 'ecology' parties I would contend that it is really only the latter who could be really defined as such from the perspective of my own typology.

Other authors were more concerned with trying to establish why such parties should arise in the first place and what were the social and cultural roots of these parties. Their views extended from a clear identification with the student rebellions of the 1960s, to the issue of unemployment and its effect on young people as a political force. The alienation resulting from unemployment led radicals to search for an anti-establishment party, with for example the far right benefiting in Germany almost as much as the left or the greens.

However, the green parties themselves would argue that what was being created was a new politics for the twenty-first century. Their criticism of the above analysis would tend to be based on the way in which they were analysed from a left/right perspective. Instead what they were presenting was a break away from such a perspective which they considered to be a dead nineteenth century phenomenon. Instead, they frequently argued that the division was no longer between left and right, but rather between those who believed in progress through economic growth and those who wished to see an end to, or redefinition of, growth:

> Complementary arguments have been propounded in specific regard to the environment, with suggestions that the traditional

yardstick by which the progress of industrial societies has been mea-
sured – economic growth – is no longer appropriate. Among others,
Ophuls, Pirages, Rifkin and Robertson argue that many of our social
beliefs, formed in times of abundance, have needed reassessment in
the light of growing ecological scarcity.

(McCormick, 1995, pp. 218–19)

While the essence of the above statement was correct it did not need to
be identified as having 'specific regard to the environment'. Rather, the
questioning of economic growth went beyond simply a concern with
the environment and raised questions concerning the redistribution of
wealth, doubts about the nature of progress, a questioning of industrialization and of the western scientific and rationalist tradition.

Rudolph Bahro, as a leading figure in the German Green Party (*die
Grünen*) had written explicitly about this situation and his own transformation from out of a Marxist tradition. In a draft election manifesto
in 1983 Bahro contended that,

> Not only have we reached the end of our economic system, but also
> we and our whole industrial civilisation have reached a state of cri-
> sis which will prove terminal if we are not prepared to change our
> total course.

(1986, p. 30)

His proposed manifesto included solidarity with third world countries,
peace as the objective of foreign policy, an ecologically sound economic policy, redistribution of wealth and democratic structures (*ibid.*,
pp. 30–44).

Such an effort to establish Die Grünen as a party with a coherent
range of policies based on sound ecological principles was the basic
task facing all such parties. The problem they encountered was the
image projected by the mainstream media of parties with a single issue
agenda, whereas their leadership and policy formulators argued that
ecology was holistic and presented a new way of looking at all public
policy issues.

## The German Green Party

The German Green Party (*die Grünen*) has often been identified as the
most significant force in European ecological politics as they are the
party that has been closest to power and electoral success. However, for

*die Grünen* the problems began with their successful attainment of a degree of power unknown to any other ecology party. Once this had been achieved the divisions that were evident but tolerated began to emerge more significantly. The divisions were along the so-called realists versus fundamentalists split and centred on the validity or otherwise of developing a coalition with the more mainstream parties. Another dispute centred on the issue of the nature of the state and its claim to the monopoly of legitimate force, strongly associated with the criticism emerging from the peace movement and the anti-nuclear debate. As Thomas Poguntke pointed out, this was also associated with the choice of political strategy:

> Activists who have no confidence in piecemeal reform tend to prefer radical extra-parliamentary action ... Consistently, Radical Ecologists and Eco-Socialists tend to be extremely critical of possible coalitions with the SPD and prefer extra-parliamentary mobilization over governmental responsibility. Realists and the small group of Eco-Libertarians are to be found on the moderate reformist side of internal Green battle lines.
>
> (1990, p. 34)

Bramwell (1994, p. 101) had also noted that the very openness and democratic procedures of *die Grünen* meant that these splits within the party were made very public.

Poguntke argued that one of the significant problems facing *die Grünen*, and I would contend all such parties, was that the electorate were concerned about the issues highlighted and did not necessarily have a strong loyalty to the party as such. Consequently, their survival was 'dependent on their ability to maintain a firm place in the centre of political debate' (*ibid.*, p. 43).

However, the public's attention became more focused on the internal squabbles which marked the party in the late 1980s and into the 1990s, including the discovery of the bodies of Petra Kelly and Gert Bastian, two of *die Grünen*'s leading figures, 'one, at least, murdered' (Bramwell, 1994, p. 109). In particular, there were disputes over the support for violent opposition to the nuclear power industry by anti-nuclear campaigners. While the Fundis supported such activities the Realos objected because of potential damage to their public support. This was made even more open when it was found that some Fundi leaders were channelling money to other activist groups (Zirakzadeh, 1997, pp. 88–9).

The reason for this apparent failure of *die Grünen* to capitalise on their success, as with other Green Parties, was that the electorate tended to see the environment in its most basic terms and did not identify with the deeper, lifestyle and more holistic conceptualization of radical ecology. As a result, the adoption of green issues by the mainstream parties, which Bramwell (1994, p. 110) argued particularly upset Petra Kelly, was evident in most major western democracies. Few members of the electorate identified the Greens as having anything to say on the economy that was significant, and evidence coming from the newly emerging Eastern European states meant that state led planning and environmental regulation came under suspicion of being tainted by the failures of other planned systems. The market was to be the way out of our environmental problems.

However, the German Greens have maintained a hardcore electoral base as a minority party. Through the electoral system and the success of the Social Democratic Party in the October 1998 elections, the Greens gained a place in the government of Germany. As part of the arrangements for establishing a coalition government the two parties have agreed to the winding-down of the nuclear power industry in Germany. However, interest will now centre on how the Greens cope with power at national level. The strains in the Party between Realos and Fundis may well re-emerge as new areas of conflict and compromise arise.

## European parties

The development and range of countries with ecological parties throughout Europe was significant, as were the dates they were founded. It was noticeable that in Western Europe the development of most green parties took place in the early 1980s when issues associated with the peace movement and in particular the arrival of cruise missiles on European soil revived the radicalism of the late 1960s and early 1970s.

In addition, the perception that single issue pressure group politics did not really acknowledge the wider significance of the lessons provided by the science and philosophy of ecology led many to argue the need for a wider challenge to existing power structures.

It is particularly noticeable from scanning Table 8.1 that by and large the parties were established in a very short space of time and this had little to do with the cultural traditions of these various countries. The development of green parties in Central and Eastern Europe followed quickly on from the collapse of the Soviet Union, although there are

*Table 8.1*   The rise of European green parties (by year of foundation)

| Country | Party | Founded |
|---|---|---|
| Switzerland | Ecology Party | 1972 |
| UK | Green Party | 1973 |
| Belgium | Anders Gaan Leven (Agalev) | 1976 |
| | Parti Ecologiste (Ecolo) | |
| Germany | Die Grünen | 1980 |
| Finland | Vihreat (The Greens) | 1980 |
| Italy | Liste Verdi (Green List) | 1980 |
| Sweden | Miljopartiet (Environmental | 1981 |
| | Party) | |
| Ireland | Green Party | 1981 |
| Portugal | Os Verdes | 1881 |
| France | Les Vertes | 1982 |
| Austria | United Greens of Austria (VGO) | 1982 |
| | Austrian Alternative List (ALO) | 1982 |
| Luxembourg | Alternative Lescht-Wiert Ich | 1983 |
| Denmark | De Gronne | 1983 |
| | Federation des Patis Ecologistes | 1983 |
| Switzerland | de Suisse | |
| | Federation Verte | 1983 |
| Luxembourg | Green Alternative | 1983 |
| Netherlands | De Groenen | 1983 |
| Spain | Los Verdes | 1984 |
| Austria | Green Alternative | 1986 |
| Poland | Green Party | 1988 |
| Greece | Alternative Ecologists | 1989 |
| Czech Republic | Green Party | 1989 |
| Moldova | Green Movement (Actiunya Verde) | 1989 |
| Lithuania | Green Party | 1989 |
| Slovenia | Slovene Greens | 1989 |
| Romania | Ecological Movement | n.a. |
| | Ecology Party | 1989 |
| Bulgaria | Ecoglasnost | 1990 |
| | Green Party | 1990 |
| Albania | Green Party | 1990 |
| Slovakia | The Greens | n.a. |
| Croatia | Green Action | n.a. |
| Latvia | Green Party | 1990 |
| Estonia | Green Movement | 1991 |
| Georgia | Green Party | n.a. |
| Ukraine | n.a. | n.a. |

*Source*: Adapted from McCormick (1995) *The Global Environmental Movement*, (2nd edn) (London: John Wiley), pp. 205–6.

notable absences in this table of groups emerging from the states of the former Soviet Union itself.

Bramwell argued that the development of an ecological movement in Eastern Europe had a number of factors that were of significance in revealing their differences as well as similarities to those of the West. From the perspective of similarity, the emergence of the movement could be traced back to the late 1960s, and in particular the Prague Spring of 1968 when political liberalism led to the development of a wider political and cultural critique of socialist systems.

Secondly, the role of the intelligentsia was significant in the development of scientific ideas and the social/political aspects of ecology. However, Bramwell pointed out important distinctions between the East and West in the way the issues had developed. Firstly, environmental awareness grew out of a worsening economic situation rather than the post-materialist glut of the West. Older industries failed in their regulation of pollution and became significant dangers for public health. The role of the Soviet Union through the economic planning system of COMECON came to be associated with deterioration in environmental quality of life and once 'liberation' from the Soviet Union occurred, then the environment became part of a wider critique:

> So environmentalism in Eastern Europe did not spring from some nebulous and unfocused sense of dissatisfaction with the modern, industrialised world *per se*, but rather from opposition to, and concern about, a quite specific form of forced industrialisation, and its too visible and tangible destructive consequences.
>
> (1994, pp. 192–3)

As the development of the green political parties has continued, their potential for electoral success may well increase (see Table 8.2). Their success at local government level and the continuing rise in the political saliency of the environment in the minds of the electorate should see their potential for sharing power in coalition governments increase over the next decade. This is even though their present levels of support are small and varied depending on national cultural and political circumstances (Richardson and Rootes, 1995, p. 20). Besides seeing the development of a wide range of national ecological parties, Europe has also witnessed the growth of environmental pressure groups and become a central area for major international organizations.

*Table 8.2*    Latest electoral figures for Green parties in the European Union

| Country | Party | Election date | %age vote |
|---|---|---|---|
| Austria | Grune Alternative | 17 December 1998 | 4.81 |
| Belgium | Ecolo | 21 May 1994 | 4.00 |
| | Agalev | | 4.40 |
| Denmark | Enhedslisten | 11 March 1998 | 2.70 |
| Finland | Vihrea Liitto | 13 April 1995 | 6.5 |
| France | Verts | 1 June 1997 | 1.63 |
| Germany | Die Grünen | 27 September 1998 | 6.70 |
| Greece | Ecologist Union | 22 September 1996 | 0.29 |
| | Greek Ecologists | | 0.06 |
| Ireland | Comhaonteas Glas | 6 June 1997 | 2.80 |
| Italy | I Verdi | 21 April 1996 | 2.80 |
| Luxembourg | Dei Greng | 12 June 1994 | 10.30 |
| Netherlands | Groen Links | 6 May 1998 | 7.30 |
| Portugal | C.D.U. Coalition (Green/Communist) | 1 October 1995 | 8.60 |
| Spain | Three small parties | 3 March 1996 | 0.35 |
| Sweden | Miljoparteit de Grona | 20 September 1998 | 4.50 |
| United Kingdom | Green Party | 1 May 1997 | 1.38 |

*Source*: Adapted from *The Independent*, London, 31 October 1998.

## International organizations

The initial development of international NGOs working on environmental issues was a phenomenon of the late 1970s and 1980s where the continued expansion in the number of global and international conferences created a need for new organizations. According to Thomas Princen there was an important role for groups that bridged the gap between national issues and global concerns. In particular, Princen argued that within the areas covered by international diplomatic negotiations the role of NGOs was to develop expertise in areas that were neglected by mainstream diplomats, in particular 'immediate community needs':

> It is influence gained from speaking when others will not speak, from espousing something more than narrow self-interest, from sacrificing personal gain for broader goals, from giving voice to those who otherwise would not have it, from rejecting pessimism and looking for signs of hope.

(1994, p. 41)

Finger saw the role of NGOs being one of setting an example and providing alternatives to traditional politics as part of communal or 'social learning'. Finger identified a post-modernist perspective in which traditional politics had given way to a fragmented method with solutions that were equally 'scattered, fragmented and incoherent' (1994, p. 61).

Perhaps the most renowned and significant ecological organizations that have an international impact are Friends of the Earth and Greenpeace. Their reputations for well-organized events and their ability to highlight issues through the use of the media have been commented on as characteristic of post-modern new social movements. Both these organizations were established as part of the new wave of ecological groups, FoE being founded in San Francisco in 1969. Greenpeace was born directly out of the peace and anti-nuclear movements by a Canadian team of protesters concerned with French and US nuclear testing in 1971 (McCormick, 1995, pp. 172–3).

As the 1970s progressed, FoE began to develop a significant degree of scientific expertise supporting a range of media events and direct action methods. Greenpeace centred much more directly on confrontational techniques with whaling ships and French naval vessels in their protests against nuclear testing. Greenpeace, while encouraging support groups with more than three million members, have kept their core membership limited for reasons of expertise and discipline in carrying out their activities. FoE has also allowed the development of national groups using the title, pursuing their own local agendas but within centrally agreed policies:

> they are not membership based organizations. Rather, they have institutional relationships with national organizations which bear the same name and are, in effect, affiliates.
>
> (Elliott, 1998, p. 136)

This form of organizational structure has allowed these organizations to become large, well-financed and influential with some of the resulting problems of bureaucratization. Greenpeace International, for example, had an annual budget of $US25.9 million in 1996 (Elliott, 1998, p. 138).

David Brower who was disillusioned with the more limited aims and tactics of the Sierra Club founded FoE. Under the typology utilized above it can be seen that the Sierra Club may be regarded as environmentalist, but Brower's position and FoE are more in tune with an ecological perspective. Brower wanted to adopt a more radical approach to protest than the Sierra Club. However, Garner (1996, p. 66) noted that FoE itself became more moderate and Brower again found himself out of tune with the organization. He moved on to help establish Earth First! with a more explicit eco-warrior approach. FoE's tactics have developed further with a much more specialist approach to the development of technical evidence for industry as well as government.

This research base resulted in FoE becoming increasingly an insider pressure group, working with government departments in a number of countries providing expertise and alternative sources of information. With the ending of the Communist system in Eastern Europe FoE has also established a presence in a number of ex-Soviet bloc countries (Bryner, 1997, p. 192). The organizational variation that this form of federated structure allowed meant that FoE has established a range of differing relationships with government, although this was related to the relative importance of environmental issues in the particular state.

The high salience of environmental issues in Norway, for example, resulted in FoE Norway being included in the corporate decision-making process:

> Thus Friends of the Earth Norway is both partially funded by government and its leadership welcomed into the inner sanctums of policy making. This situation is very different from that in the United States and Britain, where Friends of the Earth is a campaigning group which tries to influence government, but has no privileged access to policy making beyond the pressure that any interest groups can apply.
>
> (Dryzek, 1997, p. 140)

Greenpeace increasingly found itself to be outside the realm of government as it pursued a consistent policy of direct action. In the UK, Greenpeace moved outside the mainstream democratic process as it became disillusioned with formal planning procedures in the area of nuclear power stations and reprocessing plants. In the USA their distrust of the formal political procedures and the federal government meant that they were excluded from the development of the so-called G10 groups of environmentalist organised by Robert Allen of the Kendall Foundation. Allen had invited only those organizations which had established and regular meetings with Congressional members and industry (Dowie, 1996, p. 69). Indeed, according to Dowie the later inclusion of representatives from both FoE and Greenpeace appeared to have undermined the coherence of a rather conservative group (p. 74), although Greenpeace's use of direct action was one of the main factors in making them the largest mass-membership group in the US.

## The United States

The United States had already a well-established conservationist and environmentalist movement with a major set of concerns centering on issues of wilderness and animal conservation. The Audubon Society, the Sierra Club and the National Parks movement had all contributed to a wealth of support for preserving significant areas of the United States and keeping out commercial exploitation.

However, the development of a more radical ecological approach had a major effect on these more traditional organizations. As was noted above, the desire to engage in a more hard-edged form of political lobbying had led Dave Brower to part company with the Sierra Club. Indeed, as McCormick noted (1995, p. 171), his political lobbying against the damming of the Grand Canyon led to the loss of charitable status for the Club. The development of a more direct action approach through the establishment of Friends of the Earth was a significant move. It made way for a newer ecological perspective that went beyond the traditions of conservation embodied in the Sierra Club and the National Parks movement. However, it also reflected back on the activities of the Sierra Club and their pivotal role in the production of the Limits to Growth book placed them within the newer realm of environmentalism.

The development of Greenpeace as a major international force also propelled the US environmental movement towards an ecological radicalism. But perhaps the most significant force radicalising the movement was that of nuclear power. While opposition to nuclear power was a significant element of all ecological movements, in the US it took on a central role because of a number of events:

> ... safety was a more important issue than it had been in Britain. Non-violent opposition was adopted by protesters at a site in Seabrook, New Hampshire, in October 1976, more than 1400 were arrested. Public suspicion was raised in 1974 by the unexplained death in a car crash in November of that year of Karen Silkwood, an employee at the Kerr–McGee plutonium plant in Oklahoma.
>
> (McCormick, 1995, p. 175)

The nuclear accident at Three Mile Island was a foretaste of the Chernobyl accident. It instilled in the US environmental movement a particular concern because of the level of secrecy involved, its association with the military in an industry developed by the public sector, but now within the private sector subjecting it to policies of risk-taking.

For Bramwell, the problem with the US environmental movement was its association with the counter culture identified by Roszak, with its mix of New Age lifestyle concerns and New Left radicalism:

> The political split behind the environmental movement – essentially New Left versus New Age – dominates other divisions, such as that between radical, direct action and legal action, or deep versus reform ecologists.
>
> (Bramwell, 1994, p. 57)

However, she argued that they were one of the most influential movements in respect of the development and implementation of environmental legislation. This was despite the lack of a green party, such as existed in Europe, but built on a tradition of lobbying in which the State or locality takes precedence in many instances over the needs and actions of the Federal Government based in Washington.

For Dowie, this localism embodied the hope for the future of the ecology movement in the United States. While he argued that the mainstream environmental movement had lost itself in the lobbying processes of government in Washington, the new wave was concerned with the development of a more localized form of action:

> Meanwhile, the movement is losing ground on the issues it does focus on – toxics, wilderness preservation, takings, risk assessments, unfunded mandates, clean air, and clean water. Yet the rationale for lobbying is not being questioned; it has become so central to mainstream environmental strategy that shifting resources away from it would seem like a retreat from battle.
>
> (Dowie, 1996, p. 194)

As a result, the problems faced by mainstream environmentalists have resulted in the development of Dowie's Fourth Wave of environmentalism, where locality and a sense of the need to defend the ecological community resulted in new approaches to ecological activism. In particular Dowie used the example of the Native Americans and their struggles to defend their communities:

> The battles and lawsuits fought by native communities … are emblematic of fourth-wave activity. They are independent expressions of the

need for protection of community health and direct action against polluters and are based on the conviction that neither government nor the traditional environmental movement can be relied upon to deliver environmental justice.

(p. 221)

Such an approach emphasized the role of local communities, the diversity of environmental action and perceived need. Dowie's hopes lay in the development of a highly decentralized and disparate movement without any claims to a single ideological position.

However, this localism was problematic for the movement, as the USA was unlikely to move down the road towards a breakdown of the nation, even though there may be important social and cultural differences throughout the country. Indeed, as Bramwell argued,

Short of war or similar catastrophe, the USA is unlikely to break up. 'Strong' areas would find it hard to break away from declining areas. Romans do not voluntarily give up their empire. It may be that the arguments of environmentalists will do what other tensions and economic problems have failed to do: shatter the political homogeneity, the unified sovereignty of the United States of America.

(Bramwell, 1994, p. 92)

Such a prospect appeared both unlikely and questionable as to its value to the cause of ecological improvements. However, the development of local, small groups activism and the apparent disillusionment with the larger ecological and environmental groups is revealing of the future direction of the movement. Dowie's Fourth Wave may well be one of community opposition and the use of direct action to defend local environmental causes, leaving the larger issues to the stuttering international summits attended by national governments.

## The United Kingdom

The development of the environment as a political issue has been a long-standing concern in the UK. Many significant groups emerged, largely as amenity organizations, in the nineteenth century. In particular, groups concerned with the protection of rural amenity and animal protection emerged out of the period of rapid urban and industrial growth in the mid to late-nineteenth century (Lowe and Goyder, 1983, pp. 15–23). This concern with the apparent neglect or threat to the countryside and in turn a concern with the built environment where old buildings were being destroyed as new Victorian developments went ahead, can be identified with the perception of industrialization as a threat.

Indeed, according to Lowe and Goyder, the self-same questioning of progress and a rejection of the themes of rational improvement associated with the enlightenment were evident in this criticism:

> What was different [from earlier concerns] was a new evaluation of the features being obliterated and a new orientation towards the forces and motives which wrought these changes. In particular, there was a reversal of the rationalist, progressivist outlook deriving from the 'Enlightenment' which, with its confidence in the perfectibility of all things, had looked always to the improvement of nature and society through the exercise of human reason and ingenuity.
>
> (1983, p. 19)

For Lowe and Goyder the modern concerns with the environment and the underlying ideology were not new in the UK context. In addition, McCormick noted that the most important aspect or policy area of environmental concern within the UK was protection of the country-side (1995, p. 161). Consequently, it may be argued that in many ways, while the tactics and the link with lifestyle may be new, the anti-roads lobby and even the protests against live animal exports, are more directly related to the traditions of British conservation than with a new concept of political ecology.

In turning to the Green Party, there are significant problems associated with the development of new political parties in an electoral system based on 'first past the post'. Such a system required that in order to succeed a party had to have a significant geographical concentration of support rather than a wide, diffuse support across the country. The relative success of the Greens in the south-west of England was largely associated with local government success rather than any particular groundswell of environmental protest.

In his study of the Green Party, Frankland (1990, pp. 7–28) argued that environmentalism or 'light green' politics in the form of significant pressure group membership does have a place in the future of British politics. However, the more radical, deep green ecology position of the Green Party was more limited in its appeal and the electoral system worked against its success. While he was less sanguine than

Bramwell, internal factions had held back the development of the Green Party since the 1989 European election.

As with its German counterpart, the Green Party were preoccupied by the means of decision-making within the Party. Consequently, their attachment to a non-hierarchical leadership system meant that the Party chose to adopt a 'triumvirate' to give focus to debates. The party conference also adopted a system of workshops in which small groups of activists would brainstorm new ideas and policies for debate by the whole conference. The problem for the Party was that, as with all eco-logical groups, great importance was attached to access by the media and the conference itself was a media event. While they aimed at a par-ticipatory form of decision making, the media frequently subjected the process to ridicule, comparing it unfavourably with the efficiency of the machine politics of the mainstream parties.

As a consequence of these difficulties the various ecological and more traditional pressure groups have benefited from the growth in membership and staffing throughout the 1980s and 1990s at the expense of the Green Party itself. McCormick has analysed the growth in both these factors and discovered that, while many different groups have benefited significantly from the growth in environmental aware-ness it has been the more radical ecological groups such as Greenpeace, FoE and WWF which have profited most from this growth (1991, pp. 151–7).

The 1980s saw a change in tactics with traditional environmental groups adopting more professional lobbying techniques, and groups such as FoE became 'more conservative'. McCormick argued that the radical groups had become less confrontational:

> more centrally part of the 'establishment' environmental lobby ... Greenpeace ... has not only seen a remarkable growth in its size, sup-port and wealth, but it has also become less confrontational, and more inclined to use the same tactics of lobbying and discreet polit-ical influence once reserved by the more conservative groups. Much the same has happened to Friends of the Earth.
>
> (McCormick, 1991, p. 158)

This potential for an increasingly mainstream role for the largest eco-logical groups has always been there due to their greater concern with the scientific basis of their challenges to government policy and the activities of industry in particular.

Within the UK the more radical developments have centred on the growth of the animal rights movement and the anti-roads lobby. As noted above, these combine within themselves the traditional concerns of British conservation with the New Ageism of many activists. Consequently, the social mix and the support given to pro-testers at places such as the 1997 site of the Newbury by-pass and the 1998/9 opposition to a second runway at Manchester International Airport, reflect this combination in a unique way. The sight of New Age travellers being supported with food and drink from middle-class homeowners was a significant development in the transformation of protest groups activity in the UK. Similar alliances were also evident in the efforts to block the transport of live animals for export, where direct action led to the death of one of the protesters.

## Conclusions

For critics such as Dowie it may be thought that environmentalists have become the victims of their own success in that their ideas have been taken up, in a watered down sense by the mainstream and that the major environmental players have become 'indecisive and irres-olute' (1996, p. 261). Whether it be Mrs Thatcher expressing concern with global warming, or vice-President Al Gore publishing on environ-mental issues, we are all green now. Even the World Bank asserted the need for environmental impact assessments to be carried out before it supported the development of any major capital projects (Adams, 1990, pp. 160–3).

In the US as in the UK while the major groups established in the 1970s, notably FoE and to a lesser extent Greenpeace and national organizations such as the Sierra Club, have become less of a vanguard, local groups have become much more active and radical. While many of these activities may be criticized as examples of NIMBYism ('Not In My Backyard') at its most vociferous there are also much more important examples of resistance to development:

> In the towns and villages surrounded by our national forests, and populated by families dependent on logging and milling, hun-dreds of citizens have formed organizations to stop clearcutting of the last few ancient trees on the continent. They withstand the anger of loggers whipped up by junk-bond corporados and Wise Use vigilantes.

> (Dowie, 1996, p. 261)

Dowie also noted that the large national organizations in the US tended to be dismissive of these local group activities as parochial, temporary and lacking professional media skills.

In the UK the most significant new directions in the environmental movement are associated with the animal rights movement, the anti-roads lobby and anarchistic activists such as the 'Reclaim the Streets' movement. Along with protests against the transportation of live animals for export it was the development of local activity that brought together the 'eco-warriors' and the middle class. In line with the concept of thinking globally, acting locally these developments are seen by Dowie as hopeful, in which the activities of such groups are so integrated with questions of life-style and culture they penetrate every aspect of life rather than just political activity.

However, such a perspective was problematic as it made it extremely difficult to establish a coherent system of thought or ideology. This was not surprising since as we have seen there was a great diversity in thinking on the environment over and above the three-fold typology utilized here. In addition, the widespread concern with a commitment to diversity and the range of understandings of nature found amongst traditional societies undermined the development of a comprehensive ideology. As John Young (1990) asserted,

> Some of those who seek to preserve hedgerows and bunny rabbits may do so for relatively trivial reasons, even while supporting the national economic policies which lead to their destruction. Their reasons do not therefore form part of a coherent environmentalist philosophy.
>
> (p. 145)

The diversity of environmental and ecological thinking also permitted the development of a wide range of political ideologies utilizing the environment as part of their wider interests and views. In relation to deep ecology, Young contended that while it was becoming a sophisticated concept, 'its implications for humans are not dissimilar. Its logic leads to an extreme position either on the Right or the Left' (p. 146). Such an assessment was also complicated by the divisions that existed between the political 'realists' who developed their ideas and tactics in relation to the existing political system, and the fundamentalists who find such efforts compromising. In the US this was associated with the way groups such as FoE supported Democratic candidates against Republicans as a least worst case. In Germany, the classic divisions between 'Realos' and 'Fundis' within *die Grünen,* as they tried to grapple with the problem of potential access to political power, was a reflection of these difficulties.

It does appear, then, that if we are considering the distinction between those who support a more democratic form of action and a decentralized society the Fundis may be in favour of a more participatory form of democracy. The acceptance of a reformist approach by the Realos and their equivalent was linked to the belief that action was needed quickly on some specific issues. The transformation of society into an ecologically sound state through the development of an ecological consciousness was a much more long-term project. In addition, realists may tend to feel that the political or ecological purity of a more fundamentalist perspective was too idealist for the present crisis and perhaps too morally exclusive. The more fundamentalist position however, may well have felt that realists were simply tinkering at the edges and moving the deck chairs around on the Titanic.

As far as the effectiveness of pressure group activity the situation is ambivalent. The green parties in various countries have gone into decline since their high point at the end of the 1980s and early 1990s. The adoption of environmentalist attitudes by various mainstream political parties has undermined their credibility in the eyes of the electorate. However, the locality and community-based approaches adopted by many within the new social movements and ecological pressure groups involved in direct action present a different problem. The very diffuse nature of their activity and the association with NIMBYish attitudes may be a double-edged sword. While they raise the issues amongst local people and politicize them in the process it is difficult to see how long lasting this impact is when the issue has been resolved one way or the other. Once the activists have moved on to the next major project what have they really left behind? The diffuse and locally based nature of the protests appeal to the instincts of the activists but given the scale of the problems they argue we are having to contend with it is difficult to see the extent of their impact. Nor can it be said that the emergence of such alliances is really leading towards the creation of an ecologically sound society.

# 9
# The Green Party and Party Politics in the UK

The purpose of this chapter and the next is to examine the ideology and the methods of a number of organizations who may be said to comprise part of a community or movement whose concern is centred upon environmental issues. The material was gathered between 1978 and 1998, and includes publications, interviews with members and items published on the Internet. The views expressed, except where these come from pamphlets and other publications, are the personal views of those interviewed.

## The Green Party

The idea of establishing an ecological or green party resulted in a serious debate over tactics. In 1978 there were three groups associated with the mainstream political parties, the Liberal Ecology Group (LEG), the Conservative Ecology Group (CEG), and the Socialist Environment and Resources Association (SERA). These organizations acted as internal pressure groups and consultative bodies to the mainstream parties. The groups affiliated to parties felt that better results could be gained by developing ecological ideas within already established parties with their large membership and popular vote. Jonathan Porritt, who in the late 1970s was the Ecology Party's Vice-Chairman, dismissed such a view as for him ecology was very much an alternative ideology covering all aspects of the political, social and economic scene. This being so he felt that there was a need to transcend traditional left/right politics, as these were becoming increasingly anachronistic. A major criticism of the other groups was that their position inevitably led to compromise. However, he saw them having a role in propagating ecological ideas within the parties in order to ameliorate the effects of their traditional ideologies. The Ecology Party allowed the development of alternative policies from a truly ecological perspective and presented these to a mass audience in the form of an election manifesto.

For Porritt this was the task that was set the party by entering elections, even though success was not a realistic prospect and he did not contemplate the possibility of winning a seat. The aim was to gain access to the public through the media and raise the profile of the party. Their low membership had disappointed Porritt and a high profile election campaign was seen as improving this situation:

> It has always been strangely paradoxical that this of all countries should have proved so hostile an environment for the growth of an ecological party. For no country in the world has a higher percentage of its population pursuing hobbies or supporting pressure groups which in one way or another, from Friends of the Earth and the Conservation Society through to the Ramblers Association and the Royal Society for the Protection of Birds, demonstrate some degree of environmental awareness.

> (Porritt, 1979)

And yet he answered this 'paradox' when he told me that he saw the need for environmentalists to think through to the political consequences of their position, something that many just did not consider.

The Party itself had been forced to perform such a rethink due to the nature of the composition of the membership. Established in 1973 as a response to the publication of the 'Blueprint for Survival' in the Ecologist, as the 'People Party', its major source of recruitment was initially politically active people who, dissatisfied with membership of the three major parties, came together on this new project. This led to a situation whereby the party received the experience and expertise gathered from party activity, but members had obviously brought with them the remnants of those traditional party view points. There was some conflict and a fairly rapid turnover in membership in the early period, but as the Party developed a clearer identity was established.

Their membership was also a largely middle-class, intellectual party which was essential in order that a degree of expertise was rapidly established and to attract the 'big names' of the ecology movement such as Edward Goldsmith. A problem with this approach was the development in the early stages along possibly elitist lines, and Porritt agreed that this had led in some quarters to, what he termed, 'eco-fascism', those centralist ideas based upon an expert oligarchy of ecologists. This was because the problems of the environment appeared so large that the temptation of a centralized, authoritarian solution was an easy way out. But again, he did feel that the conflicts and discussions within the Party executive had developed democratic lines of thought much more explicitly.

For this reason a major statement in the Party's election manifesto was concerned with the decentralization of government:

> Consistently apply the golden rule of decentralization – 'That nothing should be done at a higher level which can be done at a lower level' – Participation is the key to success in any democracy.
>
> (Ecology Party, 1979)

The restricted social formation to their membership was also reflected in the difficulties Porritt saw with the term 'Ecology'. He saw it as being initially clouded in a scientific mist and access to the media was essential to throw some light on their ideas before the public. However, this was to prove fruitless and the success of the German greens, as well as their own faltering position in UK elections, led the Party to change its name to the Green Party in 1985.

Porritt's concern that the democratic elements within ecology should take a lead was supported with a major emphasis placed on the development of the local community as a more self-supporting system. The 1979 election manifesto stated that the policy was to,

> Work towards a fully decentralized society. Make it a priority for Central Government to set up legislative and administrative structures to facilitate all local initiatives in this direction.... We believe that the greatest task of our democracy is to transfer responsibility away from Central Government back to the people of this country. It is only by doing this that we shall restore the balance between the individual, the community and the nation.
>
> (Ecology Party, 1979)

This was the main problem for a Party committed to decentralization in a centralized state, and the efforts put into local government by the Ecology Party revealed a greater confidence in local politics than in national elections.

Frankland noted that apart from the electoral system itself, the other barriers to success included the antagonism of the more traditionalist pressure groups that dominated the conservation and environmentalist sections of the UK scene. They did not like to be associated with the deep green elements of the Party (1990, pp. 9–10). As McCormick has noted, there has been little contact between the Green Party and the more traditional environmentalist groups in the UK. He noted that a study of membership overlap in 1984, not surprisingly, showed that Green Party members were often members of ecological groups such as Greenpeace, Friends of the Earth and CND (1991, p. 123). The British public also had a sense that the environment was a single-issue problem rather than a new politics. The Party's own anti-bureaucratic sensibilities militated against their organizational development at the expense of any significant political impact.

This revealed itself in the potential for disputes within the Party over the formulation of policies. During the successful campaign in the 1989 European Parliament election, in which they gained 15 per cent of the vote, members complained about the lack of consultation over the drafting of the manifesto (Frankland, 1990, p. 22). Grassroots opposition to reform to increase their effectiveness, notably at their 1986 Party Conference, revealed an ambiguity towards the whole political process and the very idea of parliamentary party politics. Indeed, as McCormick (1991, pp. 122–3) has noted, their success in the 1989 European elections was a surprise and the greater media attention they received raised questions about their goals and abilities as a serious political force. However, Garner has also added the point that the Green Party in the UK has been more strictly deep green, with the attendant tendency towards ideological purity, than other European green parties (1996, p. 131).

This problem gave rise to a series of conflicts between the main wings of the Party over the issue of organizing for electoral success. Garner discussed some of the major events in which those in favour of reform in the pursuit of success struggled against the more fundamentalist tendencies of deep green activists (*ibid.*, pp. 132–3). However, even after the reformers were able to transform the structure they were not able to turn around the Green Party's continuing slide in elections. By the end of the 1990s the Party had reformulated themselves and changed their organization. However, as a political force they had declined significantly as the mainstream parties had taken on board some of the challenges of the environmental agenda. The Party had further developed their approaches to the issues of ecological politics and the structure of an ecologically sound society. In particular, the Party had developed a detailed set of proposals on the principles of government and public administration.

As with their earlier statements, the Greens concentrated on the development of the concept of decentralization. However, there were some significant problems in the detailed proposals, in particular the concept of subsidiarity and how this should operate. Essentially, the idea of subsidiarity was that if any decision making can be done 'equally well or better' locally then it should be performed locally. In addition, any body which feels that it can perform a task better than a higher authority can make a claim to take over that task:

> Any democratic and accountable authority may judge for itself which functions carried out at a higher level it can do equally well or better.
>
> (Green Party, Internet Website, 1998)

The problem with this approach was the potential for an uneven and unequal distribution of powers around a state. As each locally-based authority made a different claim to jurisdiction and competence the issue of how decisions should be made by the superior authority about the devolving of that power to one locality rather than another was unclear.

Further support for decentralization was provided through the concept of self-reliance in which localities are able to satisfy most of their needs. As part of this process, there was support for the devolving of tax raising powers to the locality in order that the economic structure was available to support the political arrangements. However, the difficulty facing the Green Party was still that of arriving at an ecologically sound system and in order that this was achieved the Party proposed the establishment of a constitutional convention allied to a Bill of Rights that would enable all the citizenry to participate in an harmonious way. Such an arrangement was still vague and utopian and was couched in terms of 'harmony with the planet':

> Divisions, power-relations, intolerance, prejudice, wide inequalities and failures in communication all weaken communities and preclude such co-operation. A Bill to enshrine rights and responsibilities must exist to help protect against this; positive action to build a tolerant, global awareness and to empower oppressed groups is also necessary.
>
> (Green Party Website, 1998)

A major problem facing such transference of power down to the locality was the question of how would the existing holders of power react to such developments. In particular, the Green Party was operating within the context of the United Kingdom where they contended that the existing state was one of the most hierarchical and centralized of all democratic societies. The system they proposed was one of participatory democracy which was significantly at odds with the traditions of representative democracy in the UK. The existence of the European Union was a complicating factor where the role of a 'European Community of the regions' would, according to the Greens, seek to implement such proposals across the whole of Europe.

While they sought to establish a system of tax raising powers which enabled all the various localities to carry out their functions they argued the case for allowing such areas to choose whether they utilized such power at all, while placing no restrictions on the level raised by each locality. This variation in taxation between levels may create problems associated with the migration of peoples between localities and the decision to try and ensure some redistribution of wealth between regions. If a region can rely on money coming from a central fund to raise their economic base who will decide how this was done and would it act as a disincentive to employ revenue powers locally if they could expect funding from a higher authority?

The philosophical principles on which these proposals were based had changed very little from those that were developed in the 1970s. At the heart of these principles was the questioning of economic growth and the search for a sustainable society. Indeed, in some ways the policy statement of the Green Party appeared to go back to some of the early fundamentals of the search for zero-growth. The policy statement argued that selective growth might be needed to improve conditions in the developing world, but that the maintenance of the affluence of the industrialized world was not possible within the context of a sustainable society. In a future in which resource limits were reached then, the Green Party argued, the 'industrial importing nations will suffer most and to pursue tactics now which require increases in resource consumption will only hasten the day' (Green Party Website, 1998).

For the Green Party the main elements of a sustainable society were:

(a)  minimum disruption of ecological processes;
(b)  maximum conservation of materials and energy – or an economy of stock rather than flow;
(c)  a population in which recruitment equals loss;
(d)  a social system in which the individual can enjoy, rather than feel restricted by, the first three conditions;

(e)  a social system where spirituality is recognized and respected.
(Green Party Website, 1998)

The manifesto also turned to a consideration of the issues surrounding science and technology. Here the ambiguous position of the green movement towards science was very evident. While there was an aim to establish a series of Ethical Boards to evaluate all research utilizing criteria which would emerge from public debate, the manifesto also spoke of science as being essential to 'force political acceptance' of environmental policies. This sense that science should actually force government to act is very revealing of a deep-seated distrust of democratic governments which may not be ecologically sound. Such a lack of trust seems to overcome the concern over the aims and activities of science itself.

In other areas where there is some debate within the movement the manifesto does throw some light on the debate over animal rights. Here a cautiously worded discussion aimed to introduce significant controls on the use of animals for a range of activities. While there was substantial evidence of the influence of animal rights campaigns the section was comparatively short and reformist. Indeed, while the obvious bans on circuses and hunting were there the use of animals for racing were simply stated in terms of improved welfare. Perhaps the most radical proposal in terms of rights, rather than protection, was the aim to lobby for an Animal Rights Division within the UN.

Consequently, while the Green Party had moved on in developing some detailed recommendations for the administration and government of a sustainable society it was not significantly advanced in terms of the basic principles of the Party. While some of its proposals concern the transition towards a sustainable society there was little recognition of the obstacles which may be presented to such a change. The process was based very much on the goodwill of the existing centres of power in giving up access to that power to those lower down the hierarchy. In addition, while decentralized structures were developed and the issue of inequality between localities may be raised there was little about how such a system could be maintained once established and whether population movements and differing tax regimes would have a tendency to make the system unbalanced.

## Party affiliated groups

The groups ranged under this heading were those whose activists worked within or through the main channels of the major political parties to raise awareness of ecological issues. From these groups the main stumbling block was the issue of economic growth in the main political parties. The Conservative Party presented Richard Williams with special problems by its nature as a hierarchical party. CEG was set up in order to complement the work of LEG and the Socialist Environment and Resources Association (SERA). It seemed pointless to him for ecologists to consider the Conservative Party as beyond the pale. The task, therefore, set the group was to influence the party hierarchy, as it was difficult to have any effect upon constituency parties without the aid of the parliamentary party. The nature of the Conservative Party was such that the leadership was very much the purveyor of right thinking. Williams felt that the only way through was by contacting MP's and asking for articles on pet topics concerned with environment, which were then distributed to the various constituency groups.

Williams saw the future of politics centring upon a growth/anti-growth debate rather than the traditional left/right one. There was, he believed, a firm alliance of people developing on green issues and that ecology was a philosophy upon which to build across the old ideological divisions. Ecology was a radical challenge to the existing system of organizing society and its productive forces that created environmental degradation and alienation. Ecology aimed at rooting out the causes of pollution rather than treating the symptoms.

It was this area of the agenda that was the greatest problem for Williams in presenting these issues within the Conservative Party. The environment was something that many Conservatives were concerned with, traditionally along the lines of conserving the countryside and the amenities it offered, whether these were large estates, agriculture or game. But for them it was seen as an aspect of life into which politics stepped when decisions were required, while ecology was the perspective from which politics was to be viewed holistically rather than as a single issue.

The Conservative Ecology Group's effect on the Conservative Party was very difficult to consider. The written statements by Conservative MPs for the Group, revealed a wide variety of subject matter and perspective. On the one hand there were the statements put together by the group itself that were obviously produced from an ecological perspective with its concentration upon the 'steady-state' economy (Conservative Ecology Group, 1978) while on the other hand those written by MPs looked upon these matters differently. For instance, where Ian Lloyd MP touched upon the steady-state economy, it was only seen as the reward of growth. Tim Sainsbury MP (1978) saw environmental protection as a way of removing an obstacle to growth rather than vice versa. Indeed this appeared to show just how limited knowledge was of ecology as a social and economic alternative, and the view that it was just a science of 'clearing-up' the detritus of progress.

Ian Lloyd's piece was an attempt to integrate ecology into the Conservative philosophy and concerned itself with attempting to dissociate ecology from what he called 'the ideological riff-raff who seeks every opportunity to dominate and take over the political debate under the banner of ecology' (Lloyd, 1978).

It was difficult to see the idea of ecology in its purest form penetrating deeply into the Conservative consciousness, while at the same time environmental concerns, in the form of conservation, continued as a central theme in Conservative policy-making. The aim was the development of a green, anti-growth grouping within each party, giving rise to a growth/anti-growth debate within a new parliamentary situation. However, this was not to be and the Conservative Ecology Group was not to survive for long as an active part of the Conservative Party. The Conservative Party itself as with all mainstream parties adopted some of the environmental agenda. This was mainly due to the impact of the major international issues such as the depletion of the ozone layer and the greenhouse effect. Consequently, issues such as vehicle emissions and improvements in water quality were included in their policy statements, but all with the proviso of affordability by industry and the maintenance of high levels of growth.

However, one of the most significant periods in the development of green issues in the UK was the acceptance of the evidence for ozone depletion and global warming by the Conservative Government. This was an important change and appeared to be a major change of heart:

> Because of the Thatcher government's insensitivity to such problems as acid rain and nuclear wastes, Britain had become known during the 1980s in environmentalist circles as 'the dirty man of Europe'. But in her September 1988 speech to the Royal Society, Mrs Thatcher abruptly put herself on the side of 'sustainable economic growth' and against atmospheric pollution.
>
> (Frankland, 1990, p. 13)

For Mrs Thatcher there was no conflict between economic growth and environmental protection and she identified the traditions of the Conservative Party with that of conservation. This statement placed the environment in the mainstream but also undermined efforts to present an alternative political position to that of the mainstream parties, making radical positions untenable within the Conservative Party itself.

The feeling of struggling against unfavourable odds expressed by Williams was less obvious when speaking to Tony Beamish of LEG. He felt that they had made very good early running since their foundation in the summer of 1977 with early recruitment reaching three figures at the Liberal Party Conference that year. By 1978, members of the party hierarchy were beginning to consult with LEG, although they acted as an independent group of Liberals acting as a policy pressure group. The groups aims were:

(a) To draw attention to the direct links between expansionist policies and the world ecological crisis;
(b) To promote debate about the principles which must underlie the development of a post-expansionist society;
(c) To encourage the adoption by the Liberal Party of policies based on sound ecological principles;
(d) To encourage Liberals to consider and take full account of the ecological impact of any decisions made;
(e) To encourage environmentally-aware people to join and give support to the Liberal Party.

(Personal correspondence, 1979)

Speaking of the anti-growth thesis, Beamish considered that both this area and others of concern to ecology had broadened out. With the end of the 'doom' scenario and ecology's original iconoclasm, areas of communication with the mainstream parties were now being opened up. Previously the ideas of ecologists were so far removed from orthodoxy that they were misunderstood and dismissed. The more positive elements were now being explored and they opened up great possibilities for the movement.

Beamish argued that all means should be used to explain and develop the movement and its ideas. For this reason he saw no conflict with other groups, and that the foundations of ecology were believed to be strong enough to override traditional political differences once its ideals were accepted. Beamish saw a common aim existing in the ecological movement, and ecology as a natural science providing lessons concerning humanity's social being. Beamish often used religious terminology, for he believed that during the past 400 years we had achieved remarkable material and technical progress but that now we had entered a transitional period from which an equivalent era of moral and spiritual progress would occur.

Beamish welcomed all those who wished to promote the ecological perspective, but he acknowledged there were the dangers of authoritarian solutions being promoted. He considered that James Robertson's book *The Sane Alternative* and the five recipes for future development with which he begins that book provided an essential guide:

> business as usual; disaster; the totalitarian conservationist (TC) future; the hyper expansionist (HE) future; and the sane, humanitarian ecological (SHE) future.
>
> (Robertson, 1978, p. 9)

The task was for the ecology movement to promote the SHE future as strenuously as possible and to reject the TC future which was the centralist, authoritarian thread which was tempting to some in the ecology movement.

In relation to the Liberal Party itself, Beamish felt that while there had been significant advances the issue of economic growth was still a problem (Beamish, the *Guardian*, 1978). The Liberal Party Resolution 'Ecology and the Quality of Life' passed at Southport in 1978 was held to be deficient by LEG. It stated that we had to,

> take account of the long-term consequences of today's economic and planning decisions by giving prime importance to environmental factors ... express fundamental opposition to an economy based primarily on material objectives.
>
> (Liberal Party, 1978)

But Beamish felt that even this very general statement was 'streets ahead of anything that Tories or Labour would agree on'. Beamish saw the most promising areas to be within the Liberal Party, notably in the area of 'community politics', and he referred to David Steel's speech at the 1978 conference in which he stated that 'Small is not just Beautiful, it works better'. This speech lacked the economics of the steady-state to support any view that it was part of the 'ecological perspective' as Beamish saw it, certainly gave LEG members grounds for hope.

The perceived success of LEG in advising the Liberals was continued after their merging with the Social Democratic Party to form the Liberal Democrats. Of the three mainstream parties in the UK, the Liberal Democrats have become the most committed to radical action on the environment. However, this position is made less gratifying for ecologists because of their distance from power as a minority party.

With the merging of the Social Democratic Party and the Liberals in 1988, the new party presented itself as the main green force in party politics. Paddy Ashdown stated that green ideas were at the centre of the new party and the most significant aspect of the Liberal Democrats programme has been a long-standing commitment to overhauling the tax system to benefit the environment. The proposals in their 1997 election manifesto were based on the idea of shifting the tax burden away from consumption and income towards taxing pollution and energy use at source. The view was that this would increase the costs of production using high levels of energy through the use of an energy tax. The use of income from such taxation to introduce energy conservation schemes in homes and industry would reinforce the move towards a reduction in climate change. The Liberal Democrats have also adopted some of the major terminology of the green movement, most notably the concept of 'thinking globally, acting locally' (Liberal Democrat manifesto, 1997, pp. 21–5).

With the creation of the Liberal Democratic Party, the Liberal Ecology Group was superseded by the Green Democrats who continued with the same tactic of trying to promote green values and develop contacts throughout the green movement. They were still highly critical of the Green Party because of its lack of realism and pragmatism that acted as a barrier to electoral success. They were also concerned about the 'authoritarian and illiberal implications' of some of the writing emanating from the Green Party (Frankland, 1990, p. 14).

In contrast to Beamish, Paul Robson of SERA agreed with only some ecological approaches, but was critical of their ideas as deterministic, whether geographic or technological. For Robson, the environment was to be seen from a different ideological angle that was more socialist than deep green. Robson acknowledged the importance within the labour movement of the Labour Party but the Association was a much more radical group, aimed at the grassroots within the trade unions and the community life of working people. The aim was to work from the individual's experience in their working environment and then spread outwards to wider issues. For Robson the environment was an aspect of traditional politics in that it was a question of the distribution of resources. Socialist thought can encompass this within its traditions, Robson believed, as the earliest concerns with the environment were expressed by socialists over the conditions suffered in the inner city areas of the industrial revolution. It was the expansion of these problems into the lives of the middle-class that had led to the upsurge in environmentalism. He found that the word environment was a term towards which all politicians had to 'give a ritual genuflexion'. But this did mean that some MPs who had an early association with SERA either dropped out later, or reduced their activity once they discovered the radical nature of the association and its aims.

This concern with the grassroots of the Labour movement led Robson to a feeling that too often discussions centred around technical matters, especially on the nuclear issue, and could have become tied up in esoteric discussions between differing experts. While not dismissing this line of approach he felt that it should be extended to the social and political effects of nuclear power and its impact on civil liberties. Too often the technical matters were weighted in favour of British Nuclear Fuels Ltd. and the Atomic Energy Authority due to the tie-up between civil and military uses of nuclear power. The need was to reveal how the system adversely affected peoples' environment in the most immediate ways.

Tony Webb, of SERA's Energy group, backed up this approach. His concern was very much with the way in which capitalism, by its very nature promoted a type of technology that was both capital intensive and centralized, and nuclear power highlighted these issues. For Webb, capitalism was a system where competition meant that the most successful firms were those best able to unload their costs onto the community as externals. This was done either by using equipment that unloaded effluent into the atmosphere and the soil, or by the use of equipment lacking adequate safety controls, thus placing the operator at risk. In this way the community suffered as a direct result of industry cutting corners in search of profits.

SERA's aim was to destroy the myths surrounding such technologies as nuclear power and exposing the political and social forces underlying their promotion and use. The task was to promote a social order based upon technologies of a different nature, that were environmentally less damaging, operated on a smaller scale, allowing control and decision-making to rest with the producers. This was seen as a political activity as much as merely technological change. At present the two main methods being advocated were the use of market forces and legislation. The first was to use financial disincentives to force changes, but Webb felt that this resulted in added costs to the consumer and in matters such as energy costs this usually meant the less able suffered the worst effects of a higher priced market. The other was to legislate against specific forms of pollution. Webb was critical of the European Union, in that they promoted the former at the expense of the latter, which Britain had employed previously.

Both Robson and Webb felt that there was a gap between SERA and the other political groups that could not be bridged by an ecological philosophy. They could obviously find common ground in the areas of practical opposition to environmentally degrading activities, but the perspectives from which these issues were approached by the different groups created too great a gulf. Robson believed that as things developed in the future the more traditional political attitudes of activists in the movement would come to the fore. For him the idea of developing a social theory from a natural science like ecology was reminiscent of the way Darwin's ideas had been used to promote a conservative ideology in social Darwinism. Tony Webb was even more critical, and when the question of differences in the terms 'environmentalism' and 'ecology' was raised he was very dismissive, finding that such philosophical niceties were fine for a discussion over a drink in a pub but had little relevance to the problems facing SERA. For him, contact with other groups on the environmental scene was a necessary evil as too often the ecological movement was overly concerned with the construction of an ideology rather than acting from a practical base. Robson said that in reading ecological material he felt that he was being preached a form of 'moral rearmament'.

In an article in Undercurrents SERA's strategy was outlined and the concern with the need to start from concrete needs was expressed:

> We must start where people are at rather than with our favourite issue … This approach need not mean diluting your principles. It means *listening* to the ideas and principles of others first, so that they are more likely to listen to you.
>
> (Emerson, 1978)

The need was to discover the problems being faced by working people, listen to what they felt to be their real needs and then develop practical solutions which were environmentally sound and through this try to show the links between specific problems and the total picture.

The Labour Party had also begun to take note of the problems associated with the environment. In its statement to the annual conference in 1978, the NEC declared, under the heading 'Labour and the Environment' that,

> We are concerned here not merely with the prevention of pollution and the protection of our cities and countryside from spoliation – important though these are. For the problem of the environment goes far wider than issues of this kind: it concerns the very values and priorities which determine the nature of our society.
>
> (Labour Party, 1978)

The Socialist approach to the environment was clearly linked to the methods used by SERA and the aims which were set out for a future, ecologically sound society:

> Our approach is characterised by three principles: to emphasise the relevance of environmental issues to working class life;
>
> To help achieve more jobs and more secure jobs through the attainment of a better environment;
>
> To expose and fight against the shallow acquisitive goals and values of our present society and to pose, sharply, a relevant, attainable, more democratic alternative.

> (*Ibid.*)

In the important area of growth, where others have found the parties lacking most decisively, there was support for a 'selective' approach. This was in line with the ideas expressed by Webb who believed that the concept of zero-growth was a non-starter from the beginning, and that growth must be selectively re-directed.

SERA saw its task as a 'consciousness-raising' group, having members working to highlight such matters as health and safety at work and the environmental dangers of production techniques. They would work within their individual capacities as Trade Union members and Labour Party activists as well as acting in their capacity as a consultative group within the Labour Party. As Paul Robson stated, by conceiving environmental problems within the framework of a socialist critique such apparent contradictions as between jobs and the environment disappear:

> The policies we propose are job creating, involve minimal environmental and resource impact, and reject the greed and waste of the big business consumer society.

> (SERA, 1978)

Essentially they saw themselves as being on the left of the Labour Party and for this reason their tactics and their priorities on growth and their attachment to a decentralized society were at odds with the predominant policies of their Party. Yet at the same time they distrusted the claim of the Ecology Party, that ecology had transcended the traditional socialist/capitalist division.

By the late 1990s, SERA had continued to develop a programme of environmental action from within the labour movement and from a socialist perspective. However, the balance noted above by Robson and

Webb in which most of the work was with the trades unions had apparently shifted. As the power and role of the unions had declined in the UK during the 1980s SERA had shifted its emphasis towards more directly influencing the Labour Party: 'While we work with many other bodies and individuals, our primary goal is to green the Labour Party' (SERA Internet home page, 1998).

As such they have increasingly aimed to play a part in the development of the Labour Party's policy statements on the environment. However, Richardson and Rootes (1995, p. 84) argued that it was competition from the Liberal Democrats and the Conservatives which led to the adoption of environmental issues by the Labour Party rather than pressure from SERA. The Party aimed in its manifesto to carry out a green audit of the work of all departments of state. However, while SERA could claim to have influenced some of the Labour Party's environmental policy, the extent of commitment to ecological issues was open to debate because of the low profile the issue was given in the manifesto.

However, the Labour Party had developed a number of proposals including increased regulation of industry, investigation of energy taxes and the introduction of new measures to assess economic welfare in less crude economic terms than GDP.

This last issue was particularly of interest in relation to SERA and its approach to economic growth. SERA had always revealed some tensions in its relationship with the other groups in the environmental movement, coming as it did from an explicitly socialist position. Unlike the Green Party, therefore, the issue of growth as a limiting factor played a different role. For SERA, therefore, 'the question of growth is irrelevant: it all depends on what is growing' (SERA, 1998), and this requires the establishment of new indicators for identifying the development of a country's economy. The introduction of a new system of taxation, on resource use and energy, was also advocated. This was perhaps the most significant aspect of their policy statement as economic issues were seen as crucial to the development of a sustainable society and where their proposals were potentially most influential. They argue for a greater emphasis on public transport, the ending of major developments which were seen as potentially ecologically damaging, and economic growth through the encouragement of the environmental industries:

> The market for environmental industries is already enormous. For pollution abatement alone the global market is $250 billion, and

will be worth over $300 billion by the end of the decade, which is more than the global aerospace market.

(SERA, 1998)

Like the Liberal Democrats, SERA supported the reform of the tax system with the introduction of a tax on energy and pollution, but with associated reductions in taxation on labour to ensure employment. One model they promoted was a carbon/energy tax being developed by the Commission of the European Union. However, they also argued that such a tax system could not be introduced without considering the social implications of such a development on inequality. Finally, their mission statement gave prominence to the need for democratic processes in decision making. SERA was critical of the market-based system of decision making in which people were too narrowly conceived of as consumers. They argued in favour of the wider, democratic view of people as citizens in a 'healthy, sustainable and more equal society'.

## Conclusions

While some changes had emerged in the policy proposals and the influence of these groups, their fortunes have been very varied. With the Conservative Ecology Group their demise was largely foreseen, while for the Green Party the relatively low profile in the late 1990s was less predictable given their earlier successes. However, what was significant for all the groups was their commitment to decentralized political processes, while there was to a large degree an absence of information on the transition to such a society.

While the Green Party had produced a detailed study of the structure of such a future society a great deal was dependent on the good will of existing power structures and their willingness to dismantle themselves. The other groups centred their proposals on the introduction of various policies by their supporting parties within the context of the existing economic and political system. This was inevitably the case for groups that had to operate within such a context, while the Green Party had the freedom of independence from such ties. The mainstream parties themselves had inevitably developed policies to cope with the continuing environmental crisis, but all still operated within the constraints provided by a commitment to continued high economic growth. As such they also saw the environment as a single-issue problem rather than a comprehensive political philosophy.

On the overall concepts and philosophy provided by the environmental movement and ecology there was little significant change in the views expressed between these groups over the twenty year period. The material gathered in 1978 revealed a significant degree of similarity in style and approach to those in 1998. While some thought appeared to have been given to some of the detailed policy ideas and the agenda on specific issues had changed slightly, the fundamental beliefs revealed a large degree of consistency, particularly over economic growth, industrialization and decentralization.

# 10
## Ecological Pressure Groups

Turning from those groups attached to the established parliamentary parties and the electoral system, the next to consider are those pressure groups active on environmental issues but which have no party political link. The range of such organizations is very wide and so the choice of groups discussed below is a small section of the total number in existence. Some of the groups have emerged in response to the environmental crisis and are associated with the radical concept of ecology. Other groups discussed include ecological research groups and recent developments surrounding the anti-roads lobby and their association with life-style changes.

A number of ideas emerged during a series of interviews carried out in the late 1970s which revealed a very profound set of views that have withstood the test of time. Many are still dominant within the theoretical literature and the publications of the pressure groups themselves. Organizational issues, philosophical debates and tactical questions revealed a strong sense of continuity in the last quarter of the twentieth century. As with the theoretical literature, there were various areas of debate and dispute as well as consensus and co-operation, but there were few signs of the establishment of a single view on how we can move towards an ecologically sound society.

### Ecological pressure groups

The organizations considered under this heading are those which have the most developed sense of an ecological identity, although the Conservation Society was the one with most links to previous, less green, roots. Established in 1966, the major concern of the Conservation Society was the booming UK population and the resource depletion resulting from this, notably the encroachment of urban areas on agricultural land. This position broadened and developed as the environmental debate matured. John Davoll as Director identified problems such as technology and affluence which were largely political. For these reasons an important goal for the future was the establishment of a steady-state society. Davoll stated in a pamphlet, 'Options for Political Action',

> It has been suggested by some members of Council that the Society need nevertheless concern itself only with the maintenance of environmental quality, without expressing an opinion on such highly political matters as the distribution of income and wealth (inter- and intra-nationally).

> (Davoll, 1978)

Davoll supported the aims of the ecology movement and argued that the political consequences of such a position should be realized. He considered that the authoritarian path could become more prevalent as the easiest to establish at a practical level. Inertia in society's institutions and its people, predisposed it to business-as-usual, so that any radical change which was not brought about by some form of ecological collapse may be difficult to engineer. Many writers, such as James Robertson, were over optimistic and catchphrases such as 'Breakdown and Break-through' and 'Decolonization' betrayed a comfortable background of middle-class consensus politics (see Robertson, 1978, pp. 55–6, 104–13). However, he also felt that the promotion of acts of civil disobedience as promoted in the anti-nuclear cause, was not the right response.

The varied membership of the Conservation Society did not exclude direct action by individuals and in a letter to *The Ecologist* the Chairman, Leonard Taitz wrote on such civil disobedience:

> Please count me personally among those who would support such a campaign if this proved to be the only way in which we can bring the nation to its senses.

> (Taitz, 1978)

Davoll disagreed as he considered the threat of nuclear power was not as great as that posed by civil disobedience if it escalated to violence. The need was to continue to discuss rationally, and maintain contacts, with those on the other side of the fence. Although direct action was obviously a part of any popular movement the problems of organization and the care required when confronted by the state were enormous.

Davoll considered that the need was for research into the problem areas in order to propose adequate alternatives. Modern society was so complex that without expertise it cannot function, therefore it was equally important to establish counter expertise in order to convince opponents as well as laying a foundation for a popular movement. Although the Society had committed itself to an anti-nuclear stance, Davoll personally had doubts as there were too many unknowns on both sides and also there were problems with the soft energy path, in that the period available may not allow its full development and it did not guarantee a more open form of government.

The structure of the Society was one of regional branches working on local issues as well as giving aid to the National Office and being represented on the Council, and Working Parties, which perform research and propaganda work on various topics including Economics, Energy, Pollution, Population, the Sustainable Society and Transport. The working parties prepared papers of their own and represented the Society at conferences on topics within their sphere and in representations to government.

On the green movement, Davoll did not believe it was strong enough to withstand the problems which would inevitably arise with increased access to decision-making. He considered that it was such a disparate grouping of political perspectives that these difficulties would arise both between and within the groups under the environmental umbrella. Although environmental questions may colour all political questions it was just one aspect of a wider politics.

A favourable development was the growing interest of some scientists and technologists with alternatives. Mainly conservative in their approaches to social problems and with a scientific training, they were predisposed to the technical fix. Also, once again because of the complexity of society and the advance of science, the need to keep up in ones own field led to a degree of narrowness of vision, even amongst those concerned with alternatives.

Davoll felt that many of the most important questions were in the international arena, where future resource depletion could lead to a North/South conflict. Civil strife was not to be ruled out as the inertia within society suddenly became confronted by the urgent questions of distribution and equality which a halt to growth would raise. He felt that societies under stress often react with amazing flexibility, and pessimism was a temptation to fight against as much as the optimism of the 'eco-freaks' or the 'technological-fixers'. However, by the late 1980s Davoll had apparently rejected the more radical aspects of the green agenda. Porritt and Winner noted that while he had been,

> one of the most influential environmental figures of the 1970s, defiantly declared that the Conservation Society was '*not* a green organization'.

> (1988, p. 61)

This linked in with the view held by Porritt and Winner that the search by the Green Party for a holistic conception which required a political view on all the traditional aspects of party politics had left more mainstream groups behind. For the Green Party 'green means the lot' while for most people green is limited to the environment (*ibid.*, p. 60).

Tom Burke who was the Director of Friends of the Earth at the time of the interview, was also opposed to direct action which involved civil disobedience. This was for two basic reasons. On the one hand there was the structure of FoE as an organization. The branches were contractually associated with the London headquarters and this allowed them to use the name in their activities, but this required them to propagate the views of central office and remain within the law. If the central office decided upon civil disobedience, as a form of illegal activity it would open their contractual arrangements to dispute. On the other hand there was the practical problem of maintaining a position of respectability in order that their voice carried weight when lobbying parliament. Civil disobedience required a large degree of discipline which was difficult to maintain. Burke also felt that direct action should be the last action as the main aim was to make government appear unreasonable.

Burke was critical of Greenpeace for their campaigns, particularly against the Seal cull off Scotland. He felt that it was an overly emotive issue which had been entered into without proper research and may have been a bad move. Greenpeace had entered areas where FoE had long been involved and through direct action may damage the work of the movement as a whole. Czech Conroy, FoE's energy spokesman:

> We have a long standing commitment to fighting environmental issues by democratic means. If you can effectively campaign within the law then that is better than using illegal means.

> (Bunyard, 1978)

By developing a large degree of expertize around specific issues allied to their experience and comparatively large numbers of local campaigners, access to the establishment and local government had increased.

Burke did not consider that there was a truly coherent philosophy, but that the environment was an aspect of politics and that the Ecology Party which saw issues from a purely environmental stance was too crude and naive. The role of the environmentalist should be that of a catalyst in politics which, in alliance with groups involved in Third World development and the Peace movement, questioned the orthodox ideas of government. The crises with the environment could not be narrowed to a single cause and simply to blame capitalism, or growth, was not enough. Although Burke felt that some emphasis should be placed on technological changes, for these had led to the ability to do everything just that much more and had its own logic which could not simply be laid at the door of private profit. There had arisen a belief that 'if it can be done, it must be done' instead of considering how it would benefit humanity.

On the nuclear issue, for example, he felt that the emphasis should be placed upon less technical matters, especially those of civil liberties and the centralization of industrial power. Burke considered that the causes of environmental degradation were those of who owns what and the relations of production, as well as the means of production and what was being produced.

FoE was established in Britain in 1970 as a member of FoE International. The local groups were established on the initiative of people around the country who contacted FoE central office in order to become associate members. By the 1990s, FoE had moved on to develop a policy which clearly identified support for participatory democracy as 'both an end in itself and as vital to the protection of the environment and the sound management of natural resources' (FoE Mission Statement, 1998). The organization of FoE was based upon autonomous groups which operated within the guidelines established by FoE International within a federated structure. In addition, they promoted ethnic and cultural diversity, equal access to resources, social and political justice, as well as their original support for sustainable development and opposition to environmental degradation. The central issue of sustainable development was one of the most significant campaigns where FoE was working increasingly with governments in various countries to develop new approaches to both development and consumption. Campaigns for Sustainable Societies and Sustainable Europe involving almost forty separate countries. This approach has increasingly linked together the national FoE groups to provide information for policy learning between states.

However, while these stated positions were evident in their literature FoE was subjected to sustained criticism by activists in the area of roads protests. They were increasingly seen as too middle-class and reformist in their approach to ecological issues. As Doherty noted, Greenpeace was also included in this criticism of the largest and most established groups of the new ecological period (Doherty, 1998, pp. 370–83). Consequently, in their study of the development of environmental groups as part of a defined new social movement, Jordan and Maloney were able to argue that,

> Critiques of the 'pureness' of mass groups or protest businesses such as FoE or Greenpeace are to a large extent social science constructs... these groups do not see themselves as being vehicles for the expansion of participatory democracy, and nor do the members themselves.
> (1997, p. 191)

However, in the 1970s Malcolm Stern of Greenpeace saw their work as complementary to FoE by the very fact of their being a popular movement based upon non-violent, direct action. The green movement needed to have a broad range of options for action and different organizations, such as FoE and the Conservation Society who had similar aims and methods, should maintain their independence. Stern felt Greenpeace had a unique role, leaving others free to continue with traditional lobbying procedures.

Established in 1970 in response to the US Atomic Energy Commissions' announcement of a testing programme in the Aleutian Islands, Greenpeace developed from the peace movements of the 1960s. Its major tactical position was that of non-violent direct action linked to an avowedly a-political stance. The structure of the movement was limited to a London Office which received support from individuals, but has not established a local branch network, or a system of membership:

> Many people have asked about the possibility of forming local Greenpeace groups. We have had long discussions on this subject and have decided that the administration involved would be counter-productive in achieving our goals. People who would like to support the activities of Greenpeace and Rainbow Warrior are encouraged to form autonomous entities with names like 'Whale Preservation Society' or 'Environmental Action Group'. In this way

we concentrate our staff and energy on campaign organising. Supporting groups with their own identity are free to evolve their own priorities and philosophy, and to support our campaigns.

(1978b)

Greenpeace could organize quickly and with an experienced nucleus of people for their direct action campaigns. It can also maintain its a-political stance which Stern emphasized as being essential in order that they could receive support from as wide a cross-section of the pubic as possible.

Twenty years later, the organization of Greenpeace was under review again to maintain the effectiveness of their direct action operations. The balance between centralization of certain functions and relative autonomy for the national organizations was still the key to the structure of the organization. In 1996 the Articles of Association were changed with the objectives of ensuring 'fast, uncompromising decisions based on participation and consultation; rigid centralisation of some functions and widely distributed responsibility for others' (Greenpeace, 1997). The aim was also to ensure transparency about the use of resources received from supporters through an annual report.

This organizational structure was aimed at ensuring that effective direct action was unhindered by the involvement of untrained individuals who may be difficult to control in difficult and dangerous circumstances. This problem was highlighted most notoriously with the sinking of the Rainbow Warrior by French secret service personnel, as well as the continued action in confronting whaling ships.

The campaigns in which they were involved were limited by this as well as by their lack of resources. Greenpeace was concentrating on three basic issues at the time of the interview; whaling, the seal culls in Canada and the Orkneys, and nuclear power. In this way they could most effectively employ their limited resources and manpower rather than dispersing their activities. The tactics it used were problematical and the structure of the group with its a-political, non-violent, stance were necessary in order to deter the 'lunatic fringe' from entering. The possibility of an extremist action, such as 'throwing a Molotov cocktail on to a whaling ship' was obviously something to be avoided.

Stern argued that while being a populist movement and dealing in moral imperatives rather than technical considerations, this did not exclude the need to back up their arguments with some degree of expertize. In the case of the seal cull in the Orkneys they were hiring a

professional biologist to research the actual situation of the seal numbers and their effects upon fish stocks and the fishing industry.

While Greenpeace has continued to maintain their activities in those
areas they are most clearly associated with, such as anti-nuclear
weapons testing, whaling and the ecological health of the oceans,
they have expanded into new activities. These include technological
developments such as new refrigeration systems, and support for alternative technologies in the area of energy production (Greenpeace,
1998).

However, their a-political approach was breached in the area of
nuclear power. Their 'Greenpeace Nuclear Power Policy Statement'
listed their objections to the peaceful and military uses of nuclear
energy and these included the belief that

> It threatens the democratic fabric of society through excessive cen-
> tralisation of the means of production of electrical energy. It further
> entrenches society in an economic, political and social pattern
> which is in urgent need of change.
>
> (Greenpeace, 1978d)

Stern conceded that there were obviously political elements within the
debate but these were the task of other groups within the movement to
develop. In all their campaigns he maintained that the aim was to
show their opponents lack of moral credibility rather than attack such
matters which, he said, were not wrong in themselves but only if moral
issues were overlooked in their pursuit. The statements and the
method of action chosen by Greenpeace had libertarian elements
which were expressed in a feeling of inevitability over the result of the
public inquiry into the nuclear reprocessing plant at Windscale (now
renamed Sellafield):

> Unlike some groups, however, we see our policy of direct non-
> violent action as being the most likely way of successfully opposing
> nuclear power. The Parker Report on the Windscale Inquiry can
> really lead to no other conclusion.
>
> (Greenpeace, 1979)

Their interests in nuclear issues have, however, continued to centre
on their original objectives of preventing nuclear testing. While they
were able to declare relative success with the signing of the 1996
Comprehensive Test Ban Treaty, subsequent nuclear tests by Pakistan

and India, countries that had refused to sign the Treaty, revealed the continued problem of nuclear proliferation. Greenpeace therefore maintain their policy of protest against testing and support for a non-nuclear world.

The effectiveness of these groups has been varied. While the Conservation Society was the oldest established group, it was the more spectacular issue-orientated approaches of FoE and Greenpeace which have reached the media and seen significant increases in membership (see Table 10.1). The Conservation Society made its presence felt rather by careful research work and the presentation of reports to various international conferences, as well as government agencies and inquiries. FoE has developed a similar method although the larger number of members with enthusiastic local workers have worked in greater contact with the public on the street, with such campaigns as those in support of recycling waste and the attempts to abolish non-returnable bottles as well as the larger issue of nuclear power. Greenpeace's success has been varied, although their high profile campaigns resulted in their emergence as one of the best supported green organizations in the UK and internationally.

Problems arise once the organizations are confronted by more powerful vested interests. If the organizations against nuclear technology are proposing radical social change by confronting the orthodoxy of technological progress and economic growth, their efforts are going to be less rewarding. The problems they face mean that although these pressure groups have had some success they appear slight alongside the depth of their analysis: 'In all our activities, the aim is to attack the cause of the problem, rather than cope with the symptoms' (Friends of the Earth, 1979).

While successes were particularly evident in the early period of their development, both Greenpeace and FoE have become large and bureaucratic in the eyes of some of their critics. They seem to be too close to the government and the establishment as they have developed their role as expert advisors rather than as rigorously confrontational as the more radical activists would like to see. As a result, the nature of FoE and Greenpeace as environmental pressure groups is one increasingly associated with the traditional forms of pressure groups activity in the United Kingdom. Those ecological activists who want a more direct link between the nature of their activism and the ethical transformation of society to an ecocentric position have moved on to the more lifestyle-oriented groups associated with eco-warriors and new-age travellers.

*Table 10.1* Membership trends among selected UK environmental and campaigning organizations (000s)

| | 1971 | 1981 | 1984 | 1986 | 1987 | 1988 | 1989 | 1990 | 1991 | 1992 | 1993 | 1994 |
|---|---|---|---|---|---|---|---|---|---|---|---|---|
| Council for the Protection of Rural England | 21 | 29 | – | – | 32 | 32 | 40 | 44 | 45 | 46 | 45 | 46 |
| Friends of the Earth | 1 | 18 | 27 | 28 | 55 | 65 | 140 | 110 | 114 | 116 | 120 | 112 |
| Green-peace | – | 30 | – | – | – | – | 320 | 380 | 408 | 411 | 410 | 300 |
| Royal Society for the Protection of Birds | 98 | 441 | 466 | 506 | 561 | 540 | 771 | 844 | 852 | 850 | 850 | 870 |
| World Wildlife Fund for Nature | 12 | 60 | 76 | 106 | 124 | 147 | 200 | 247 | 227 | 209 | 207 | 187 |

*Source*: Adapted from Jordan and Maloney (1997) p. 13.

## The ecological research groups: the search for alternative expertise

The above groups felt that because they were dealing with matters that are often technical and are faced by the resources of large corporations, they needed a source of counter-expertise. While there are criticisms over the possibility of establishing the power of experts, the majority feeling was that charges of irrationality and lack of informed comment needed to be responded to.

FoE had felt the need to establish an independent research body, Earth Resources Research (ERR), in 1973. David Baldock, Executive Director of ERR stated that the main problem was that of resources. The number of staff they employed was limited by the amount of work they were sponsored to take up. The hope was that by establishing themselves as an independent organization they would begin to receive requests for research from home and abroad.

Baldock did not consider that ecology was an adequate philosophy on which to found the cultural and social movement as a whole. Rather, it was part of a trend in society which involved a change in social and personal morality which found an expression in the many cultural liberation movements including feminism and gay liberation. Also dissatisfaction with materialism and the work environment were major aspects with an historical link to the New Left and the counter-culture of the 1960s.

The problem Baldock saw was that this link with the counter-culture meant that the majority were often very young and although obviously enthusiastic, they lacked the experience of their opponents. However, this was changing as a growing number of scientists and technologists were beginning to be interested in these matters, particularly though the technical project of radical technologies and this was of great importance for the development of the movement's information and technical work. The task for ERR was not just to produce information counter to the present orthodoxy but also to oppose the centralist, authoritarian trends within the movement itself by showing the possibilities of rational development to an ecologically sound society.

The main problem faced by ERR as a research organization was that of access to information as people often refused to speak, because they felt that the inquiries were seeking to attack their livelihood and their profession. There was also the problem of access to information due to commercial confidentiality covering products and production processes.

This was emphasized in the case of the nuclear power industry because of the blurred boundaries between peaceful and military uses.

Martin Stott of the Political Ecology Research Group (PERG) also saw this as the major problem in the investigation of the nuclear industry because it restricted rational discussion. PERG was established in 1976 in Oxford with, as its main task, that of becoming an alternative research centre. Stott felt that the role of such organizations was to act as a back-up for a more populist movement which lacked the time and the resources to carry out the research. The need was for counter-expertize with a staff of trained researchers who tried to inform the public on the matters where information was scarce. The desire was to allow rational and informed discussion of the problems in order to promote an ecologically sound society (Oxford Political Ecology Research Group, 1977, p. ii). The nuclear power debate was a typical issue where this problem emerged:

> It is often said that a majority of the public are incapable of understanding many of the issues related to energy. This presumption is dangerous and must be resisted…Only then will a public debate about nuclear power be meaningful.
>
> (Oxford Political Ecology Research Group, 1978c, pp. 2–5)

The nuclear power debate for Stott was important to the movement as a whole. If it was developed as many of its proponents suggested we would embark on the road to a form of 'super-capitalism' within a highly technical, centralized system. Opposing a nuclear future would mean a reliance on 'soft paths' with a move away from the fossil fuels on which we now rely. This would necessitate a change in the way we lived and the questioning of the quality of life was an important part of the movement. However, the development of a soft energy path need not entail a spiritual reform and Lovins, for example, was proposing a form of 'soft-energy' capitalism with the large corporations adopting alternative projects with relish.

Stott saw the issue of nuclear power as being important also in that it brought together different groups which allowed the cross-fertilization of ideas. There had developed an alliance between ecologists and the libertarian socialists who had emerged from the late 1960s. This alliance would come under strain, as would the whole movement, if things developed and ecologists get closer to decision-making in society. The fragmentary nature of the movement would reveal itself more as the different perspectives of people were forced to the surface. Baldock of ERR though thought differently in this respect. The very fact that the alternative movement was fragmentary and entered many areas of social protest and cultural thought was a strength. It could react in a very plastic way, concentrating its forces in new areas and therefore failure in one area was not crucial.

Such flexibility did not prevent these organizations from being disbanded in the 1980s. However, the need for such research organizations has not gone away and so new bodies have emerged. FoE itself has undertaken more research increasingly alongside industrial concerns and trades unions. The growth of the green movement has resulted in an increasingly diverse source of information and expertize. This has been particularly evident in the growth of research centres and courses within the University sector. Geography and environmental studies have therefore transformed the whole area of green research. The increasing role of scientific research into the problems of ecological balance and environmental degradation is evident in the emergence of international agreements on the environment.

A further group considered under the heading of alternative expertize was the Intermediate Technology Development Group (ITDG). Established in 1965 by E.F. Schumacher to give technical advice on technologies to developing countries and develop appropriate technologies themselves, giving support to appropriate technology centres in the developing world. The aim was to supply a source of expertize which has an alternative approach to development from the traditional importation of highly capital-intensive technologies in aid programmes and by foreign capital (ITDG, 1978).

The group was a registered charity made up of technical sections of expert volunteers who provide an advisory service to the permanent staff and are a communications channel for other individuals and organizations. The technical services involved such matters as Building and Building Materials, Forestry and Transport, as well as advice on cooperatives and homesteads. These were supported by permanent units based in the UK who collated information and published on appropriate technology. The group established itself as an important aid and information source for many countries, including practical projects in association with charities such as Christian Aid. They developed practical projects such as a brick and tile factory in the Sudan, and consultation projects throughout the developing world. Because of this work and its importance the ITDG maintained a non-political stance. Steven Bonnist, their Information Officer, argued that any statement of political commitment could see them losing access to certain areas of the world. He believed the work they were involved in was too valuable as practical help to the poor to be lost in such a manner.

Essentially, the aim of ITDG was to give information not normally available so that simple techniques could be spread to solve the basic problems which developing countries need to tackle (McRobie and Carr, 1977, p. 15). In the past aid was too often an attempt to reproduce the industrial position of the northern hemisphere, without any thought for the immediate needs of employment and rural development. The need was to allow a greater self-sufficiency and independence, both inter- and intra-nationally:

> Decentralised, relatively small scale production units, which enable very large numbers of people to get more productive jobs, can maximise local (and national) self-sufficiency, and open the way for further development of local skills.
>
> (*Ibid.*, p. 21)

An interesting development within the group was the establishment of the 'Appropriate Technology–UK Unit (AT–UK)' whose aim was to promote the ideas of Schumacher and ITDG within the UK. This was provided through Local Enterprise Trusts which could contribute 'to the revival of a spirit of independence and enterprise in a community' (Davies, 1978, p. 10).

Davies contended that this was a civilizing process in which development in both the northern and southern hemispheres would be 'on a convergent course'. Such an approach was overly deterministic, because when matters concerning the socioeconomic structure were discussed they were seen as dependent on technical change:

> It is a choice which affects the whole pattern of income distribution and the fabric of the economic and social structure. It determines *who* works and who does not; *where* work is done and therefore the urban/rural balance; *what* is produced: and for whose benefit resources are used.
>
> (ITDG, 1978)

Obviously their task as a source of information and expertise was essentially a technical one, but it was founded upon a philosophy which, because of its reliance upon technical change as the source of social change, may only lead to the alleviation of the worst side effects

of the present social structure. However, their continued work and relative success has meant that ITDG has become an established part of the
development scene.

## The 1990s and lifestyle changes

The above discussion has centred on the changes affecting some of the
organizations that were established in the early period of the ecological
movement. While some of these organizations have disappeared they
have been replaced by new ones but more particularly there has been
the significant emergence of lifestyle groups, notably the New Age travellers and eco-warriors. The main change affecting such loosely com-
bined individuals was the movement from a decision to pursue a
particular lifestyle to a direct action approach to protest against environmental degradation.

As Dobson noted,

> Disillusionment with mainstream political parties and the agendas
> they promote has given rise to a form of do-it-yourself politics:
> groups of (mostly) young people organize around a squat, a sound
> system, a drug, a piece of land, and try to live a self-reliant life.
>
> (1995, p. 146)

The development of these 'tribes' has not been associated with formal
environmental campaigns as their main focus of attention. Rather, a
moral and spiritual view of their relationship with nature, which was
at times directly linked to an ecological sensibility, plays a central part
in their lifestyle choices. This includes an anti-industrial, decentralist
approach to community and political action. As such the relationship
with the planet and the concern with the destruction of nature are
inevitable areas of concern and a focal point for organization and contact. As such the links between a range of disparate groups reveals a
rejection of some of the philosophical and ideological differences that
exist within the literature of green politics and ecological thought.

An example of this is provided by the activities of Earth First! in the
United Kingdom. They argue consistently for non-violent direct action
as the best means to bring the ecological crisis to the attention of the
media and as a means of consciousness-raising:

> You can't hope to change people's minds or put pressure on politi-
> cians without calling attention to the damage. Civil disobedience or

a clever banner-hanging exposes the issue on the front pages of the papers that normally hide a single paragraph about ecological catastrophe on the back pages next to the ads and obituaries.

*(http://www.enviroweb.org/ef/primer/DA.html*, 1998)

The range of activities reported on this site revealed the areas of support for environmental and related campaigns. These included the continuing support for the Women's Peace Camps around various US military bases in the UK, anti-nuclear activity, support for the Reclaim the Streets movement and acknowledgement of the work of animal rights campaigners. The publication on the internet of action updates allows for considerable cross-fertilization of ideas and activity both nationally and internationally.

However, this does not wholly overcome the existence of such differences even at this level. The Earth First! site reveals the way in which these debates have entered the activists territory. On their web site they also define the nature of deep ecology as the foundation for their organization's activities:

> All natural things have intrinsic value, inherent worth...They are. They exist. For their own sake. Without consideration for any real or imagined value to human civilization. Even more important than the individual wild creature is the wild interconnected community – the wilderness, the stream of life unimpeded by industrial interference of human manipulation.
>
> *(http://www.enviroweb.org/ef/primer/Deep.html*, 1998)

As such, while there are grounds for supposing that environmentalists, animal-rights campaigners and others will organize together against a perceived common enemy there are significant areas of potential conflict. In the publication, while actions are seen as specific to a particular issue they are also identified as part of a global campaign against 'suicidal progress' and in support of 'the will of the planet'.

In addition, they also exhibit a dismissive attitude towards the formal operation of public inquiries into major planning decisions over roads and runways (Griggs, Howarth and Jacobs, 1998, p. 363). The belief is that such inquiries are futile and inevitably operate in favour of the road builders and established interests. This attitude is associated with a moral certainty in their cause which cannot be detached from their lifestyle choices and separated them from its more mainstream allies in such protests as the Manchester Second Runway. Here, the local support from the community was more concerned with their quality of life rather than the wider environmental issues, while the eco-warriors 'sought to operate completely outside the formal channels of representation and interest mediation' (Griggs *et al.*, 1998, p. 367). However, their activities and the use of the media significantly highlighted the issues associated with these campaigns and also drew largely sympathetic attention to the lifestyles of the eco-warriors. Their more affinity-style approach to nature and their commitment to a radical direct action position also placed them in opposition to the more reformist approaches now associated with the longer standing groups of the green movement.

Whether this can establish such groups as part of a specific concept of New Social Movements, associated with post-modernist ideas of political action, is questioned by Jordan and Maloney (1997). They noted the work of Kuechler and Dalton as identifying new social movements as,

> characterized by alienation and integration, a radical critique pursued through 'unconventional' methods by a largely middle-class constituency materially benefiting from the existing order, and a negativist ideology which knows what it doesn't want, but not really what it does.
>
> (Jordan and Maloney, 1997, p. 65)

However, Jordan and Maloney argue that the groups they survey from the ecological movement are not very different from their conservationist predecessors. They contended that as groups such as Greenpeace and FoE have aimed to expand their influence within governments they have come to adopt the tactics of traditional pressure groups such as the Council for the Protection of Rural England and the RSPCA (*ibid.*, p. 195).

Clearly, the discussion above has shown that both these groups have moved on from their earlier more radical positions. But this change occurred very early on, particularly in the case of FoE who quickly saw the need to develop alternative research and expertise to counter the activities of their opponents. However, the nature of the green movement is such that the need for a new ethical relationship with nature and the desire to overcome alienation through a more ecocentric ideal will always result in the development of a radical alternative. The critique of rationality and material progress is associated with this ethic in such a way that ecological groups will reject the economic and political values of a society which is founded upon the very ideals that they see as the heart of the problem.

Such groups are part of a tradition within the ecological movement stemming from the counter-cultural critiques of the 1960s identified by Theodore Roszak. For a time in the late 1970s and 1980s in particular these individuals appeared to take refuge in the hills of Wales and the development of alternative approaches to living. However, as the state began to take an interest in their movement, and to some extent criminalise their lifestyle choices, some of them have re-emerged to challenge mainstream society on a variety of fronts, including the environment.

## Conclusions

As with the Green Party and the party-affiliated groups, the various organizations reviewed above reveal a significant degree of continuity in their thinking and approaches to green issues and action. While some individuals noted the problems of a tendency towards authoritarian solutions to the ecological crisis in the 1970s, by the 1990s the mainstream ecological groups were committed to decentralization, participatory democracy and a recognition of the diversity of cultures and societies.

Organizationally, however, there was a greater tendency towards direction from the centre to ensure that there was some consistency in approach when using the name of the parent group. This was particularly noticeable in the case of FoE and Greenpeace where national autonomy was tempered by the policy directives emerging from the international centre. These organizations and the various research organizations also showed a commitment to the development of expertise in order to impress their ideas on governments, industry and the public. This was a necessary tactic for groups that were trying to press governments, companies and international organizations to incorporate ecologically sound policies.

However, the eco-warriors and lifestyle groups of the 1990s adopted more radical approaches to direct action, such as the anti-roads campaigns, the campaign against the second runway at Manchester International Airport, and the campaign against live animal exports. While some of the larger groups, most notably FoE, were involved in some of these campaigns, it was the eco-warriors and new age individuals who promoted the issues through the example of a lifestyle change who were most prominent. As such, they have an organizational structure which appears loosely based on social networks, with distinctly anarchist tendencies, but is highly disciplined when involved in the direct action itself. Given the dangers involved such an approach is inevitable, while their political action is based on a belief in the moral superiority of their cause so that they are dismissive of the structures and decision-making procedures of representative democracy in the UK today.

In addition, these new groups may be seen as more centrally linked to the concept of 'new social movements'. FoE and Greenpeace have some elements of such an approach but throughout their history they have always maintained a more centralized organizational structure. As such Jordan and Maloney (1997, pp. 190–2) have seen them as more traditional pressure groups with a large number of passive members. However, the development of lifestyle groups reveals a dissatisfaction with the way these mainstream groups have carried forward the green cause as well as frustration with the processes of representative democracy. This may be evidence of a transformation in the movement towards more confrontational techniques and one which carries a greater risk of violence and lack of control, potentially reducing the overall effectiveness of the movement.

# 11
## Conclusions

Alain Touraine (1979) stated that the development of political ecology and the green movement, particularly in France and Germany,

> ... can be compared to a new revolutionary movement – developing within, and desperately trying to pump life into an earlier revolution that has grown cold and died.
>
> (p. 308)

As such, radical activists should work within the community and have adopted the more radical concepts of the socialist/utopian traditions in opposition to centralist tendencies within a lot of the theoretical writings. In comparing the anti-nuclear movement of the 1970s with the green movement, Touraine stated,

> The anti-nuclear movement is both united with and opposed to, a defensive campaign. The latter is, say, the threatened local population of a proposed site. Utopian protest, on the other hand, is concerned with the entire human species – mankind – as a part of nature.
>
> (p. 309)

However, tactically the development of the new social movements, most notably anti-roads campaigns in the United Kingdom, have attempted to bridge the gap and bring to the local population a sense of the wider context of their protests.

It is in the practical development of actions against specific projects that differences are overcome. Links between the peace movement, eco-feminists and the animal rights movement are established through the activities of individuals who are members of a variety of causes.

While some authors appear to see this as a contradiction, due to the areas of contention between various deep green, eco-feminist and animal rights theorists and philosophers, on the ground such disputes are frequently left behind.

Where the differences begin to resurface is amongst the green parties when they gain access to power or when they become engaged in the practicalities of government and administration. The problems of construction or policy-making are always more severe than the development of a critique. While many may have a similar position on what constitutes a sustainable society there are great differences in the identification of methods for moving towards such a society. The criticism of the 'Parliamentary road' to change by activists who see this as a diversion and compromise from the direct action they favour is just one example of these differences. Within the green parties themselves the 'realist' versus 'fundi' debate will not go away.

As the imminent threat of ecological collapse has receded the decentralist tendency has gained the upper hand. While those who saw such a collapse as imminent saw the need for large-scale state action and regulation, the decentralists supported the need for a grassroots movement developing around local initiatives and individual revolutions in consciousness. The difficulty for the latter is the need for a transformation in consciousness amongst those with vested interests in the existing system. While the centralist position sees a major role for the state and international agreements, decentralists can appear utopian. Ophuls saw that a centralist solution also required leadership,

> To steer us clear of anarchy and chaos during the transition... Next to the sheer lack of time in the face of onrushing events, the paucity of genuine leaders is probably our most serious obstacle to a better and more humane future.
>
> (1977, pp. 243–4)

The decentralist tradition, however, can rely too heavily on a voluntarism amongst existing power holders. Robertson, for example, developed the concept of 'decolonization' in which the members of the existing power centres, and those with a stake in the present system, will disengage themselves voluntarily. Central to this approach is an attachment to a form of affinity ethic which rejects rationalism and seeks to convert people to an ecological perspective through an emotional transformation.

The decentralist ideal identifies politics as an integral factor in a fully functioning ecological society in which all the community participates in decision-making. In addition, the interests of non-human members of that community will be taken into account possibly through 'surrogates' who would represent those interests. It would also have the practical consequence of reducing the reliance on large scale technologies with their associated problems of resource depletion and pollution. More importantly, the route taken by decentralist supporters also involves the reintroduction of values into the social and political sphere, but also into the technological and scientific enterprise. This is the role of critical science or 'post-modern' science which investigates problems which,

> are not the result of deliberate attempts to poison the environment. But they result from practices whose correction will involve inconvenience and money costs; and the interests may be those of powerful firms or agencies of the state itself.
>
> (Ravetz, 1973, p. 424)

For Ravetz this inevitably gives critical science, including ecology, a political element and distinguishes it from positivist science in that it rejects any efforts to be value-neutral. It is now a quarter of a century since Ravetz wrote the above, and yet there has not been an effective analysis of how such a society may be arrived at.

This problem of how to arrive at a sustainable society is aggravated by the development of an environmental ethic in which there is a tendency towards a moral absolutism. Whether it be the aim of developing an objective conceptualization of the value of the non-human world or an ethic based upon an affinity with nature which is emotional and rejects rationalism, the end product can lack tolerance. As such it can find significant problems with democratic processes and lead to the use of direct action and non-parliamentary forms of political activity.

However, political ecology and green political thought have given to much recent social and political thought a reinvigorated moral dimension. This was largely because of its utopian edge which was summed up by Theodore Roszak:

> What we are after is a change in the quality of our lives that will lead us to see the adventure of self-discovery as our paramount cultural value... The larger that grows, the more lightly human society will rest upon the Earth.
>
> (1979, pp. 306, 317)

Ecology is a holistic science whose aim is to reveal the organic links between the parts of a whole which requires the breakdown of the artificial barriers between scientific disciplines. As a political philosophy it is an attempt to break down the artificial barriers between individuals and between humanity and nature. For this reason, the decentralist participatory strand appears to be the most consistent within an ecological approach. However, in addition to the need to reject the urge towards a centralist politics there should also be a note of caution expressed against the rejection of rationalism and technological change. Ecology as a science is within the rationalist tradition and what it overcomes is the artificial, and essentially socio-political divisions between scientific disciplines which have emerged in the twentieth century. While it helps inform our understanding of the world its use as the basis of a moral and political philosophy is a questionable project.

The alternative though is linked to the rejection of rationalism, the questioning of the scientific method and its links to technological development. Such an approach includes the spiritual approach to the issue of alienation from nature and the eco-feminist concept of affinity through feeling and emotion. Such a rejection of rationalism has provided an important critique of the assumptions contained within the modernist tradition. However, it also leads to a possible end to debate in that such views can contend that rational debate is part of the problem. The search for an environmental ethic also betrayed such a tendency in that the concept of an objective value for nature was rejected by some because of the difficulties involved. This view that developing a perspective on nature from within the tradition of ethical discourse was rejected because of the link with the western rational tradition.

The alternative was the possibility of developing an eco-centric approach to an environmental ethic which displaced humanity from the centre of the ethical universe. The problems associated with such an approach included the difficulty of establishing what were the interests of the non-human world. Naess and the concept of deep ecology attempted to do this through empathy with nature, and by asserting the superiority of thinking in such terms compared to the reformism of shallow ecology. This is problematic in that empathy with the non-human world is centred on the idea of relegating the interests of humanity, while at the same time granting to the natural world very human attributes.

The embracing of all the non-human world into such an ethic moved green thinking beyond the more limited and individualistic concepts contained within the animal rights movement. Like the animal rights movement, some green thinking has rejected human interests altogether, in that the non-human begins to take precedence. This was explicit within the writings of some early environmental writers such as Ehrlich and their belief in the need to substantially reduce the global population. More usually now, the belief manifests itself in a rejection of anthropocentric approaches to the environment which identify human interest as being the foundation for reform. Such anthropocentric positions would tend to see the preservation of the environment as instrumental to the survival of humanity, including the need for biodiversity because of the potential discovery of new medicines from rare plant species etc. Eco-centric views would concentrate on the idea that nature should be protected for its own sake and that humanity should leave the natural world alone, rather than even adopting a benign approach to conservation.

The history of the movement itself reveals some of these problems and how they have affected the development of ideas on organization and democracy. There is within the movement a major problem in how it should confront the issues of environmental action. While the movement is committed to decentralization and democracy in its statements of principle, in practice the organizational demands of radical action as well as traditional lobbying activities has led to the maintenance of centralized structures. The main groups considered included Greenpeace and FoE which have very large memberships and have been the most high profile in the development of the movement. However, as Jordan and Maloney (1997) have argued and is supported above, that mass membership organizations such as these have not redefined public participation. Rather, they have sought to maintain a quiescent membership who contribute funds but where the decision-making is highly centralized. With their development as major national and international pressure groups they become bureaucratized:

> they become large, centralised, national groups lacking local sub-units through which individual members can influence group decision-making...large scale 'new politics' groups in the United Kingdom have added very little to the enhancement of participatory democracy associated with their characterization within a new social movement paradigm.
>
> (Jordan and Maloney, 1997, pp. 194–5)

While it may be argued that the disillusionment of the New Age groups and eco-warriors with the failures of established green organizations is opening up a new phase, it is doubtful that such groups are wholly democratic. With their association with lifestyle change and the assertion of a moral rather than a traditional political agenda, they reject formal systems of inquiry in the, not unfounded, assumption that they will lose the case.

At the international level, this may also prove to be a problem as the constraints on state action are even more difficult to overcome than those affecting the state internally. The maintenance of national sovereignty over resources and their exploitation was central to the programmes of action arising from the international arena. As such they have led to a large degree of suspicion and scepticism amongst green activists. However, without the imposition of regulatory controls on one nation by another or the establishment of an authoritarian world government such procedures will continue to be slow moving and will encounter major problems of implementation.

As in the case of the lifestyle movements and their criticism of mainstream green pressure groups, the problems associated with the international arena for ecological activists are the slow procedures and apparent compromise on issues deemed to be fundamental to the survival of the planet. As such there are dangers of critics of the process turning towards a more anti-democratic stance.

The main problems in considering the theories and activities of the green movement are associated with its diversity. This is also the case with its approach to democracy and is the prime reason for the uncertainty contained in the title of this book. It is difficult to come to a hard and fast conclusion as to whether the green movement is committed to democracy or is liable to fall for more dictatorial means to achieve its ends. As Taylor has stated,

We find liberal environmentalists like US Vice-President Al Gore, radical participatory democrats like Murray Bookchin, theorists like Christopher Stone who are more concerned with legal issues than citizen participation, and out-and-out anti-democrats such as some in the Earth First! Movement. Most Greens claim to respect democratic diversity, while others retreat into the racist and native intolerance of an Edward Abbey. Likewise, some environmentalists follow theorists like Mark Sagoff in their respect for democratic diversity, while others ... have abandoned this respect and place their hopes in the enlightened rule of eco-philosophers.

(Taylor, 1996, p. 102)

What the above has argued is that while it is certainly true to say that the green movement portrays all possible variations in its approach to politics and democratic forms, there are some trends which present a less-welcome stance than others. Deep ecology, with the sense of moral superiority implicit in the name, lifestyle approaches and anti-rational affinity approaches with their New Age spirituality contain within them a sense of intolerance to alternative positions so that their claim to democratic sensibility is suspect. The incremental changes and the painstaking research employed by reformist tendencies, with their utilization of existing democratic systems may be more frustrating and time-consuming, but its validity in maintaining the values of rational discourse and the democratic framework are essential. Their success in engaging with the mainstream political parties and governments may smack of compromise to many, but the long-term prospects may well be defended better by such approaches than the tactics employed by more confrontational groups. The problem with anti-democratic or extra-parliamentary methods is that it provides the opposition to ecological change with the excuse and the methods to counter the aims of the movement through similarly anti-democratic but also repressive measures.

# Bibliography

Adams, W.M. (1990) *Green Development: Environment and Sustainability in the Third World*, London: Routledge.

Agarwhal, B. (1992) 'The Gender and Environmental Debate', *Feminist Studies*, vol. 18/1, pp. 119–58.

Allaby, M. (1977) *Inventing Tomorrow*, London: Sphere/Abacus.

Allen, R. (1972) 'Down with Environmentalism', *The Ecologist*, vol. 2, no. 12.

Bahro, R. (1986) *Building the Green Movement*, London/Baltimore: GMP Publishers.

Balibar, E. (1978) 'Irrationalism and Marxism', *New Left Review*, vol. 107.

Barry, B. (1995) *Justice as Impartiality*, Oxford: OUP.

Barry, J. (1996) 'Sustainability, Judgement and Citizenship', in B. Doherty and M. de Geus (eds), *Democracy and Green Political Thought*, London: Routledge.

Barry, J. (1999) *Rethinking Green Politics*, London: Sage.

Beamish, T. (1978) Letter to *the Guardian*, 9 November.

Beckerman, W. (1976) *In Defence of Economic Growth*, London: Jonathan Cape.

Beckerman, W. (1979) 'Small is Stupid', *Times Higher Education Supplement*, 23 November.

Bell, D. (1976) *The Coming of Post-Industrial Society*, Harmondsworth: Penguin.

Benton, T. (1996) 'Animal Rights: An Eco-Socialist View', in R. Garner (ed.), *Animal Rights: The Changing Debate*, London: Macmillan.

Berlin, I. (1978) *Against The Current*, London: Hogarth Press.

Berlin, I. (1990) *The Crooked Timber of Humanity*, London: John Murray.

Berlin, I. (1998) 'The Counter Enlightenment', in I. Berlin (ed.), *The Proper Study of Mankind*, London: Pimlico Press.

Bobrow, D.B. (1977) 'The Politics of Co-ordinated Redistribution', in D.C. Pirages (ed.), *The Sustainable Society*, San Francisco: Freeman.

Bookchin, M. (1974) *Post-Scarcity Anarchism*, London: Wildwood House.

Boulding, K. (1970) *Beyond Economics*, Michegan: Ann Arbor.

Bradshaw, A. (1978) 'Looking Back to the Future: Utopian Ecology', *The Ecologist Quarterly*, Winter, pp. 336–53.

Bramwell, A. (1994) *The Fading of the Greens*, New Haven/London: Yale University Press.

Bryner, G.C. (1997) *From Promises to Performance: Achieving Global Environmental Goals*, New York/London: W.W. Norton.

Bunyard, T. (1978) 'Attitudes to Civil Disobedience', *New Ecologist*, vol. 8, no. 4, July/August, pp. 134–36.

Byrne, P. (1998) 'Nuclear Weapons and CND', *Parliamentary Affairs*, vol. 51/3, pp. 424–34.

CND (1978) *Nuclear Weapons, Nuclear Energy and the Dangers of Proliferation*, Campaign for Nuclear Disarmament, May.

Callicott, J.B. (1992) 'Animal Liberation: A Triangular Affair', in E. Hargrove (ed.), *Animal Rights/Environmental Ethics Debate: The Environmental Perspective*, Albany: Suny Press.

Callicott, J.B. (1993) 'The Search for an Environmental Ethic', in T. Regan (ed.), *Matters of Life and Death*, New York: McGraw-Hill.

Cameron, B. (1989) 'Do Future Generations Matter?', in N. Dower (ed.), *Ethics and Environmental Responsibility*, Aldershot: Avebury Press/Gower.

Carter, A. (1993) 'Towards a Green Politcal Theory', in A. Dobson and P. Lucardie (eds), *The Politics of Nature*, London: Routledge.

Clark, S.R.L. (1997) *Animals and Their Moral Standing*, London: Routledge.

Commoner, B. (1970) *Science and Survival*, New York: Ballantine.

Commoner, B. (1974) *The Closing Circle*, New York: Bantam.

Commoner, B. (1977) *The Poverty of Power*, New York: Bantam.

Conley, V.A. (1997) *Ecopolitics: The Environment in Post-Structuralist Thought*, London: Routledge.

Conservative Ecology Group (1978) *Broadsheet: Statement of Policy*, London.

Conservative Party (1997) *Election Manifesto*, London: Conservative Party.

Cook, T.E. and Morgan, P.M. (1971) *Participatory Democracy*, London: Cranfield Press.

Cook, S., Pakulski, J. and Waters, M. (1992) *Postmodernism: Change in Advanced Society*, London: Sage.

Cotgrove, S. (1976) 'Environmentalism and Utopia', *Sociological Review*, vol. 24.

Cuomo, C. (1996) 'Towards Thoughtful Eco-feminist Action', in K.J. Warren (ed.), *Ecological Feminist Philosophies*, Indianapolis: Indiana U.P.

Daly, H. (1973) *Towards a Steady-State Economy*, San Francisco: Freeman.

Davies, J. (1978) 'Appropriate Technology for the U.K.', *Newsletter*, no. 5 Jan/July.

Davoll, J. (1978) *Options for Political Action*, Conservation Society, 5 September.

de Geus, M. (1996) 'The Ecological Restructuring of the State', in B. Doherty and M. de Geus (eds), *Democracy and Green Political Thought*, London: Routledge.

de-Shalit, A. (1995) *Why Posterity Matters: Environmental Policies and Future Generations*, London: Routledge.

Dickens, P. (1996) *Reconstructing Nature: Alienation, Emancipation and the Division of Labour*, London: Routledge.

Dickson, D. (1974) *Alternative Technology*, London: Fontana.

di Zerega, G. (1997) 'Empathy, Society, Nature and the Relational Self: Deep Ecology and Liberal Modernity', in R.S. Gottlieb (ed.), *The Ecological Community*, London: Routledge.

Dobson, A. (1995) *Green Political Thought*, (2nd Edition) London: Routledge.

Doherty, B. and de Geus, M. (1996) *Democracy and Green Political Thought*, London: Routledge.

Doherty, B. (1998) 'Opposition to Road Building', *Parliamentary Affairs*, vol. 51/3, pp. 370–83.

Dower, N. (1989) *Ethics and Environmental Responsibility*, Aldershot: Avebury Press/Gower.

Dowie, M. (1996) *Losing Ground*, Cambridge, Mass: MIT Press.

Dryzek, J.S. (1997) *The Politics of the Earth: Environmental Discourses*, Oxford: OUP.

Dubos, R. (1976) *A God Within*, London: Sphere/Abacus.

Dubos, R. (1959) *Mirage of Health*, New York: Anchor Books.

Dudley, G. and Richardson, J. (1998) 'Arena Without Rule and Policy Changes: Outsider Groups and British Roads Policy', *Political Studies*, vol. XLVI, pp. 727–47.

Eastlea, B. (1973) *Liberation and the Aims of Science*, London: Chatto & Windus.

Eckersley, R. (1992) *Environmentalism and Political Theory*, London: UCL Press.
Ecology Party (1979) 'Ecology Party Manifesto', *New Ecologist*, vol. 9/2. March/ April, pp. 59–61.
Ehrlich, A.H. and Ehrlich, P.R. (1970) *Population, Resources, Environment*, San Francisco: Freeman.
Ehrlich, P. (1971) *The Population Bomb*, London: Pan/Ballantine.
Ehrlich, P.R. and Pirages, D.C. (1974) *Ark II*, San Francisco: Freeman.
Ehrlich, P.R. *et al.* (1973) *Human Ecology*, San Francisco: Freeman.
Elliott, D. and Elliott, R. (1976) *The Control of Technology*, London: Wykeham.
Elliott, D. (1977) 'The Lucas Aerospace Workers' Campaign', *Young Fabian Pamphlet*, no. 46.
Elliott, D. *et al.* (1978) *The Politics of Nuclear Power*, London: Pluto Press.
Elliott, L. (1998) *The Global Politics of the Environment*, London: Macmillan.
Ellul, J. (1965) *The Technological Society*, London, Jonathan Cape.
Emerson, T. (1978) 'Ripple Revolutionism', *Undercurrents*, 22, pp. 36–7.
Enzensberger, H.-M. (1974) *A Critique of Political Ecology*, New Left Review, 84.
Finger, M. (1994) 'Environmental NGOs in the UNCED Process', in T. Princen, and M. Finger (eds), *Environmental NGOs in World Politics*, London: Routledge.
Flood, M. and Grove-White, R. (1977) *Nuclear Prospects*, Lodon: FOE.
Friends of the Earth (1978) *Introductory Broadsheet*, London: FOE.
Fowler, R.B. (1972) 'The Anarchist Tradition in Political Thought', *Western Political Quarterly*, vol. 25, pp. 738–52.
Fox, W. (1995) *Towards a Transpersonal Ecology: Developing New Foundations for Environmentalism*, Totnes: Green Books.
Frankland, E.G. (1990) 'Does Green Politics Have a Future in Britain?', *Green Politics One*, Edinburgh: Edinburgh U.P.
Fromm, E. (1963) *The Sane Society*, London: Routledge & Kegan Paul.
Fromm, E. (1979) *To Have or To Be*, London: Sphere/Abacus.
Fry, C. (1976) 'Marxism vs. Ecology', *The Ecologist*, vol. 6, no. 9.
Gandhi, M. (1975) 'Excerpts from the Writings and Speeches of Mahatma Gandhi', *The Ecologist*, vol. 5, no. 8, p. 308.
Gare, A.E. (1995) *Postmodernism and the Environmental Crisis*, London: Routledge.
Garner, R. (1996) *Environmental Politics*, London: Harvester Prentice-Hall/ Wheatsheaf.
Gergen, K.J. (1992) 'Organisation Theory in the Post-Modern Era', in M. Reed and M. Hughes (eds), *Rethinking Organisations*, London: Sage.
Gershuny, J. (1978) *After Industrial Society?* London: Macmillan.
Goldsmith, E. (1974) 'The Ecology of War', *The Ecologist*, vol. 4, no. 4, pp. 124–35.
Goldsmith, E. *et al.* (1972) *A Blueprint for Survival*, Harmondsworth: Penguin.
Goldsmith, E. *et al.* (1978) 'Reprocessing the Truth', *The Ecologist*, vol. 8.
Goodin, R. (1992) *Green Political Theory*, Cambridge: Polity Press.
Gorz, A. (1994) *Capitalism, Socialism, Ecology*, London: Verso Press.
Gould, N. (1974) 'Peter Kropotkin-The Anarchist Prince', *The Ecologist*, vol. 4, no. 7, pp. 261–64.
Green Party (1997) *Election Manifesto*, London: Green Party.
Greenpeace (1978a) *History of Greenpeace*, Broadsheet, Greenpeace Ltd.
Greenpeace (1978b) *Newsletter* November, Greenpeace Ltd.
Greenpeace (1978c) 'What are Whales?', *Broadsheet*, Greenpeace Ltd.

Greenpeace (1978d) *Nuclear Power Policy Statement*, Greenpeace Ltd.

Greenpeace (1979) *Nuclear Campaign at Torness*, Greenpeace Ltd.

Greenpeace (1998) *Greenpeace Website, http://www.greenpeace.org*

Gribben, J. (1979) *Future Worlds*, London: Sphere-Abacus.

Griffiths, D. and Smith, D. (1977) *How Many More?* London: CND.

Griggs, S., Howarth, D. and Jacobs, B. (1998) 'Second Runway at Manchester', *Parliamentary Affairs*, vol. 51/3, pp. 358–69.

Hardin, G. (1977) 'The Tragedy of the Commons', in G. Hardin and J. Baden (eds), *Managing the Commons*, San Francisco: Freeman.

Hayward, A. (1994) *Ecological Thought: An Introduction*, Cambridge: Polity Press.

Heilbroner, R.L. (1977) Business Civilisation in Decline, Harmondsworth: Penguin.

Heilbroner, R.L. (1975) *The Human Prospect,* London: Calder & Boyars.

Higgins, R. (1980) *The Seventh Enemy*, London: Pan.

Hildyard, N. (1979) 'Green Crosses', *The Ecologist,* vol. 9, no. 3, p. 103.

Hoyle, F. (1977) *Energy or Extinction*, London: Heineman.

Hurrell, A. and Kingsbury, B. (1992) *The International Politics of the Environment*, Oxford: OUP.

ITDG (1978) *Introductory Pamphlet*, London: Intermediate Technology Development Group.

Illich, I. (1974) *Energy and Equity*, London: Marion Boyars.

Illich, I. (1973) *Tools for Conviviality*, London: Fontana.

Jäger, J. and O'Riordan, T. (1996) 'The History of Climate Change Science and Politics', in T. O'Riordan and J. Jäger (eds), *Politics of Climate Change: A European Perspective*, London: Routledge.

Jagtenberg, T. and McKie, D. (1997) *Eco-impacts and the Greening of Postmodernity*, London/Beverly Hills: Sage.

Jordan, G. and Maloney, W. (1997) *The Protest Business? Mobilizing Campaign Groups*, Manchester: Manchester U.P.

Kahn, H. *et al.* (1978) *The Next 200 years*, London: Sphere/Abacus.

Kleining, J. (1991) *Valuing Life*, Princeton: Princeton U.P.

King, Roger J.H. (1996) 'Caring About Nature: Feminist Ethics and Environmentalism', in K.J. Warren (ed.), *Ecological Feminist Philosophies*, Indianapolis: Indiana U.P.

Kohr, L. (1976) 'The City as Convivial Centre', *Tract*, 12, Gryphon Press.

Kraft, M. (1977) 'Political Change and the Sustainable Society', in D.C. Pirages (ed.), *The Sustainable Society*, San Francisco: Freeman.

Kropotkin, P. (1974) *Fields, Factories & Workshops Tomorrow*, London: Allen & Unwin.

Labour Party (1978*) National Executive Committee: Statements to Annual Conference*, London: Labour Party.

Labour Party (1997) *Election Manifesto,* London: Labour Party.

Lafferty, W.M. and Meadowcraft, J. (1996) *Democracy and the Environment: Problems and Prospects*, London: Edward Elgar.

Leahy, M.P.T. (1991) *Against Liberation: Putting Animals in Perspective*, London: Routledge.

Lee, K. (1993) 'To De-industrialise – is it so irrational?', in A. Dobson and P. Lucardie (eds), *The Politics of Nature,* London: Routledge.

Leopold, A. (1949) *A Sand Country Almanac*, Oxford: OUP.

Liberal Party (1978) *Ecology and the Quality of Life*, London: Liberal Party.

Liberal Democratic Party (1997) *Election Manifesto,* London: Liberal Democratic Party.

Lindner, C. (1997) 'Agenda 21', in F. Dodds (ed.), *The Way Forward: Beyond Agenda 21,* London: Earthscan.

Lipietz, A. (1995) *Green Hopes: The Future of Political Ecology,* London: Polity Press.

Lloyd, I. (1978) 'Ecology and the Conservative Philosophy', *Broadsheet,* London: Conservative Ecology Group.

Love, S. (1977) 'Redividing North America', *The Ecologist,* vol. 7, no. 7.

Lovins, A.B. (1975) *World Energy Strategies,* Cambridge: Ballinger.

Lovins, A.B. (1977) *Soft Energy Paths,* Harmondsworth: Penguin.

Lowe, P. and Goyder, J. (1983) *Environmental Groups in Politics,* London: George Allen & Unwin.

Luke, B. (1997) 'Solidarity Across Diversity: A Pluralistic Rapprochement of Environmentalism and Animal Liberation' in R.S. Gottlieb (ed.), *The Ecological Community,* London: Routledge.

Macpherson, C.B. (1962) *The Political Theory of Possessive Individualism,* Oxford: OUP.

Maddox, J. (1972) *The Doomsday Syndrome,* London: Macmillan.

Mandel, E. (1978) *Late Capitalism,* London: Verso.

Marcuse, H. (1968) *One-Dimensional Man,* London: Sphere/Abacus.

Marcuse, H. (1972) *Counter-Revolution and Revolt,* Harmondsworth: Allen Lane.

Martin, B. (1978) 'Soft Energy, Hard Politics', *Undercurrents,* no. 27.

Marx, K. (1975) *Early Writings,* Harmondsworth: Penguin.

Marx, K. (1976) *Capital Volume I,* Harmondsworth: Penguin.

McCormick, J. (1991) *British Politics and the Environment,* London: Earthscan.

McCormick, J. (1995) *The Global Environmental Movement,* London: John Wiley & Sons.

McRobie, G. and Carr, M. (1977) *Mass Production or Production by the Masses?,* London: ITDG Ltd.

Meadows, D. *et al.* (1972) *Limits to Growth,* London: Pan/Earth Island.

Mellor, M. (1997) *Feminism and Ecology,* London: Polity Press.

Meszaros, I. (1970) *Marx's Theory of Alienation,* London: Merlin.

Midgley, M. (1992) 'Towards a More Humane View of the Beasts?', in D.E. Cooper and J.A. Palmer (eds), *The Environment in Question,* London: Routledge.

Mies, M. and Shiva, V. (1993) *Eco-feminism,* London/New Jersey: Zed Books.

Mills, M. (1996) 'Green Democracy', in B. Doherty and M. de Geus (eds), *Democracy and Green Political Thought,* London: Routledge.

Milton, K. (1996) *Environmentalism and Cultural Theory,* London: Routledge.

Mishan, E.D. (1969) *The Costs of Economic Growth,* Harmondsworth: Penguin.

Muller-Rommel, F. (1982) 'Ecology Parties in Western Europe', *West European Politics,* vol. 5/1, pp. 68–74.

Mumford, L. (1967) *The Myth of the Machine: Technics & Human Development,* London: Secker & Warburg.

Mumford, L. (1971) *The Pentagon of Power,* London: Secker & Warburg.

Naess, A. (1973) 'The Shallow and the Deep, Long-range Ecology Movement', *Inquiry,* vol. 16, pp. 95–100.

Naess, A. (1989) *Ecology, Community and Lifestyle,* Cambridge: Cambridge U.P.

Needham, J. (1976) 'History and Human Values', in H. Rose and S. Rose (eds), *The Radicalisation of Science,* London: Macmillan.

Newell, P. (1997) 'A Changing Landscape of Diplomatic Conflict: The Politics of Climate Change Post-Rio', in F. Dodds (ed.), *The Way Forward: Beyond Agenda 21*, London: Earthscan.

Norman, C. (1978) 'Soft Technologies, Hard Choices', *Worldwatch*, Washington, no. 21, June.

Norton, B.G. (1984) 'Environmental Ethics and Weak Anthropocentrism', in *Environmental Ethics*, vol. 6, pp. 133–48.

Odum, E.P. (1971) *The Fundamentals of Ecology*, Philadelphia: W.B. Saunders.

Odum, E.P. (1977) 'Ecology – the common-sense approach', *The Ecologist*, vol. 7, no. 7, pp. 250–53.

OECD (1974) *Energy Prospects for 1985*, Paris: OECD.

OECD (1977) *World Energy Outlook*, Paris: OECD.

O'Neill, J. (1993) *Ecology, Policy and Politics*, London: Routledge.

Ophuls, W. (1977a) *Ecology and the Politics of Scarcity*, San Francisco: Freeman.

Ophuls, W. (1977b) 'The Politics of the Sustainable Society', in D.C. Pirages (ed.), *The Sustainable Society*, San Francisco: Freeman.

O'Riordan, T. and Jäger, J. (1996) *Politics of Climate Change: A European Perspective*, London: Routledge.

Orr, D. and Hill, S. (1978) 'Leviathan and the Crisis of Ecology', *Western Political Quarterly*, December.

Oxford Political Ecology Research Group (1977) 'Use and Abuse of Information in the Nuclear Power Debate', *Oxford Report*, no. 2, 1977.

Oxford Political Ecology Research Group (1978a) The Windscale Inquiry and Safety Asessment, *Oxford Report*, no. 4.

Oxford Political Ecology Research Group (1978b) 'A Potential Fast Breeder Accident at Kalkar in West Germany', *Oxford Report*, no. 5.

Oxford Political Ecology Research Group (1978c) *Public Participation and Energy Policy*, Oxford.

Paddock, W. (1968) *Famine – 1975!*, London: Weidenfeld & Nicolson.

Passmore, J. (1974) *Man's Responsibility for Nature*, London: Duckworth.

Pearce, D. (1989) *Blueprint for a Green Economy*, London: Earthscan.

Pearce, D. *et al.* (1991) *Blueprint 2*, London: Earthscan.

Pepper, D. (1993) *Eco-socialism*, London: Routledge.

Pirages, D.C. (ed.) (1977) *The Sustainable Society*, San Francisco: Freeman.

Plumwood, V. (1994) 'Nature, Self and Gender', in L. Gruen and D. Jamieson (eds), *Reflecting on Nature*, Oxford: OUP.

Poguntke, T. (1990) 'Party Activists versus Voters: Are the German Greens Losing Touch with the Electorate', *Green Politics One*, Edinburgh: Edinburgh U.P.

Pole, N. (1973) 'An Interview with Paul Ehrlich', *The Ecologist*, vol. 3, no. 1.

Porritt, J. (1979) 'Gearing Up for the General Election', *New Ecologist*, vol. 9. no. 1.

Porritt, J. (1997) 'Introduction', in F. Dodds (ed.), *The Way Forward: Beyond Agenda 21*, London: Earthscan.

Porritt, J. and Winner, D. (1988) *The Coming of the Greens*, London: Fontana.

Princen, T. (1994) 'NGOs: Creating a Niche in Environmental Diplomacy', in T. Princen and M. Finger (eds), *Environmental NGOs in World Politics*, London: Routledge.

Quigley, P. (1992) 'Rethinking Resistence, Environmentalism, Literature and Post-structuralist Theory', in *Environmental Ethics*, vol. 14, pp. 291–306.

Regan, T. (1983) *The Case for Animal Rights*, London: Routledge.

Regan, T. (ed.) (1993) *Matters of Life and Death*, London: McGraw-Hill.

Richardson, D. and Rootes, C. (1995) *The Green Challenge: The Development of Green Parties in Europe*, London: Routledge.

Ridgeway, J. (1971) *The Politics of Ecology*, New York: Dutton.

Roach, C. (1996) 'Loving Your Mother: On the Woman-Nature Relationship', in K.J. Warren (ed.), *Ecological Feminist Philosophies*, Indianapolis: Indiana U.P.

Robertson, J. (1978) *The Sane Alternative*, London: James Robertson.

Rolston III, H. (1994) 'Environmental Ethics: Values and Duties to the Natural World', in L. Gruen and D. Jamieson (eds), *Reflecting on Nature*, Oxford: OUP.

Ross, G. (1974) 'The Second Coming of Daniel Bell', *Socialist Register*, London.

Roszak, T. (1971) *The Making of a Counter Culture*, London: Faber.

Roszak, T. (1974) *Where the Wasteland Ends*, London: Faber.

Roszak, T. (1976) *Unfinished Animal*, London: Faber.

Roszak, T. (1979) *Person/Planet*, London: Gollancz.

SERA (1978) *Membership Statement*, London: SERA.

Sainsbury, T. (1978) 'In Place of Palliatives', *Broadsheet,* London: Conservative Ecology Group.

Saward, M. (1996) 'Must Democrats be Environmentalists?', in B. Doherty and M. de Geus (eds), *Democracy and Green Political Thought*, London: Routledge.

Sessions, R. (1996) 'Deep Ecology versus Ecofeminism: Healthy Differences or Incompatible Philosophies', in K.J. Warren (ed.), *Ecological Feminist Philosophies*, Indianapolis: Indiana U.P.

Schumacher, E.F. (1974) *Small is Beautiful*, London: Sphere/Abacus.

Sen, G. (1995) 'Women, Poverty and Population', in K. Conca *et al.* (eds), *Green Planet Blues*, Colorado: Westview Press.

Simmons, I.G. (1997) *Humanity and Environment: A Cultural Ecology*, London: Harlow.

Singer, P. (1991) *Animal Liberation*, (2nd Edition) London: Thorsons/Harper-Collins.

Singer, P. (1993) 'Animals and the Value of Life', in T. Regan (ed.), Matters of Life and Death, New York: McGraw-Hill.

Singer, P. (1994) *Rethinking Life and Death*, Oxford: OUP.

Singh, N. (1976) *Economics and the Crisis of Ecology*, Delhi: OUP.

Skolimowski, H. (1976) 'Ecological Humanism', *Tract,* no. 19–20.

Skolimowski, H. (1976) 'The Earth and its Friends', *The Listener,* 19 December, pp. 702–3.

Smith, M. (1993) *Pressure, Power and Policy,* London: Harvester/Wheatsheaf.

Stavrianos, L.S. (1974) *The Promise of the Coming Dark Age*, San Francisco: Freeman.

Steel, D. (1978) 'Speech to Liberal Party Assembly', 16 September.

Stillman, P.G. (1974) 'Ecological Problems, Political Theory and Public Policy', in S.S. Nagal (ed.), *Environmental Politics*, New York: Praeger.

Stoneman, C. (1972) 'The Unviability of Capitalism', in K. Coates (ed.), *Socialism and the Environment*, London: Spokesman Press.

Stretton, H. (1977) *Capitalism, Socialism and The Environment*, Cambridge: Cambridge U.P.

Taitz, L. (1977) 'Chairman's Introduction', *Annual Report*, London: Conservation.

Taitz, L. (1978) *New Ecologist*, vol. 8, no. 4, p. 144.

Taylor, B.P. (1996) 'Democracy and Environmental Ethics', in W.M. Lafferty and J. Meadowcraft (eds), *Democracy and the Environment: Problems and Prospects*, London: Edward Elgar.

Taylor, P. (1994) 'Respect for Nature: A Theory of Environmental Ethics', in L. Gruen and D. Jamieson (eds), *Reflecting on Nature*, Oxford: OUP.

Tester, K. (1991) *Animals and Society: The Humanity of Animal Rights*, London: Routledge.

Thompson, E.P. and Smith, D. (1978) *Protest and Survive*, Harmondsworth: Penguin.

Thompson, P.B. (1995) *The Spirit of the Soil,* London: Routledge.

Touraine, A. (1979) 'Political Ecology: A Demand to Live Differently – Now', *New Society*, 8 November 1979.

Tyler, J. (1979) 'The New Ecologist Interviews Jonathan Tyler', *New Ecologist*, vol. 9, no. 2, March/April, p. 62.

Undercurrents (1979) '1.5% Swing to Ecology Party', *Undercurents*, no. 34, p. 3.

Vogal, S. (1997) 'Habermas and the Ethics of Nature', in R.S. Gottlieb (ed.), *The Ecological Community*, London: Routledge.

Von Moltke, K. and Rahman, A. (1996) 'External Perspectives on Climate Change: A View from the United States and the Third World', in T. O'Riordan and J. Jäger (eds), *Politics of Climate Change: A European Perspective*, London: Routledge.

Walker, H.J. (1979) 'Ecological Limits and Marxian Thought', *Politics*, vol. XIV no. 1, May.

Wallace, M.J. (1997) 'Environmental Justice, Neopreservationism and Sustainable Spirituality', in R.S. Gottlieb (ed.), *The Ecological Community*, London: Routledge.

Warren, K.J. (ed.) (1996) *Ecological Feminist Philosophies*, Indianapolis: Indiana U.P.

Weale, A. (1992) The New Politics of Pollution, Manchester: Manchester University Press.

White Jr., L. (1973) 'The Historical Roots of Our Ecological Crisis', in I.G. Barbour (ed.), *Western Man and Environmental Ethics*, Cambridge: Addison-Wesley.

Woodcock, G. (1974) 'Anarchism and Ecology', *The Ecologist,* vol. 4, no. 3, pp. 84–8.

World Commission on Environment and Development. (1987) *Our Common Future (The Bruntland Report)*, Oxford: OUP.

Yearley, S. (1992) *The Green Case*, London: Routledge.

Young, J. (1990) *Post Environmentalism*, London: Belhaven Press.

Young, N. (1977) *An Infantile Disorder?*, London: Routledge & Kegan Paul.

Zimmerman, M.E. (1997) 'Ecofascism: A Threat to American Environmentalism?', in R.S. Gottleib (ed.), *The Ecological Community*, London: Routledge.

Zirakzadeh, C.E. (1997) *Social Movements in Politics: A Comparative Study*, London: Addison Wesley Longman.

# Index